scienceblind

scienceblind

Why Our Intuitive Theories About the World Are So Often Wrong

Andrew Shtulman

BASIC BOOKS

New York

Published by Basic Books, an imprint of Perseus Books, LLC,
a subsidiary of Hachette Book Group, Inc.

Books published by Basic Books are available at special discounts for
bulk purchases in the United States by corporations, institutions, and
other organizations. For more information, please contact the Special
Markets Department at Perseus Books, 2300 Chestnut Street, Suite 200,
Philadelphia, PA 19103, or call (800) 810-4145, ext. 5000, or e-mail
special.markets@perseusbooks.com.

DESIGNED BY LINDA MARK

Library of Congress Cataloging-in-Publication Data
Names: Shtulman, Andrew.
Title: Scienceblind : why our intuitive theories about the world are so
   often wrong / Andrew Shtulman.
Other titles: Science blind
Description: New York : Basic Books, [2017] | Includes bibliographical
   references and index.
Identifiers: LCCN 2016050643| ISBN 9780465053940 (hardcover) |
   ISBN 9780465094929 (ebook)
Subjects: LCSH: Science—Methodology. | Errors, Scientific. | Fallacies
   (Logic) | Intuition. | Reasoning.
Classification: LCC Q175.32.R45 S48 2017 | DDC 501—dc23 LC record
   available at https://lccn.loc.gov/2016050643

10 9 8 7 6 5 4 3 2 1

To Katie, Teddy, and Lucy

Contents

1 | WHY WE GET THE WORLD WRONG

MOST PEOPLE TODAY WOULDN'T CLASSIFY MILK AS A HEALTH HAZARD. To us, it's an innocuous form of nutrition, poured over cereal or consumed with cookies. Milk was not always so innocuous, though. Only a century ago, it was a leading cause of food-borne illness in the industrialized world. Drinking cow's milk is not inherently dangerous—humans have been doing so for millennia—but it becomes dangerous if too much time has passed between when the milk is collected and when the milk is consumed. Milk is typically consumed without heating, and heat is what kills the bacteria inherent in our food. Milk is also high in sugar and fat, which makes it a perfect medium for bacterial growth. The negligible amount of bacteria present in milk when it is collected grows exponentially with each passing hour—a biological fact that milk consumers never really grappled with until the dawn of the Industrial Revolution, in the latter half of the nineteenth century.

The industrial revolution changed the landscape of where people worked and thus where they lived. As the population of Europe and the United States shifted from the country (where people worked on farms) to the city (where they worked in factories), people no longer lived close to the cows that produced their milk. Dairy farmers began transporting milk farther and farther from its source, which meant that people began drinking milk longer and longer after it had been collected. This combination

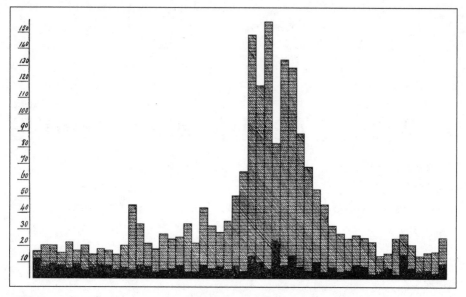

This graph depicts Parisian infants in 1903 who died of gastrointestinal disease within the first year of life, from week 1 to week 52. Breastfed infants (solid bars) were significantly less likely to die than were bottle-fed infants (hatched bars).

of factors—that milk is consumed cold, that milk is an ideal incubator for bacteria, and that milk was being consumed days after its collection—led to several mass epidemics of milk-borne disease in Europe and the United States; the epidemics included outbreaks of tuberculosis, typhoid, scarlet fever, and cowpox. Milk in the nineteenth century was, according to one medical expert, "as deadly as Socrates' hemlock."

The problem of how to safely consume milk several hours (or days) after its collection was solved in the 1860s with a relatively simple process: heating milk for long enough to kill most of the bacteria within but not so long as to alter its sensory qualities or nutritional value. This method of food treatment, devised by Louis Pasteur, came to be known as *pasteurization*. The health consequences of pasteurization were immediate and immense. Those most at risk of milk-borne disease in the nineteenth century were infants, as infants fed cow's milk were several times more likely to die than those fed from the breast. After pasteurization was introduced, however, infant mortality rates in urban centers dropped by around 20 percent.

Today, pasteurized milk is considered one of the safest foods to consume, associated with less than 1 percent of all food-borne illnesses. Oddly, however, people are increasingly opting to drink *unpasteurized* milk, and as a consequence, the rates of milk-borne disease are rising. Between 2007 and 2009, the United States experienced thirty outbreaks related to the bacteria *Campylobacter*, *Salmonella*, and *E. coli*—outbreaks linked to the consumption of unpasteurized milk. Between 2010 and 2012, that number rose to fifty-one. People are increasingly buying raw, unpasteurized milk for a variety of reasons: the belief that raw milk tastes better than pasteurized milk, that raw milk has higher nutritional content than pasteurized milk (which it does not), that raw milk is what humans were intended to drink, and that consumers should have the right to choose whether their milk is pasteurized or not. Those who reject pasteurized milk in favor of a more "natural" alternative do so seemingly blind to the fact that, before the advent of pasteurization, thousands of people suffered organ failure, miscarriage, blindness, paralysis, and even death at the hands of milk-borne diseases.

Do people fully understand what they are rejecting when they reject pasteurizing? Probably not. Pasteurization is counterintuitive. It's counterintuitive because germs are counterintuitive. Germs are living things that cannot be seen; they are passed from one host to another without detection, and they make us ill several hours or days after we come in contact with them. Also counterintuitive is the idea that germs transform our food from sources of nutrition to sources of disease but that we can stop germs from doing so by killing them with heat. Heating food to kill germs is a widespread practice in the food industry. Several types of food are pasteurized (or otherwise heat-treated) before they hit the shelves—beer, wine, juice, canned fruits, canned vegetables—not just milk. It is ironic that advocates for unpasteurized milk are seemingly okay with pasteurized beer and canned peaches. Either they believe that forgoing pasteurization is a justified risk for milk but not for other foods, or, more likely, they fail to understand what pasteurization is and why it is a necessary safeguard against food-borne illness.

The science behind pasteurization is as sound as science gets, but many people reject this science. They reject not just the science behind pasteurization but science in general, from immunology to geology to genetics. A recent survey of American adults found that only 65 percent believe that humans have evolved over time, compared with 98 percent of the members of the world's largest scientific society, the American Association for the Advancement of Science (AAAS). Only 50 percent of American adults believe that climate change is due mostly to human activity, compared with 87 percent of AAAS members. And only 37 percent of American adults believe that genetically modified foods are safe to eat, compared with 88 percent of AAAS members.

Science denial is not a modern phenomenon. Most people denied that the earth orbits the sun, that the continents are drifting, or that disease is caused by germs when those ideas were first proposed. Still, resistance to science in today's age—an age flush with scientific information and science education—requires explanation. Many scholars and media pundits point to ideology as an explanation, either political ideology or religious ideology. Others point to misinformation, as when vaccines were falsely linked to autism or when genetically modified foods were falsely linked to cancer. All these factors have been shown to play a role in science denial. Conservatives are less likely to accept science than liberals, religious individuals are less likely to accept science than secular individuals, and misinformation breeds skepticism and hostility toward scientific ideas. But these factors are not the only causes of science denial. Psychologists have uncovered another: *intuitive theories.*

Intuitive theories are our untutored explanations for how the world works. They are our best guess as to why we observe the events we do and how we can intervene in those events to change them. Intuitive theories cover all manner of phenomena—from gravity to geology to illness to adaptation—and they operate from infancy to senescence. The problem is, they are often wrong. Our intuitive theory of illness, for instance, is grounded in behavior (what we should and should not do to stay healthy), not microbes. Thus it seems incredible that heating milk could render it safer to drink or that injecting dead viruses into our bodies, as done in vaccination, could confer immunity to live strains of the disease. Likewise, our intuitive theory of geology assumes that the earth is a static object, not a dynamic system, and thus we find it inconceivable that humans could be changing the earth itself, causing earthquakes though hydraulic fracking or global warming though carbon emission.

Intuitive theories are a double-edged sword. On one hand, they broaden our perspective of the phenomena they seek to explain and refine our interactions with those phenomena because holding an intuitive theory is better than holding no theory at all. On the other hand, they close our minds to ideas and observations that are inconsistent with those theories, and they keep us from discovering the true nature of how things work. They can cause us not just to misconceive reality but to be blind to reality—to ignore facts and findings that definitively refute those theories. Thus, my goal in writing this book is to introduce you, the reader, to your own intuitive theories and to help you appreciate when and how those theories may lead you astray.

In this book, I hope to convince you of two main ideas. The first is that we do, in fact, get the world wrong—that our intuitive theories in several domains of knowledge carve up the world into entities and processes that do not actually exist. The second is that, to get the world right, we need to do more than just change our beliefs; we need to change the very concepts that articulate those beliefs. That is, to get the world right, we cannot simply refine our intuitive theories; we must dismantle them and rebuild them from their foundations. Galileo once decreed that "all truths are easy to understand once they are discovered; the point is to discover them," but he was wrong. There are many, many truths that are not easy to understand, because they defy our earliest-developing and most easily accessed ideas about how the world works. This book is a story of those truths: why they initially elude us and how we can come to grasp them.

✦ ✦ ✦

THE IDEA THAT we construct intuitive theories strikes many, at first, as an overly intellectualized view of how we think about the world. Why would a nonphysicist construct a theory of motion or a theory of matter? Why would a nonbiologist construct a theory of inheritance or a theory of evolution? We do so because physics and biology are inescapable aspects of human life; we are immersed in physical and biological phenomena every day.

We may not care about motion in the abstract, but we care about lifting boxes and pouring cereal, riding bicycles, and throwing balls. We may not care about matter in the abstract, but we care about melting ice and boiling water, preventing rust, and lighting fires. Likewise, we care about inheritance insofar as we want to know how likely it is we'll go bald or whether we are predisposed to cancer, and we care about evolution insofar as we want to know why bacteria develop drug resistance or where dogs came from. While few of us can articulate a detailed theory of matter that can explain both rusting and burning or a detailed theory of evolution that can explain both drug resistance and canine domestication, we have coherent and systematic ideas about those phenomena nonetheless.

Psychologists call intuitive theories *intuitive* because these ideas are our first attempt to understand the phenomena around us, before we learn scientific theories of those same phenomena. They call intuitive theories *theories* because these ideas embody a specific kind of knowledge: causal knowledge. Causal knowledge is an understanding of cause-and-effect relationships. It allows us to make inferences from our observations—inferences about why something happened in the past (explanation) or what is likely to happen in the future (prediction).

Much of the causal knowledge embodied by our intuitive theories is learned through experience, but at least some of that knowledge is innate. Whether a piece of knowledge is learned or innate is an empirical question—a question that psychologists answer by studying people of various ages and experiences. Studies with young infants, for instance, suggest that many of our expectations about motion and matter are innate. Studies with adults from different cultures, on the other hand, suggest that many of our expectations about illness and cosmology are shaped by what we hear from the people around us. Nevertheless, all of our intuitive theories are shaped both by innate expectations and by lived experiences. Infants may come into the world with expectations about the behavior of physical objects, but those expectations are further refined by their experience interacting with objects. Likewise, different cultures may subscribe to different theories of illness, but all such theories are grounded in the shared experience of what illness actually looks like (e.g., coughing, congestion, fevers).

Intuitive theories vary not just in their source but also in their assumptions about causality. Most theories posit causal mechanisms of a natural (i.e., ordinary) flavor, but some posit mechanisms of a supernatural flavor. Causal mechanisms of a natural flavor are, in principle, observable and controllable. They are often labeled with scientific terminology—for example, *heat*, *inertia*, *gene*, *natural selection*—but they do not actually correspond to scientific ideas. What scientists mean by a term like *heat* (energy transfer at the molecular level) is a far cry from what nonscientists mean by the same term (an immaterial substance that flows in and out of objects and can be trapped or contained). Causal mechanisms of a supernatural flavor, on the other hand, are beyond the observation and control of mere mortals. Those mechanisms have no counterpart in science—for example, *karma, witchcraft, souls, God*—but they still provide systematic explanations for natural phenomena (e.g., displeased ancestors) and systematic means of responding to those phenomena (e.g., sacrificial offerings). And supernatural explanations are often no less substantive than natural ones. Karma, for instance, is no less substantive an explanation for why we get sick than "cold weather" or "bad air," and divine creation is no less substantive an explanation for where species come from than "transmutation" (a sudden change in form) or "spontaneous generation."

Given that we live in a thoroughly scientific world, you might wonder whether intuitive theories are a dying breed—something we constructed in the past, for want of scientific information, but we will stop constructing in the future as scientific information becomes more available and more accessible. Rest assured, intuitive theories are *not* a dying breed. They are a permanent fixture of human cognition because they are the handiwork of children, and children are not likely to be affected by changes in the availability or accessibility of scientific information. It's not because children have shorter attention spans than adults have or because children are less interested in the natural world than adults are. It's because children lack the concepts needed to encode the scientific information we might teach them.

Take, for instance, the concept of heat. Children can sense an object's warmth—or how efficiently the object transfers heat to them or from them—but they cannot actually sense its heat, as humans have no sensory apparatus for registering the collective motion of a system's molecules. To understand the scientific concept of heat, children must learn a molecular theory of matter. We do, of course, teach children a molecular theory of matter but not until they have reached middle school, and by that time, they have already constructed an intuitive theory of heat—a theory that treats heat as a substance rather than as a process (discussed in Chapter 3). We could attempt to forestall this event by introducing a molecular theory of matter earlier in children's education, but a molecular theory is itself counterintuitive. How do you explain a molecule to a preschooler, let alone an electron or a chemical bond? And how do you forestall a child from mapping thermal language—*heat, hot, cold, cool*—to concepts that the child already understands, which, in this case, are concepts like *substance, containment,* and *flow*?

Clearly, many of us do learn a scientific concept of heat, but the task is not trivial. It requires devising an entirely new framework for thinking about thermal phenomena—a framework that differs in kind from the one we create on our own. Psychologists call this type of learning *conceptual change*. This is not your run-of-the-mill learning, like learning the traits of an unfamiliar animal or the history of an unfamiliar country. Psychologists call that kind of learning *knowledge enrichment*. What differentiates conceptual change from knowledge enrichment is whether, at the outset of learning, we possess concepts capable of making sense of the information we need to learn.

Knowledge enrichment is the process of using old concepts to acquire new beliefs, as when we use the concepts of *whales*, *breathing*, and *air* to acquire the belief that whales breathe air. Conceptual change, on the other hand, is the process of acquiring new concepts or, really, new types of concepts. If I told you that a species of mouse in the Amazon eats humans, I will have invited you to entertain a new concept—the Amazonian man-eating mouse—but that concept is just a subtype of other concepts you already know (*mouse*, which is a subtype of *animal*, which is a subtype of *living thing*). We have no trouble learning new instances of preexisting types; that's just knowledge enrichment in disguise. The trouble comes in learning new types.

An analogy with Legos is useful here. A basic Lego set consists of strictly rectangular blocks. With enough rectangular blocks, you can build anything, from a life-size giraffe to a life-size statue of Conan O'Brian (both of which have been built). But there are certain structures that you cannot build: cars with wheels that roll, planes with propellers that turn, cranes with hooks that lift. To build such structures, you need to supplement your supply of rectangular blocks with new, specialty pieces: wheels, axles, gears, and crankshafts. Any vehicle you try to build without those pieces will be ineffective or incomplete. We can approximate a car, but we can't actually build a car; wheels and axles are a necessity.

Much like building an operational Lego car, building a scientific understanding of the world requires resources that are unavailable to the novice learner—that is, to a child. Those resources are concepts like *electricity*, *density*, *velocity*, *planet*, *organ*, *virus*, and *common ancestor*. Concepts are quite literally the building blocks of thought, and like building blocks, they have particular structures and functions. Entertaining the thought "humans share a common ancestor with daffodils" is not possible without the concept *common ancestor*, and entertaining the thought "water is denser

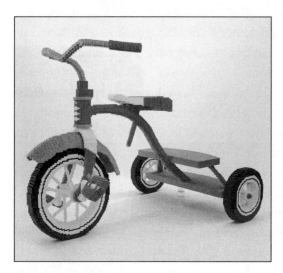

Basic Lego blocks can be used to approximate a moving vehicle, like this life-size tricycle (by artist Sean Kenney), but specialty pieces are required to build a vehicle that actually moves.

than ice" is not possible without the concept *density*. Those concepts are not part of our innate knowledge; nor are they learned from everyday experience with the physical world. They require conceptual change.

Conceptual change is a rare, hard-won achievement. It is difficult to initiate and difficult to complete, as I will try to make clear from specific instances of conceptual change presented in each chapter. At this point, however, I hope it is becoming apparent that intuitive theories and conceptual change are intrinsically linked. We construct intuitive theories of natural phenomena because constructing scientific theories of those phenomena requires conceptual change. But to achieve conceptual change, we must overhaul intuitive theories constructed in the absence of a scientific theory. Why we get the world wrong (intuitive theories) is our answer to how to get the world right (conceptual change), but getting the world right cannot happen without first getting the world wrong. It's a circular notion but not hopelessly circular. We are, after all, capable of getting the world right.

✦ ✦ ✦

INTUITIVE THEORIES ARE a prime source of misconceptions, but they are not the only source of misconceptions. Most of our misconceptions are simple factual errors—typos of the mind. Many people believe that we use only 10 percent of our brain and that the taste buds on our tongue are divided into distinct sections, but neither belief is true. These misconceptions do not signify a profound confusion about brains or tongues; they are just by-products of misinformation.

Distinguishing factual errors from deep-seated misconceptions is critical if we hope to identify (and study) intuitive theories. Many psychologists have grappled with this issue and have come to identify three hallmarks that set intuitive theories apart from other sources of misconceptions. First, intuitive theories are *coherent*; they embody a logically consistent set of beliefs and expectations. Second, intuitive theories are *widespread*; they are shared by people of different ages, cultures, and historical periods. Third, intuitive theories are *robust*; they are resistant to change in the face of counterevidence or counterinstruction.

To get a better sense of these hallmarks, consider the following two thought experiments, which are designed to pump your intuition about physical motion. First, imagine you're standing in a large, open field holding a gun. You aim the gun at the horizon and shoot a bullet parallel to the ground. As you pull the trigger, you drop a second bullet from the same height as the gun. Which bullet hits the ground first, the one you shot or the one you dropped? Second, imagine you're in the crow's nest of a ship sailing at full speed across the open sea. Next to you is a cannonball. You drop the cannonball out of the crow's nest and watch it fall. Where does it land, on the deck of the ship or in the water behind the ship?

If you're like most people, you predicted that the dropped bullet would hit the ground before the shot bullet, reasoning that the shot bullet had been imparted a forward-propelling force that would keep it aloft longer. You also predicted that the cannonball would fall behind the ship, reasoning that the ship would sail out from underneath the cannonball as it fell straight down. Neither prediction is correct, however.

The shot bullet would have no extra force keeping it aloft. As soon as both bullets were released, they would be subject to a single force—gravity—and gravity would bring them to the ground at the same time, albeit hundreds of yards apart. As for the cannonball, it would hit the deck of the ship directly below the crow's nest because the ball would have the same horizontal velocity as the ship on which it was carried. It's true that the ship would sail out from beneath the cannonball's release point, but the cannonball would not fall straight down. It would trace a parabolic path, produced by the combination of its horizontal velocity and its downward acceleration due to gravity, in the same direction as the ship.

Most people's predictions in these two situations are wrong, but that's not because there's something weird about the situations; both involve nothing more than falling objects. Our predictions are wrong because they arise from an intuitive theory of motion that assumes that objects move if, and only if, they have been imparted an internal "force," or *impetus*. The term "force" has been put in quotations here, because our intuitive notion of force is not what physicists mean by force (the product of mass and acceleration). Forces may change an object's motion, but they are not properties *of* objects. They are interactions *between* objects (as discussed in Chapter 5).

That said, our nonscientific beliefs about force and the relation between force and motion are highly coherent. Take, for instance, the two misconceptions primed above: the misconception that an object with horizontal motion (a shot bullet) will succumb to gravity less quickly than will an object with no such motion (a dropped bullet) and the misconception that a carried object (a cannonball) does not inherit the horizontal motion of its carrier (a ship). These misconceptions may seem unrelated, but they are products of the same underlying belief: that projectiles, and only projectiles, have forces imparted to them. We attribute a forward-propelling force to the shot bullet but not to the dropped bullet and not to the cannonball (which was also dropped). The force we attribute to the shot bullet is thought to keep it aloft for longer than the dropped bullet, whereas the *absence* of such a force is thought to cause the cannonball to fall straight down.

These ideas, though wrong, are internally consistent. They are also incredibly widespread. Impetus-based misconceptions have been found in students of all ages, from preschoolers to college undergraduates. They have been revealed in China, Israel, Mexico, Turkey, Ukraine, the Philippines, and the United States. And they have been revealed even in students who have taken multiple years of college-level physics. You can earn a bachelor's degree in physics and still be an impetus theorist at heart.

This consistency across individuals extends backward in time as well. People have always been impetus theorists, including professional physicists of centuries past. Galileo, for instance, explained projectile motion as follows: "The body moves upward, provided the impressed motive force is greater than the resisting weight. But since that force is continually

This drawing by sixteenth-century scholar Walther Hermann Rhyff depicts a cannonball falling straight down after its "internal force," or impetus, has dissipated—a path a real projectile would never take, as real projectiles follow parabolic paths.

weakened, it will finally become so diminished that it will no longer overcome the weight of the body." This explanation smacks of impetus, not inertia, and it is the same kind of explanation most of us would provide today, four centuries later. No one today would use the phrase "impressed motive force," but we would express those same ideas with terms like "internal energy," "force of motion," or "momentum." To a physicist, momentum is the product of mass and velocity, but to a nonphysicist, momentum is simply impetus.

What is remarkable about the sustained popularity of an intuitive theory like impetus theory, from Galileo's time to today, is that we've always had reason to doubt it. Impetus theory makes predictions that are never confirmed, because objects move in ways that do not actually accord with those predictions. When a cannonball is shot from a cannon, it traces a fully parabolic path; it never drops straight down as impetus theory predicts it should (because impetus theory predicts that the cannonball will eventually lose its impetus and succumb to gravity). Yet, if we are asked to draw the trajectory of a cannonball shot from a cannon, we draw paths that begin parabolic but end straight down—paths we have never observed, or ever could observe, in real life. Impetus theory can successfully explain some aspects of reality, but it renders us blind to the aspects it cannot.

Impetus theory is not unique in this regard. All intuitive theories are coherent (in their internal logic), widespread (across people), and robust (in the face of counterevidence), and this trifecta gives them a surprising amount of resilience. While we can learn new, more accurate theories of a phenomenon, we can't seem to *unlearn* our intuitive theories. They continue to lurk in the recesses of our minds long after we have abandoned them as our preferred theory. Intuitive theories are always there, influencing our thoughts and behaviors in subtle yet appreciable ways.

A prime example can be seen in our judgments of whether something is alive. To a four-year-old, what makes something alive is that it moves on its own. Four-year-olds thus deny that plants are alive because plants do not appear to move on their own. Eight-year-olds, on the other hand, recognize that plants are alive because children this age have stopped identifying life with mobility and have started identifying life with metabolic processes, like growth and reproduction (discussed in Chapter 8). The childish misconception that plants are not alive would thus appear to be erased from our minds within the first decade of life. Nevertheless, when college-educated adults are asked to verify the life status of plants and animals as quickly as possible, they take longer to verify that plants are alive than to verify that animals are alive. They are also less accurate for plants, judging plants as "not alive" more often than judging animals as "not alive."

Findings like these, which have been replicated in several domains of science (e.g., astronomy, mechanics, evolution) using several types of methods (e.g., perception tasks, memory tasks, inference tasks), have radically altered our understanding of conceptual change. Because conceptual change requires restructuring our knowledge, not just enriching our knowledge, it has long been assumed that conceptual change erases preexisting concepts in the same way that restructuring a house erases its preexisting floor plans. But the discovery that scientific theories never completely overwrite a person's intuitive theories suggests that a better metaphor for conceptual change is a *palimpsest*, or a manuscript in which one document has been physically recorded on top of another.

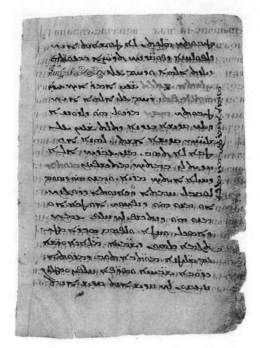

As we acquire scientific theories of the world, our intuitive theories are never completely erased from our minds. They remain etched beneath the scientific theory, similar to how early transcriptions remain etched beneath later transcriptions in a medieval palimpsest.

Palimpsests were common in the Middle Ages because parchment was scarce, and the monks who recorded documents on parchment would often reuse old pieces of parchment without fully erasing the earlier contents. Like a palimpsest, our minds record new theories (scientific theories) on top of old theories (intuitive theories) such that both theories can become active at the same time, providing competing explanations or competing predictions. Motion-based theories of life compete with metabolic theories, substance-based theories of heat compete with process-based theories, and impetus-based theories of motion compete with inertia-based theories. In some cases, our scientific knowledge may be nothing more than a veneer, thinly covering misconceptions forged decades earlier, when we were children.

✦ ✦ ✦

IN A RECENT article titled "I Know What's Best for the Health of My Family, and It's Magical Thinking," a satirist pokes fun at science denial by channeling a well-meaning yet science-denying mother. "I'm not stupid," she writes. "I went to college. I took science classes. So I know about microbiology, infection control, anatomy, physiology, and all that. I am fully aware that the scientific method—including use of a control group, randomization, double-blind studies, and the peer review method—is the best tool we humans have of unlocking the secrets of the natural world to find ways of curing disease. Science is great. It's done a lot of good for the world, to be sure. It's just not right for me or my family."

Well captured here is the paradoxical nature of science denial in a world dominated by science. Most science deniers are not ignorant of science; they are *skeptical* of science. Their skepticism arises from many sources—political beliefs, religious beliefs, cultural identity—but in this book, I hope to convince you that at least one of those sources is intuitive theories.

As someone who has chosen to read a book on intuitive theories and how they blind us to reality, you are probably not an ardent science denier yourself. But you may know science deniers, and you certainly live in a society whose policies and practices are shaped by science deniers. More importantly, you probably deny science in unintentional and unrecognized ways. Some of your attitudes are likely based on nonscientific considerations, and some of your behaviors probably run counter to sound scientific advice. No one could be an expert on all areas of science, let alone apply that expertise to all areas of life, but we can be more informed about the cognitive obstacles to doing so.

Accordingly, this book aims to show you what your intuitive theories are like and how those theories influence your beliefs, attitudes, and behaviors. The first half of the book is devoted to intuitive theories of the physical world (theories of matter, energy, gravity, motion, the cosmos, and the earth), and the second half to intuitive theories of the biological world (theories of life, growth, inheritance, illness, adaptation, and ancestry). Each theory is unique in its origin, its pattern of development, and its relation to everyday experience. Some theories are held explicitly by children but only implicitly by adults, biasing our thoughts and behaviors at the periphery of conscious experience. Others are held explicitly even by adults, biasing our thoughts and behaviors in the here and now. Together, these two types of cases underscore the pervasiveness and perniciousness of intuitive theories—how they operate across the lifespan and within the minds of even the most scientifically literate people.

To be sure, intuitive theories are not all bad. If they were, we wouldn't construct them. They furnish us with a reasonable approximation of reality and thus a reasonable basis for intervening on that reality. Intuitive theories help us *get by*. Scientific theories, on the other hand, help us *thrive*. They furnish us with fundamentally more accurate conceptions of reality and thus fundamentally more powerful tools for predicting it and controlling it. Studies have shown, for instance, that the better we understand the biological mechanisms of cold and flu transmission, the more likely we are to take precautions against catching colds and flu. The better we understand thermal equilibrium, the more likely we are to optimize our home heating and cooling practices. And the better we understand how the body metabolizes food, the more likely we are to maintain a healthy body mass index.

Failing to understand science has palpable consequences as well. Thousands have fallen ill to preventable diseases because they intentionally consumed unpasteurized milk or deliberately avoided vaccination. By blinding us to science, intuitive theories impede not just how we think but how we live—the choices we make, the advice we take, the goals we pursue. In the chapters that follow, I hope to convince you that it's not just science that's best for the health of your family; it's also *knowledge* of science that's best.

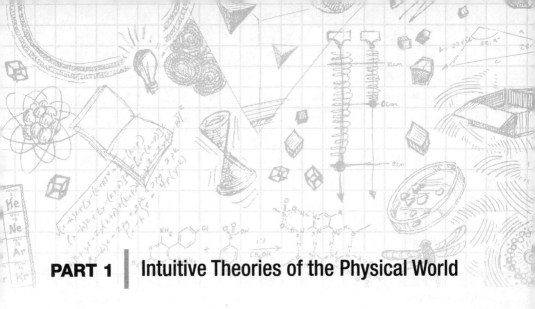

PART 1 | Intuitive Theories of the Physical World

2 | MATTER

What Is the World Made Of?
How Do Those Components Interact?

WHEN WE WATCH A CANDLE BURN OR A POT OF WATER BOIL, WE watch matter seemingly vanish into thin air. The wax disappears from the candle stick and the water disappears from the pot, but neither has truly vanished. They've just changed state, from visible wax to invisible carbon dioxide (and water vapor) and from visible water to invisible steam. Matter may appear ephemeral, but it's actually indestructible. Chemists tell us that matter can be neither created nor destroyed, but common sense tells us that matter comes and goes—here one moment, gone the next.

This commonsense view of matter is held by people of all ages, but it is most easily demonstrated in children. You can demonstrate it for yourself if you know a preschooler who can serve as a test subject. Get two transparent containers: one tall and thin and one short and squat. Fill the short, squat container half full of water, and show the child. Then pour the water from the short, squat container into the tall, thin container and ask, "Is there now more water, less water, or the same amount of water as there was before?" The water column in the second container will be higher than it was in the first, so the child will probably claim that there is now *more* water.

Preschoolers claim that there's more liquid in the tall, thin container on the right (bottom image) than in the short, squat container on the left (top image), even when they witness the liquid being poured from one container into the other.

Transferring water from one container to another is all it takes to convince the child that you've performed an impossible feat: you've made more water.

If you have ever taken an introductory psychology course, you may recognize this parlor trick as Piaget's *conservation task*. Jean Piaget was a Swiss psychologist who pioneered the study of child development in the early 1900s. He discovered several intriguing phenomena: childhood realism (mistaking appearances for reality), childhood animism (attributing life to nonliving entities), childhood artificialism (attributing human design to nature), and childhood egocentrism (assuming others know what you know). But the phenomenon he is best known for is conservation, or children's lack thereof.

There are many versions of the conservation task, and young children fail them all. In another version, children are shown two equal-sized balls of clay and are asked to confirm that they contain the same amount of clay, have the same weight, and take up the same amount of space. (If a child denies they do, he or she is asked to nullify the difference by moving pinches of clay from one ball to the other). One of the balls is then flattened into a pancake, and children are asked whether the two configurations of clay—the ball and the pancake—still contain the same amount of clay (conservation of mass), still have the same weight (conservation of weight), and still take up the same amount of space (conservation of volume). Preschoolers typically answer all three questions no, and elementary-schoolers typically answer one or two questions no. Not until middle school do children reliably recognize that flattening a ball of clay does not change its mass, weight, or volume.

Piaget's explanation for children's lack of conservation was that they have not yet acquired an operational logic of thought. He termed their thinking "preoperational," and he believed this type of thinking permeated all aspects of their mental life, not just their reasoning about conservation. Young children's inferences about physical causality and their evaluations of moral behavior were deemed preoperational as well. Psychologists today no longer endorse the distinction between operational and preoperational thought. They doubt Piaget's conclusions for a number of reasons, the most prominent of which is that children develop logical competence at different rates in different domains. For instance, children master the logic of natural language (grammar) and the logic of natural numbers (counting) before they enter school, but they master the logic of deductive reasoning (proofs) and the logic of proportional reasoning (fractions) only after a decade of formal schooling, if then.

Even within the domain of conservation, children learn to conserve mass before they learn to conserve weight, and they learn to conserve weight before they learn to conserve volume. Conservation is not a unitary notion, acquired in full or not at all. It is a consequence of knowing whether specific transformations change specific properties of specific materials. Flattening a ball of clay will not change its volume, but heating it will, and heating a ball of clay will not change its weight, but sending it to the moon will. A lot of matter-specific knowledge is required to pass conservation tasks, which makes conservation an odd task for studying cognitive development in general. Following Piaget, developmental psychologists have conducted hundreds of studies of conservation, but I doubt they would have studied conservation much at all if Piaget had not initially steered the field in that direction. Material phenomena are too mysterious and too varied to expect young children to instinctively know when material properties are conserved and when they are not.

Matter is conserved across many transformations where it blatantly appears not to be: water evaporating from an open container, steam escaping from a boiling pot, hot doors expanding in their frames, logs burning to ash. And many properties of matter are *not* conserved across transformations that conserve matter as a whole: the volume of water when frozen, the elasticity of a rubber band when stretched, the granularity of salt when dissolved, the viscosity of cake batter when baked. Preschoolers' belief that transferring water from a short, squat container into a tall, thin container increases the waters' mass can hardly be classified as a logical error, when the reality of material transformations is so opaque.

To be fair, Piaget was interested in conservation not just as it pertained to matter but as it pertained to quantities in general, including numerical quantities and spatial quantities. Rearranging a collection of toys does not change its number, in the same way that squashing a ball of clay does not change its weight, and Piaget wanted to know when and how children grasped the necessity of that conclusion. Piaget's successors, on the other hand, were often captivated by conservation errors for a different reason: those errors are incredibly persistent.

Perhaps the most straightforward approach to correcting children's conservation errors is to instruct children to attend to multiple dimensions of a material transformation—say, the spread of water in a container and not just its height. But this kind of instruction has little effect on their errors, particularly if children are tested weeks or months later. In one study, several hundred children received one of four types of instruction on conservation. Some were provided with explicit feedback on their conservation judgments; some were encouraged to make judgments before witnessing the relevant transformations; some were shown how those transformations could easily be reversed; and some were instructed on the logical reasons why mass and volume are conserved across material transformations. Children's understanding of conservation was then assessed three times over five months. The results were discouraging: children's understanding of conservation did not improve at any time under any form of instruction.

Surprisingly, the instruction used in this study, as well as the instruction used in many other studies, lacked content about matter itself. Piaget characterized children's conservation errors as failures of logic, and accordingly, many psychologists have attempted to correct those errors with logic-based instruction. An alternative approach, however, is to focus on the causes of conservation—namely, that material substances are composed of smaller particles and that those particles can be neither created nor destroyed (outside of a nuclear reaction). Any chemist asked to teach children about the conservation of matter would most likely start with molecules, not "equivalence relations" or "quantitative invariants," and taking such an approach has indeed proven effective (as discussed later on). Thus, several decades after Piaget introduced the conservation task as a measure of children's logical reasoning, we now know that children fail that task not because they are illogical but because they misunderstand the nature of matter.

✦ ✦ ✦

ATOMS ARE THE constituents of matter, comprising all solids, liquids, and gases. "Do not trust atoms," warns one internet meme. "They make up everything." Children cannot perceive atoms and are thus ignorant of their existence, as were all humans before the pioneering work of nineteenth-century chemists like John Dalton (who discovered the principles of chemical synthesis) and J. J. Thomson (who discovered the electron). Nothing about our perceptual experience of matter would suggest that matter is particulate in nature. Much of the matter around us comes in discrete, bounded packages: rocks, trees, logs, bricks, tables, chairs, shoes, hats, pencils, hammers. These objects betray no sign of their molecular composition. They appear continuous and holistic.

In addition to being unaware of the microscopic components of macroscopic objects, we also misperceive the properties of those objects. All matter has weight and volume, but humans are not built to detect weight and volume. We are built to detect *heft* (felt weight) and *bulk* (visible volume). Heft differs from weight in that it conflates weight with density; objects of the same weight can differ in heft if they also differ in density (e.g., a ten-pound piece of steel feels heavier than a ten-pound piece of Styrofoam). Bulk differs from volume in that bulk conflates volume with surface area; objects of the same volume can differ in bulk if they also differ in surface area (e.g., a blanket in a heap is bulkier than a blanket that is folded). The subjective nature of heft and bulk allows them to vary in ways that weight and volume do not. All matter has weight, but not all matter has heft (e.g., snowflakes, dust). Likewise, all matter has volume, but not all matter has bulk (e.g., helium, steam). This collection of perceptions—that matter is continuous, that matter has heft, that matter has bulk—forms the basis of children's first theory of matter: a "holistic" theory, eventually replaced in late adolescence by a "particulate" theory.

Conservation errors are consistent with a holistic theory of matter in that changing the appearance of a substance—its height, its width, its spread—is deemed synonymous with changing the substance itself. But conservation errors are not the only evidence of holistic theories. Other evidence comes from children's judgments of what is matter and what is not. When asked whether solid objects are composed of matter (e.g., rocks, trees, logs, bricks), preschoolers and elementary schoolers unanimously agree that they are. They also agree that nonsolid substances are composed of matter if those substances can be seen and touched (e.g., water, salt, juice, jelly). But they vacillate on whether less tangible material substances (e.g., dust, clouds, ink-blots, bubbles) are composed of matter. They also vacillate on whether visible, yet immaterial entities (e.g., shadows, rainbows, lightning, sunshine) are composed of matter. Children are particularly confused about air. They know that air is all around them and that they take air into their lungs, but they judge it as nonmaterial. They also claim that air has no volume—for example, that the air inside an empty box takes up no space at all. Air defies the very core of children's holistic theories of matter, as it has volume that cannot be seen (no bulk) and weight that cannot be felt (no heft).

Children's holistic theories are also evident from their predictions of sinking and floating. The primary determinant of whether an object will sink or float is its average density, but children have no sensory apparatus for gauging an object's density. They can only gauge heft and bulk, which leads to systematic patterns of error. In one study, four-year-olds were shown blocks of varying weights and sizes and asked to predict whether each would sink or float. Most children adopted a criterion based on weight: they predicted that blocks under one hundred grams would float and that blocks over a hundred grams would sink, regardless of whether the density of those blocks was above or below the density of water. Thus, children's predictions were correct for light blocks with below-threshold densities and heavy blocks with above-threshold densities, but incorrect for light blocks with above-threshold densities and heavy blocks with below-threshold densities. Other studies have found that children can be prompted to integrate weight and size, thereby approximating density, but they rarely do so on their own. Density is simply not salient on a holistic theory of matter.

MATERIAL
TANGIBLE

MATERIAL
SEMITANGIBLE

IMMATERIAL
SEMITANGIBLE

IMMATERIAL
INTANGIBLE

Children initially identify matter with tangibility. So they would correctly judge that bricks are composed of matter and that ideas are not, but they would be unsure whether semitangible entities like bubbles or shadows are composed of matter.

An even purer demonstration of children's holistic theories comes from studies in which children are asked to contemplate a material transformation that would be impossible to perceive: microscopic division. Children are shown a piece of Styrofoam and are asked to imagine what would happen to the Styrofoam's mass, weight, and volume if it were halved ad infinitum. The interview below, between a researcher and a third-grader, illustrates how children younger than ten typically respond:

RESEARCHER: Imagine it is possible to divide this tiny piece in half and in half again. If we kept dividing the tiny pieces in half and in half, would the Styrofoam matter ever disappear completely?
CHILD: Yes. After a year, it would stop. There wouldn't be anything left.
RESEARCHER: Now imagine a tiny piece of Styrofoam, so tiny that you couldn't see it. Would that tiny piece take up any space at all?
CHILD: No, because if you have really big things on a table and kept it in the corner, it wouldn't take up any space.
RESEARCHER: Would that tiny piece have any weight?

CHILD: Nothing at all.
RESEARCHER: Zero grams?
CHILD: Yes, because if you took a tiny piece off, it would just feel like your own skin because it doesn't weigh anything.

Note how this child explicitly equates volume with bulk (the tiny piece could be "kept in a corner") and weight with heft ("it would just feel like your skin"). Older children, in contrast, provide a qualitatively different pattern of results:

RESEARCHER: Imagine it is possible to divide this tiny piece in half and in half again. If we kept dividing the tiny pieces in half and in half, would the Styrofoam matter ever disappear completely?
CHILD: Half of that is still something, and half of that is very, very tiny, but it's still something. There's no one object that half of it is nothing.
RESEARCHER: If we kept dividing the tiny pieces in half and in half again, would we ever get to a piece that does not take up any space?
CHILD: No. No matter how tiny [it is], as long as it's matter, it takes up space.
RESEARCHER: Would we ever get to a piece that has no weight?
CHILD: It would be unmeasurable, but it would have weight. If a tiny person tried to pick it up, it would have weight to him.

This sixth-grader clearly views matter as indestructible, attributing weight and volume to matter even when that matter is too small to be seen. She was inclined to identify weight with heft, like the child in the previous example, but she recognized that her own perception of heft, or lack thereof, was irrelevant to whether the object still had weight (hence, the appeal to "a tiny person").

One final source of evidence for holistic theories is the confusion that children experience as they begin to learn about gases, typically in middle school. Middle-schoolers might accept that gases are composed of matter, but they have trouble connecting the macroscopic properties of gases to microscopic particles. Children initially construe gases as holistic, homogenous entities just as they initially construed solids. This notion leads them to deny that gas particles are in constant motion, that gas particles are separated by empty space, and that the spacing of gas particles depends on the volume of the gas as a whole. Many adults deny these ideas as well. We may

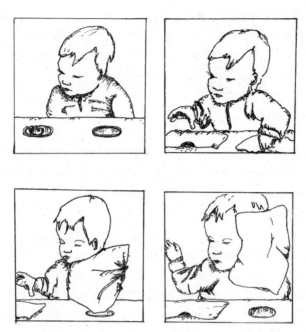

Infants under twelve months have difficulty retrieving hidden objects if the objects are hidden in different locations from one trial to the next, an error known as the "A-not-B" error. Here an infant makes that error, searching for a hidden object (a toy hidden under a cloth) in the wrong location (the right container). Curiously, infants sometimes look to an object's correct location (the left container) while reaching toward an incorrect location.

know a lot of things about the relation between a solid's macroscopic properties (e.g., buoyancy) and its microscopic properties (e.g., density), but we have to learn those ideas anew for gases.

✦ ✦ ✦

CHILDREN'S UNDERSTANDING OF matter is an outgrowth of infants' understanding of matter, and for many years, psychologists believed that infants had no such understanding at all. Infants were thought to lack *object permanence*, or the insight that objects continue to exist even when they are out of view.

The development of object permanence appeared to be slow and protracted. Below four months of age, infants make no attempt to reach for a desired object when that object is hidden behind a screen or under a cloth.

Between four and eight months, infants retrieve an object that is partly hidden from view, but they will not attempt to retrieve an object fully hidden from view. Between eight and twelve months, infants will retrieve objects that are fully hidden, but they make a curious error if those objects are hidden in the same location for several trials (location A) and then switched to a new location (location B): they search for the object in the old location before switching to the new location, a behavior known as the *A-not-B error*. Finally, between twelve and eighteen months, infants come to retrieve objects that are hidden from view, regardless of whether those objects were hidden in the same location on previous trials or in a different location.

The development of object permanence was first charted by Piaget, the same psychologist who discovered conservation errors. He concluded that infants have no innate appreciation of the permanence of matter—let alone the conservation of matter—but they develop such an appreciation over the first year of life. The problem with this conclusion is that it was based on data that conflate two types of errors: conceptual errors and motor errors. Infants may fail to retrieve hidden objects because they have forgotten their existence (a conceptual error), but they may also fail to do so because they are unable to execute a successful reach (a motor error). Watching a ten-month-old infant make the A-not-B error can convey the impression that the failure is a motor error, not a conceptual error, because infants who search for objects in the wrong location often *look to* the correct one. Their eyes reveal knowledge that their hands seemingly cannot act on.

One way to disentangle conceptual errors from motor errors is to use different methods to assess infants' expectations about objects—methods that don't require the motor skills of physically retrieving an object. Such a method was devised in the 1970s, near the end of Piaget's life, and is known as *preferential looking*. This method takes advantage of the fact that infants, like everyone else, look longer at unexpected events (e.g., one object passing through another) than at expected events (e.g., one object bumping into another). By measuring how long infants look at one set of events compared with another, psychologists have discovered that infants hold rich and varied expectations long before they are able to act on those expectations, let alone articulate them.

In one famous study, the researchers familiarized five-month-old infants with a rectangular screen that pivoted on its bottom edge, rotating back and

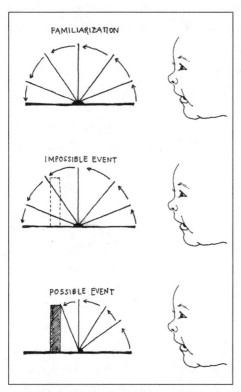

FAMILIARIZATION

IMPOSSIBLE EVENT

POSSIBLE EVENT

Infants as young as four months look longer at a rotating fan that appears to pass through a solid box (impossible event) than at one that appears to stop when it makes contact with the box (possible event).

forth like a fan. The researchers then placed a small box behind the screen, out of view of the infant, and the infant watched one of two events: either the screen stopped prematurely in its path, seemingly making contact with the box (still hidden behind the screen), or the screen continued on its path as before, seemingly passing through the box. An adult watching these two events would be surprised by the second event but unsurprised by the first and would thus look longer at the second event than at the first. Infants do the same. They look longer at the second event than at the first, which implies that they are surprised by the second event but not by the first.

This finding implies not only that infants expect objects to collide on contact (rather than pass through one another) but also that they keep track of objects hidden from view, making predictions about the behavior of visible objects (the moving screen) on the basis of their interactions with nonvisible objects (the box). Young infants thus demonstrate object permanence long before they are able to retrieve objects with their hands. In fact, infants expect a hidden box to interrupt the trajectory of a moving screen by just three months of age.

Infants of this age also expect objects to move on contact with other objects and to trace continuous paths as they move. When shown violations of these events—for example, objects moving on their own, without being contacted by other objects, or objects blipping in and out of existence—infants stare in disbelief. Such events are of course impossible, but wily researchers have figured out how to stage them using trick apparatuses or sleight of hand. Thus, contrary to what Piaget had thought, infants do hold expectations about objects—expectations that we continue to hold as adults. Infants do not, however, hold expectations about less cohesive forms of matter, like salt or sand. Their expectations about solidity, continuity, and contact are triggered only by discrete, bounded objects.

In one study, eight-month-old infants were tested on whether they could keep track of two types of entities deposited behind an opaque screen: piles of sand and solid objects that looked like piles of sand but moved cohesively (they were chunks of Styrofoam with sand glued to them). In the sand condition, the researchers poured one pile of sand behind the screen and then another. The screen was then lowered, revealing either two piles of sand or one. The infants looked equally long at both outcomes, indicating that they had no expectation about how many piles of sand should be behind the screen. In the object condition, infants watched the researchers place one object behind the screen and then another. The screen was then lowered, revealing either two objects or one. Now the infants looked reliably longer at the latter, indicating that they had expected both objects to continue to exist behind the screen.

The researchers worried that even though infants in the sand condition saw two instances of pouring (at two locations), they may have been uncertain whether the sand ended up in one pile or two. The researchers thus ran another experiment in which they poured sand behind two screens rather than one—screens separated by a sixteen-centimeter gap. When the screens were lowered, revealing either two piles of sand or one, the infants again looked equally long at both outcomes. They were not tracking the location of the sand in the way they had tracked the location of objects, even though the objects were designed to look identical to the sand (in a sand pile).

Human infants are not the only primates that track cohesive forms of matter but fail to track noncohesive ones. When the studies described above were repeated with lemurs, the results were the same: lemurs form precise expectations about the number of objects behind a screen but no expectations about the number of sand piles behind a screen.

Evolution seems to have equipped primates with the ability to track objects but not the ability to track less cohesive forms of matter. We can trace the identity of objects as they move through space, go out of view, or come into contact with other objects, but we can't even count piles of sand, at least not as infants. Of course, the abilities conferred to us by evolution are those that proved useful in furthering our survival and reproduction, and it's hard to see how tracking noncohesive substances would meet that criterion. We need to consume noncohesive substances for nourishment—milk and water in particular—but we do not need to track those substances across displacement in space. Nor do we need to perceive a connection between them and other material entities like solid objects. Conceiving of a rock as a bounded entity that can be lifted, carried, thrown, or hidden is infinitely more valuable to survival than conceiving of it as fundamentally similar to sand.

✦ ✦ ✦

So IF WE begin life thinking of matter as fundamentally holistic, how do we come to conceive of it as particulate? Telling children that matter is made of particles is not particularly helpful, because they are not prepared to engage with this information. They must first reorganize their understanding of matter—collapsing distinctions that are meaningful on a holistic theory but not a particulate theory and creating distinctions that are meaningful on a particulate theory but not a holistic theory. For instance, children must collapse the distinction between objects and noncohesive substances, coming to see both as matter, and they need to create distinctions between their perception of weight (heft) and the physical definition of weight and between their perception of volume (bulk) and the physical definition of volume. Only then can they entertain the concept of density, or weight per unit volume.

Density is, in a single property, the embodiment of a particulate theory. Only something with internal structure could be characterized as densely packed or loosely packed. But that structure is imperceptible to the naked eye, and accordingly, young children have no conception of density separate from weight. They do not use density to predict buoyancy, as discussed above; nor do they use density to differentiate types of materials. Consider the following task. You are given three blocks of metal—a block of lead measuring one inch per side and weighing 6.5 ounces; another block of lead measuring three inches per side and weighing 19.6 ounces; and a block of aluminum measuring five inches per side and weighing 7.8 ounces—and you are asked to determine which two blocks are made from the same type of metal. The blocks are covered with tape, so you can't use color as a clue.

What would you do? You would probably compare each block's weight to its size, realizing that the largest block (the aluminum block) is not as heavy for its size as the other two blocks (the lead blocks). Preschoolers and young elementary-schoolers find this task surprisingly difficult. They can discern which block is an outlier in terms of weight and which block is an outlier in terms of volume, but they cannot discern which block is an outlier in terms of weight per unit volume. Most children end up basing their judgments strictly on weight, pairing the 6.5-ounce lead block with the 7.8-ounce aluminum block.

This "mystery material" task was devised by the psychologist Carol Smith and her colleagues. Smith has studied children's intuitive theories of matter for over three decades. Most of her studies have centered on the concept of density, as children's understanding of density is a good metric of their understanding of matter in general. One approach that Smith has taken to teaching density, or mass per unit volume, is to analogize this imperceptible quantity to per-unit quantities that *can* be perceived. Pressure, for instance, is a per-unit quantity that can be detected by our skin (force per unit area). Tempo is per-unit quantity that can be detected by our ears (beats per unit time). Concentration is a per-unit quantity that can be detected by our tongue (molecules per unit volume). And crowdedness is a per-unit quantity that can be detected by our eyes (objects per unit area).

In one study, Smith introduced the concept of density by way of two other per-unit concepts: concentration and crowdedness. She and her colleagues taught seventh-graders how to differentiate the variables that enter into each per-unit quantity by having them solve two hypothetical murders. In the first murder, the victim drank poisoned Kool-Aid, and the children had to determine which suspect had prepared the Kool-Aid. They had to compare its concentration with the concentration of each suspect's preferred recipe for Kool-Aid—that is, the suspects' preferred amount of Kool-Aid mix per unit water. In the second murder, the victim ate a poisoned chocolate-chip cookie, and children had to determine which suspect had baked the cookie. To figure this out, the kids compared the crowdedness of the cookie's chips to the crowdedness of chips in each suspect's preferred recipe for chocolate-chip cookies—that is, the preferred number of chips per unit batter.

Smith assessed her students' understanding of concentration, crowdedness, and density by asking them to order, in increasing magnitude, solutions of different concentration, dot arrays of different crowdedness, and materials of different density (where each per-unit quantity was specified with easily computable values, like four teaspoons of sugar to two cups of water). Before the murder-mystery curriculum, the students were able to order the dot arrays by crowdedness but were unable to order the solutions by concentration or the materials by density. After the curriculum, students were then able to order the solutions by concentration, but they were still unable to order the materials by density. The conceptual gap between the training quantities (crowdedness and concentration) and the target quantity (density) was just too great.

In follow-up studies, Smith and her colleagues took a different approach. Rather than attempt to render density perceptible, they introduced students to material phenomena that were themselves perceptible but could only be explained in terms of density and its constituent variables: weight and volume. Over several weeks, students weighed objects too small to have heft (a fleck of glitter, a dot of ink) on a highly sensitive scale. They compared empty balloons to air-filled balloons on a balance scale. They deduced the volume of objects too small to measure with a ruler (one drop of water) from the volume of measurable quantities (one milliliter of water). They immersed objects of varying densities in liquids of varying densities. They measured the weight and volume of an iron ball before and after heating it. And they measured the weight of Alka-Seltzer tablets before and after vaporizing them.

Unlike the murder-mystery curriculum, this curriculum proved effective. Few students were able to order materials by density before the curriculum, but most could do so afterward. Likewise, few students categorized intangible substances (air, dust, smoke) as matter or attributed weight to microscopic objects (a tiny piece of Styrofoam) before the curriculum, but most did so afterward. Perhaps most noteworthy, students who failed Piaget's conservation tasks before the curriculum passed those tasks after the curriculum even though the topic of conservation was never specifically addressed.

Additional research by Smith and her colleagues has revealed that acquiring a particulate theory of matter has surprisingly widespread consequences—consequences that extend beyond the domain of matter and into the domain of number. Integers, like objects, can be divided into smaller components (fractions), yet children do not initially think of integers this way. They think of them simply as the endpoints of counting. Young children understand that numbers can be increased or decreased—by adding objects to the sets they label or removing objects from those sets—but young children have no idea that numbers can be *divided*. Numbers are seen as holistic and homogenous, similar to physical objects.

Intrigued by this parallel, Smith and her colleagues investigated whether understanding the divisibility of number develops in tandem with understanding the divisibility of matter. They did so by pairing the Styrofoam-division task described above with a number-division task. Here's a sample interview with a third-grader:

RESEARCHER: Are there any numbers between zero and one?
CHILD: No.
RESEARCHER: How about one-half?
CHILD: Yes, I think so.
RESEARCHER: About how many numbers are there between zero and one?
CHILD: A little, just zero and half, because it is halfway to one.
RESEARCHER: Suppose you divided two in half and got one, and then divided that number in half. Could you keep dividing forever?
CHILD: No, because if you just took that half a number, that would be zero and you can't divide zero.
RESEARCHER: Would you ever get to zero?
CHILD: Yes.

Some third-graders knew of the existence of fractions other than just one-half. One third-grader, for instance, noted "there's one-half, one-third, one-fourth, one over something all the way up to ten." But they denied that these fractions could themselves be divided. Older children, on the other hand, claimed not only that a fraction like one-fourth could be divided in half but also that it could be divided in half ad infinitum, as illustrated in this conversation with a fifth-grader:

RESEARCHER: Are there any numbers between zero and one?
CHILD: Yes.
RESEARCHER: Can you give an example?

CHILD: One-half or point-five.
RESEARCHER: About how many numbers are there between zero and one?
CHILD: A lot.
RESEARCHER: Suppose you divided two in half and got one, and then divided that number in half. Could you keep dividing forever?
CHILD: Yes, there always has to be something left when you divide it.
RESEARCHER: Would you ever get to zero?
CHILD: No, because there is an infinite number of numbers below one and above zero.

Critically, children's understanding of the divisibility of number tracks their understanding of the divisibility of matter. Children who claim that numbers cease to exist at some point in division also claim that material substances cease to have weight at some point in division, whereas children who claim that numbers continue to exist claim that material substances continue to have weight as well. Still, if one insight lags behind the other, it's the insight that numbers are infinitely divisible, meaning that children grasp the notion of infinite divisibility for material entities (objects) before they do so for immaterial entities (numbers).

Developing a more sophisticated understanding of matter may thus be a stepping-stone to developing a more sophisticated understanding of number. Infinite divisibility—and infinite density—are crucial insights that can be transferred from one domain to the other. Highlighting these parallels is actually a productive strategy for teaching fractions and other types of rational number, like decimals and percentages. Students taught to associate fractions with the proportion of a container filled with water (a substance) fare much better than those taught to associate fractions with pieces of a pie (objects). Objects may be useful for learning integers (as both are discrete, bounded, and unitary), but substances are more useful for learning fractions (as both are continuous, divisible, and dense). The parallels between number and matter run deeper across domains than within.

✦ ✦ ✦

WHICH IS HEAVIER, a pound of feathers or a pound of gold? Neither, of course—a pound is a pound—but the question likely gave you pause. Gold is heftier than feathers, and our conceptions of heft interfere with our conceptions of weight. Heft and bulk are perceptual experiences of matter that do not change with our conceptual understanding of matter. They interfere with our reasoning about material phenomena throughout our lives.

Take the task of deciding whether an object will sink or float in water. We adults are quick to judge that large, dense objects (e.g., an iron pan) will sink and that light, airy objects (e.g., a Styrofoam packing peanut) will float, but we are slow to judge that light-yet-dense objects (e.g., a fleck of iron) will sink and heavy-yet-airy objects (e.g., a Styrofoam crate) will float. Even though we may recognize that density is the only dimension relevant to such judgments, heft and bulk still interfere.

Heft and bulk interfere with our ability to discriminate material entities from nonmaterial entities as well. When asked to classify entities as "matter" or "not matter" as quickly as possible, we take longer to classify intangible substances (inkblots, perfume, air) as matter than we do to classify tangible ones (rocks, bricks, shoes). And when we err, our errors are consistent with children's errors on untimed versions of the task. In one speeded-classification study, adults classified inkblots as matter only 85 percent of the time, perfume as matter only 83 percent of the time, and air as matter only 75 percent of the time. Conversely, they classified thunder as matter 35 percent of the time, starlight as matter 37 percent of the time, and lightning as matter 57 percent of the time. Even Antoine Lavoisier, the founder of modern chemistry, was confused about the physical status of heat and light. He classified both as elements of matter.

We need not be under time pressure to err in our material reasoning. We err in casual situations as well. For instance, we put full bottles of water in the freezer, forgetting that they will explode when the water inside expands beyond the volume of the bottle. We pay higher prices for larger packages of food, failing to consider whether the amount of food per unit of package is equivalent across packages of different sizes. We overexert ourselves when clearing snow from our driveways, failing to see how a collection of heft-less snowflakes could yield hundreds of pounds of frozen water. And we quibble over whether a glass is half empty or half full when, in reality, it's full all the way—one part with liquid and one part with gas.

My favorite everyday example of a matter-based blunder comes from the pub. A standard pint glass is 5.875 inches tall and has a diameter of 3.25 inches at its top and 2.375 inches at its bottom. How much beer would you

The "Piaget" Beer Gauge
*Don't Get
Short Poured Again*

Glass edge

Beer surface

14 oz
13 %

12 oz
25 %

10 oz
38 %

8 oz
50 %

6 oz
63 %

web: thebeergauge.com

Conservation errors abound in daily life, even for adults. One such error is our chronic underestimation of how much beer is missing from an underfilled beer glass.

estimate is missing from a glass that is filled to 5 inches rather than the full 5.875 inches?

Nearly a quarter! A 15 percent decrement in height yields a 25 percent decrement in volume, thanks to the fact that standard pint glass is tapered and tapered glasses hold more beer at their top than at their bottom. Most of us are oblivious to how much beer we are missing when served a less-than-full glass, but now that obliviousness is avoidable. An entrepreneurial beer drinker has invented a pocket-sized device for measuring the decrement in beer volume for every decrement in beer height (available for purchase at thebeergauge.com). Its name rings true to its heritage: the Piaget beer gauge.

3 | ENERGY

What Makes Something Hot?
What Makes Something Loud?

IN THE MID-1600S, A SOCIETY KNOWN AS THE ACCADEMIA DEL CIMENTO, or the Academy of Experiment, was founded in Florence. The purpose of the academy was to explore the mysteries of nature through observation and experimentation. The members of the academy created some of the first laboratory instruments marked with standard units of measure, including alcohol-based thermometers, and they used those instruments to investigate several thermal phenomena, including the expansion of liquids on freezing, the expansion of solids on heating, and the effects of heat and cold on atmospheric pressure.

In one line of investigation, the Florentine experimenters placed vessels of different liquids—rose water, fig water, wine, vinegar, melted snow—into an ice bath to induce freezing. As the liquids froze, their expansion was recorded in relation to their temperature. Oddly, the experimenters measured temperature by placing their thermometers in the ice bath next to the vessel rather than inside the vessel. Today, over 250 years later, the practice of measuring freezing points has become a common science fair experiment for children, and all guides on how to do so direct children to place their

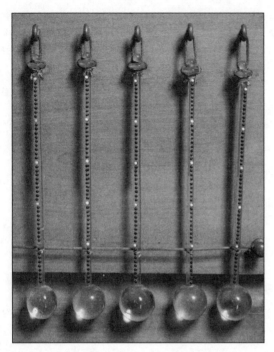

These thermometers were created by the Accademia del Cimento in seventeenth-century Florence for some of the first laboratory-based experiments on heating, cooling, burning, and freezing.

thermometers in the liquid being frozen. Why, then, did the Florentine experimenters place their thermometers in the ice bath?

It's clear from the experimenters' notebooks that they were attempting to measure changes in the liquid, not the ice bath, but their understanding of freezing was very different from ours today. They saw the purpose of the thermometer as measuring the strength of the cold flowing from the ice bath into the liquid. The vessel and its contents were viewed as passive recipients of coldness, not as equal partners in a two-way interaction. The modern view of what was happening during those experiments is that heat was transferred from the vessel to the ice bath, but this view would have been incomprehensible to the Florentine experimenters. They did not see cold as the absence of heat; they saw it as something fundamentally distinct from heat. How could heat be involved in making something colder?

The Florentine experimenters not only viewed heating and cooling as opposing processes, but also viewed heat and cold as kinds of substances, on par with water, alcohol, or oil. Heat was thought to be composed of fire particles, and the process of heating something was thought to infuse the substance with fire particles, which then pushed the substance apart (hence, the phenomenon of thermal expansion). Heat was also thought to be emitted only from heat sources: candles, coals, bonfires, the sun. A liquid at room temperature was not viewed as having heat, let alone capable of transferring that heat to a system with less heat (the ice bath).

The Florentine experimenters' view of thermal phenomena has been dubbed a *source-recipient* theory, as it drew a sharp distinction between heat sources and heat recipients, as well as a sharp distinction between cold sources and cold recipients. This theory informed how the experimenters studied all thermal phenomena, not just artificial freezing. In another line of studies, they demonstrated that brass, bronze, and copper expanded on heating and contracted on cooling. They compared the extent of this expansion to the expansion of wood as it absorbed water—a bizarre comparison on modern views of thermal expansion but a sensible one on the source-recipient view, as absorbing water particles was seen as physically analogous to absorbing fire particles (the supposed constitutes of heat).

The Florentine experimenters also compared how water freezes when placed in an ice bath ("artificial freezing") with how water freezes when placed outdoors on a cold day ("natural freezing"), looking for differences in the rate of freezing, the completeness of freezing, and the clarity of the frozen ice. These experiments were based on the idea that different kinds of cold had different effects. The results, however, were inconclusive. The experimenters never bothered to check whether the temperature of the outdoor air in the natural-freezing experiments was the same as the temperature of the ice bath in the artificial-freezing experiments. They were focused instead on characterizing the nature of different "cold sources" and their effects.

In 1761, more than a century after the founding of the Accademia del Cimento, the Scottish chemist Joseph Black discovered that adding heat to a substance did not always change its temperature. In particular, he discovered that adding heat to a mixture of ice and water did not raise its temperature but rather increased its proportion of water to ice. Only after all the ice had melted did the water's temperature begin to rise. Black discovered that the same was true for a mixture of boiling water and steam; adding heat to the mixture did not raise its temperature until all the water had turned to steam.

Black's discovery—that heat is distinct from temperature—could not be accommodated by the source-recipient theory of heat, the prevailing theory at that time. Everyone before Black had assumed that thermometers measure heat, not temperature, and they had no explanation for the dissociation between heat and temperature at a phase change.

Black's discovery necessitated a new theory of thermal phenomena, but it was not the kinetic theory of modern thermodynamics. Black's theory differentiated heat and temperature but continued to treat heat as a kind of substance. This substance, termed *caloric*, was believed to pool inside substances at their melting points or their boiling points, changing the chemical composition of those substances but not their temperature. It wasn't for another century that scientists abandoned caloric in favor of a kinetic (energy-based) view of heat, but nonscientists have never abandoned caloric. This notion underlies most of our thermal reasoning, even if we've forgotten its original name and simply call it *heat*.

✦ ✦ ✦

HEAT IS A form of energy—the collective energy of the molecules in a physical system—but we intuitively view heat as a kind of substance, in line with the historical theories described above. Our intuitive theories of heat parallel historical theories in many ways, beginning with the language we use to talk about heat. We describe heat as something that moves on its own ("heat is *escaping* from your head," "all the heat has *drained from* the tub") and that can be trapped or contained ("greenhouses *trap* the sun's heat," "close the door to *keep* the heat outside"). For some people, this language is merely metaphorical. It's easier to say "all the heat has drained from the tub" than "the water in the tub has reached thermal equilibrium with its surroundings." But for most people, this language is literal, as literal as saying "all the water has drained from the tub" or "close the door to keep the smell outside."

One reason we know this language is literal is that people who use it make qualitatively different predictions about thermal phenomena than people who do not—a finding discussed later. Another reason is that when pressed to explain substance-based language, many people articulate a fully substance-based theory, as in the following conversation between a physics education researcher and a student in a college-level level physics course:

RESEARCHER: You just used the verb "flow" to describe the process of heat conduction. Can you tell me how you envision heat transfer in this question?

STUDENT: Just like water. Just like water flows from a higher place to a lower place. It is because heat flows from a hotter area to a colder area. I think it acts like water.

Another similarity between intuitive and historical theories of heat is the distinction they both draw between heat and cold and, by extension, heat sources and cold sources. Cold is nothing more than a perceptual state. Substances that draw heat away from our bodies are perceived as cold, whereas substances that transfer heat to our body are perceived as hot. Yet we reify these distinct perceptual states as distinct substances. Consider the following explanations provided by introductory physics students when asked why a cup of tepid water dropped in temperature on contact with an ice cube or a metal table:

- "Some of the cold left the ice cube and went into the water."
- "The instance the cup touched the metal table, the molecules in the table added coldness into the cup."
- "When the cup got colder, the table transferred cold molecules to the cup. The cup transferred hot molecules to the table. So when it is done, the table will be hot and the cup cold."

The last explanation assumes not only that cold is distinct from heat but also that it is composed of a different kind of substance: "cold molecules." It may be tempting to interpret this explanation in terms of energy states—"hot molecules" are high-energy particles and "cold molecules" are low-energy particles—but this person clearly thinks that molecules themselves are transferred across substances, not their energy. This dueling-substance view of hot and cold was well articulated by another participant in the same study, who defined temperature as "a measure of the mixture of heat and cold inside an object."

A third point of similarity between intuitive theories and historical theories—the source-recipient theory in particular—is their failure to differentiate heat from temperature. Black discovered that heat is distinct from temperature through careful observation of phase changes. A more common situation in which heat is observably distinct from temperature is when objects at the same temperature convey different amounts of warmth. In a bathroom, for instance, cotton towels feel warmer than the ceramic tiles beneath them. In a hot car, metal seatbelts feel warmer than the vinyl upholstery on the seat. And in an oven, aluminum pans feel warmer than the air surrounding those pans. The reason that different materials at the same temperature convey different sensations of warmth is that some materials are better at transferring heat than others, and those that transfer heat more efficiently (conductors) are perceived as more extreme than those that transfer heat less efficiently (insulators).

Thus, to make sense of why two materials at the same temperature feel different to the touch, a person must differentiate heat—and heat transfer—from temperature. But most of us do not. Most of us assume that an object *feels* hot because it *is* hot, either because some objects are intrinsically warmer than others (e.g., towels are intrinsically warmer than tiles) or because some substances are better at trapping heat than others (e.g., cotton is intrinsically better at trapping heat than ceramic). We are inclined to interpret our fingers as heat sensors, but fingers do not measure heat. They do not even measure temperature. They measure something entirely more subjective: whether our skin is gaining heat or losing heat, and how quickly. This property matters the most from an evolutionary point of view because it determines whether we are in danger of being burned or in danger of being frostbitten. Heat is not the critical factor in a thermal injury; *heat transfer* is. If heat were the critical factor, in and of itself, we would never be able to remove a pan from a hot oven, because the air in the oven would burn the skin off our arms before we reached the pan. Our skin is safe because air transfers heat significantly slower than metal does. We can tolerate contact with 400° Fahrenheit air even if we cannot tolerate contact with a 400° Fahrenheit pan.

Arguably, then, our perception of heat (warmth) is more remote from heat itself than our perception of weight (heft) is from weight itself. Both types of perception are affected by the material at hand, but differences in material affect our perception of heat significantly more than they affect our perception of weight. Consider, for instance, the difference between aluminum and cork. Pound for pound, a piece of aluminum would feel heavier than a piece of cork of the same weight (because the cork would be larger and our perception of its weight would be calibrated for its size), but at no point would the cork be liftable and the aluminum unliftable. The warmth of those two objects, on the other hand, quickly diverges with each additional unit of heat. At 200° Fahrenheit, the cork could still be touched but the aluminum would burn our skin immediately.

✦ ✦ ✦

SUPPOSE YOU HAD two balloons filled with helium, one balloon made out of paper and the other made out of rubber. Both balloons are sealed tightly. If you left them floating inside a closet for several hours, which balloon would remain more buoyant: the paper balloon or the rubber balloon? Now suppose you had two cups of coffee, one cup made of Styrofoam and the other made of ceramic. Both cups are sealed with airtight lids. If you left the cups sitting on a table for twenty minutes, which drink would remain hotter: the coffee in the Styrofoam cup or the coffee in the ceramic cup?

From a scientific point of view, these two thought experiments are about qualitatively different phenomena: the diffusion of gas and the transfer of heat. The first problem entails a dispersion of matter, whereas the second entails an exchange of energy. Accordingly, physics experts base their answers to these two problems on different considerations: porousness (of paper versus rubber) in the first problem and thermal conductivity (of Styrofoam versus ceramic) in the second.

Physics novices, on the other hand, base their answers to both problems on the same consideration: porousness. In other words, physics experts and physics novices agree that the rubber balloon will remain more buoyant than the paper balloon, but they disagree about which cup of coffee will remain hotter. Physics experts claim that the coffee in the Styrofoam cup will remain hotter because Styrofoam is a better insulator than ceramic, but physics novices claim that coffee in the ceramic cup will remain hotter because ceramic is less porous than Styrofoam.

This pair of problems was one of several devised by the psychologist Michelene Chi and her colleagues. In each pair, they pitted a material transformation against a structurally analogous instance of energy transfer. Some of the energy problems involved heat, some involved light, and some involved electricity. Regardless of the type of energy under consideration, physics novices (in this case, ninth-graders) judged the outcome of each energy transfer to be the same as the outcome of each closely matched material transformation. And the language they used to justify their judgments was the same across the two types of problems. They used verbs that imply containment (*keeps, traps, blocks*), absorption (*soaks up, takes in, absorbs*), or macroscopic motion (*leaves, flows through, escapes*) when discussing both matter and energy.

Physics experts, on the other hand, used qualitatively different language across the two types of problems. They referred to containment, absorption, and macroscopic motion when discussing matter, but they referred to molecular interactions (*collide, contact, excite*), system-wide processes (*altogether, in parallel, at the same time*), and equilibrium-seeking processes (*propagates, transfers, becomes the same*) when discussing energy. Why do physics novices treat heat, light, and electricity as if they were substances? Chi and her colleagues think it's because we can conceptualize "things" more easily than we can conceptualize processes. Things are concrete; processes are abstract. Things are static; processes are dynamic. Things are enduring; processes are ephemeral.

Of course, not all processes are difficult to conceptualize. We have no trouble conceptualizing intentional, goal-driven processes like cooking, painting, or sewing. Chi and her colleagues term those processes *direct* and contrast them with processes they term *emergent*. Emergent processes differ from direct processes in four main respects. Emergent processes are *system-wide*, meaning they have no clear cause-and-effect explanation. They are *equilibrium-seeking*, meaning they move toward a balanced configuration of their components. They are *simultaneous*, meaning their components operate in tandem. And they are *ongoing*, meaning they have neither a beginning nor an end, even if they arrive at an equilibrium.

Heat is a prime example of an emergent process; it emerges from the collective motion of independent molecules. Other examples include pressure, which emerges from the collective force of independent gas particles; weather, which emerges from the collective movement of independent air masses; and evolution, which emerges from the collective reproduction of independent organisms. Emergent processes can also be found in the social world. Traffic emerges from the collective decisions of independent drivers, stock prices emerge from the collective decisions of independent of investors, and cities emerge from the collective decisions of independent developers. We often prefer to think of these phenomena as caused by a single agent— one dawdling driver, one irrational CEO, one visionary city planner—but

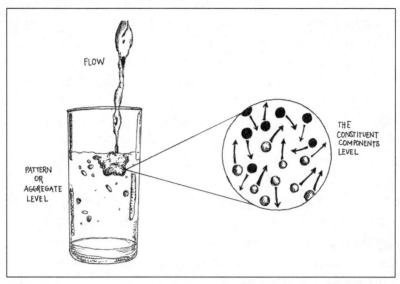

Diffusion is an emergent process, where random interactions at one level of a physical system (e.g., the microscopic level) lead to systematic patterns at a higher level of that system (e.g., the macroscopic level) such as when ink diffuses in water.

they emerge without the help (or hindrance) of a leader. Certainly, in the domain of heat, there is no single molecule leading the charge. Complex and seemingly directed patterns of change at one level of a system emerge from simple, undirected interactions at a lower level of that system.

Understanding heat from a scientific point of view requires understanding it as an emergent process. But how can we conceptualize heat as an emergent process if emergent processes themselves are difficult to grasp? Chi and her colleagues have tackled this chicken-and-egg problem by introducing physics novices to the concept of an emergent process in general before showing them how heat is an emergent process in particular. They devised a computer-based tutorial that walked students through four defining features of emergent processes: that they are system-wide, equilibrium-seeking, simultaneous, and ongoing. Chi and her colleagues measured the effectiveness of this tutorial using the task described above in which each of several energy-based problems is compared to an analogous matter-based problem.

The tutorial proved highly effective. While few students differentiated energy-based problems from matter-based problems before the tutorial in either their predictions or their explanations, most did so after the tutorial. In other words, teaching physics novices about emergent processes allowed them to think about heat as they had never thought about it before—as something that emerges from matter but is not itself matter, that affects the things around us but is not itself a thing. Such is the nature of energy.

✦ ✦ ✦

SOUND IS A form of energy, just like heat. It travels through matter—or, more precisely, by way of matter—but is not matter itself. It is a pressure wave: peaks of compressed molecules followed by troughs of rarified molecules, set in motion by a vibrating body. Most people do not think of sound as energy, however. They think of it as a substance.

Sounds clearly pass through a medium—we can hear them through solids, liquids, or gases—but they are thought to permeate the medium, slipping through the empty space inside. Many people actually think that the medium is a hindrance to sound and that sound would propagate faster if no medium were present at all. But sound cannot travel through empty space. That's why the tagline of the movie *Alien* was "In space, no one can hear you scream."

Substance-based views of sound are common and easily elicited. Consider these explanations for how sound propagates through air, provided by introductory physics students in an interview on the nature of sound:

- "As the sound moves, like as the sound comes through the air . . . it might find the spaces in between the air particles, but I think eventually it might also hit one. I mean it's not like it knows exactly where it's going."
- "It travels through just a little stuff. It just kind of works its way through . . . finding any of the little open areas that it can, until it gets to the listener."
- "Well, I would say that it's somewhat like a maze for the sound. It just kind of works its way through until it gets to the other side. I don't think sound can move the particles of the wall. I think sound just moves around them."

I've noticed the people around me make similar remarks. While watching a television show set in outer space, my wife once griped, "Don't they know there's no sound in space? There's no air particles for the sound to bounce off." She was right that there's no sound in space, but for the wrong reason. Sound is carried *by* air particles, not bounced off of them.

Children's conceptions of sound are even more substance-based than adults'. In one study, children between six and ten were asked whether sound has mass, permanence, and weight. Sample questions included "How can we hear sounds through walls?" (which is a real mystery, if sound has mass); "How far do sounds travel from their source?" (which could be quite far, if sound has permanence); and "Does a clock become a little bit lighter each time it chimes?" (which it should, if sound has weight). Almost all children attributed mass to sound, claiming that sound travels *around* walls, not through them, or that sound travels through the cracks in a wall, not the actual wall. Some children also attributed weight and permanence to sound, claiming that sounds travel forever and that clocks become lighter with each passing chime.

These attributions are not capricious; they follow a regular developmental pattern. Children initially attribute all three properties—mass, weight, and permanence—to sound until they begin to rethink those attributions, one property at a time. First, they stop attributing permanence, then they stop attributing weight, and then they stop attributing mass (if ever). Apparently, an impermanent substance is more conceivable than a weightless one, and a weightless substance is more conceivable than a massless one. What would a substance be, after all, without mass? The same pattern holds for children's conceptions of heat. Children initially assign mass, weight, and permanence to heat, followed by only mass and weight, followed by only mass. These developmental parallels make it clear that children conceptualize both sound and heat as substances, not energy. Children initially think of them as fully akin to matter and later conceptualize them as something more abstract (but still substance-like).

Children's beliefs about how we perceive sound betray substance-based views as well. The scientific process of sound perception is relatively straightforward. Sound waves enter the ear and impinge on our ear drums, causing them to vibrate. These vibrations propagate along a series of bones to the cochlea, an organ that converts them into a neural signal. How might sound perception work if sound were a substance? One possibility is that the ear acts as a funnel for "sound particles," collecting those particles and channeling them into our brain. This possibility is not, however, commonly endorsed. A more commonly endorsed possibility is that our ears actively detect sound rather than passively receive it, that they reach out and sample the sounds imbued in our environment through some kind of invisible emission. This view, known as "extramission," is well articulated in the following conversation between a science-education researcher and a ten-year-old child:

RESEARCHER: [Hits a glass beaker with a metal object] Why was a sound produced?
CHILD: The two hard objects make a sound when they hit.
RESEARCHER: Why do the objects produce a sound?
CHILD: I'm not sure. I think it has something to do with sound waves.
RESEARCHER: Can you explain what you mean by sound waves?
CHILD: Not really. They come from your ear.
RESEARCHER: How do you think the sound travels from the beaker to your ear?
CHILD: Your ear sends out sound waves and when the sound hits the waves it comes back to your ear.

This child knows the term *sound wave* but applies the term to something leaving the ear rather than entering it. If sounds are particles, traveling in or through the materials that create them, then we must have some means of sampling those particles—some kind of emission detects them and registers them. This child glommed on to the term *sound wave* as the name for that emission.

Extramissionist beliefs about auditory perception are common among children but not particularly common among adults. Extramissionist beliefs about visual perception, on the other hand, are common even among adults. Visual perception works similarly to auditory perception except that light is the relevant form of energy. Light enters our eyes, just as sound enters our ears, and it impinges on our retinas, just as sound impinges on our eardrums. Light is more ubiquitous than sound, however, and therefore less appreciated as a form of information. We recognize that we need light to see, but we don't recognize that light is the medium of sight itself—that every object in our visual field is known to us through light waves that

The superhero's X-ray vision is an exaggerated version of how most people perceive ordinary vision, as if the eye emitted rays that interact with the environment.

bounce off those objects and enter our eyes. Even great thinkers like Plato, Ptolemy, and Da Vinci misunderstood the role of light in vision. Like most adults today, these great thinkers considered light some kind of ray or wave that exits the eye and interacts with objects externally.

The conviction of our extramissionist beliefs is quite remarkable. When given a choice between intromissionist explanations of vision (e.g., rays or waves come into the eye) and extramissionist ones (e.g., rays or waves go out of the eye and then back in), we reliably endorse the latter. When given a picture of an eye and asked to draw arrows depicting the flow of information in vision, we reliably draw arrows pointing away from the eye, not toward it. And when asked to explain how we perceive a luminescent object, like a lit bulb, we acknowledge that light from the bulb enters our eyes but deny that anything enters our eyes when asked to explain how we perceive a nonluminescent object, like an unlit bulb. This last finding is particularly telling: while we accept that light enters our eyes in the presence of a light source, we don't see light as critical to vision.

The role of light in vision is not covered in a standard physics course. Only psychology courses cover such material, and they rarely refute extramissionist beliefs directly. Moreover, the experience of vision provides no clues to its intromissionist nature. Perhaps, then, it's not surprising that most adults hold extramissionist beliefs. Perhaps we've simply never been told otherwise. Researchers have looked into this possibility and found that telling people how vision works is not sufficient to correct their extramissionist misconceptions. Those misconceptions are highly resistant to instruction. In one study, the researchers devised a tutorial that specifically articulated and then refuted extramissionism. It stressed the role of light in vision and mentioned more than twenty times that light enters the eye. The tutorial concluded with the following message: "Remember, nothing leaves your eyes in order for you to see. The only thing that enters your eyes is light rays, and nothing ever goes out of your eyes when you see. Although Superman may send rays out of his eyes to help him see, real people don't send anything out of their eyes to help them see."

This tutorial was administered to fifth-graders, eighth-graders, and college undergraduates, and all groups appeared to learn from it. They espoused significantly fewer extramissionist beliefs after the tutorial than before. Three months later, however, the participants provided just as many extramissionist explanations as did students who had received no instruction at all. The participants had reverted to their earlier belief in ray vision.

Studies like these demonstrate that extramissionist beliefs exhibit all the core elements of an intuitive theory. They are historically ancient. They are robust across ages, tasks, and contexts. And they are difficult to eliminate with instruction. Accordingly, extramission is more than just a false belief; it's a by-product of a nonscientific understanding of light and its role in vision. Studies that have directly probed students' intuition about light (as opposed to our perception of light) have found that light is viewed not as a form of energy but as—you guessed it—a substance.

+ + +

LIVING LIFE AS an extramissionist is unlikely to cause much grief. Whether we believe that waves flow into the eye or out of the eye, we still know that if we are to see an object, the path between us and it must be unobstructed. But extramissionist beliefs betray fundamental misconceptions about the nature of energy, and misconceptions about energy in other contexts can have serious, or even fatal, consequences. Substance-based theories of energy assert that energy sources are distinct from energy recipients (as epitomized by the Florentine experimenter's source-recipient theory of heat). This erroneous distinction can lead to unsafe behavior around thermal or electrical systems. We may be vigilant toward the objects we view as energy sources, but we are less vigilant toward the objects we view as mere recipients.

Consider the following statistics. Most burns each year are caused not by contact with fire (the prototypical heat source) but by contact with other hot substances, like heated cookware or scalding water. Most cases of frostbite are caused not by contact with ice (the prototypical cold "source") but by prolonged exposure to cold air. And most cases of household electrical injuries are caused not by contact with outlets (the prototypical electricity source) but by the misuse of electric appliances. These statistics may be due, in part, to how frequently we encounter some hazards relative to others, but they may also be due to an underestimation of the danger posed by objects (or substances) viewed as mere energy recipients.

Acquiring a scientific understanding of heat and electricity may safeguard us against some energy-related hazards, but it's not easy to integrate scientific knowledge with everyday behavior. You may know, for instance, that electricity is an emergent property of electrons moving through circuits, but you still probably think of electricity as a substance ("juice") that flows out of an outlet and down a wire whenever you plug an electric device into the wall. Even scientists default to nonscientific intuition when they reason about energy in nonscientific contexts. In one study, individuals with PhDs in physics were asked qualitative questions about heat and heat transfer. While all the participants demonstrated an appreciation for how microscopic processes give rise to macroscopic phenomena, they often differed in their preferred explanation for those phenomena. Asked to explain why a hot platter cools when left on an open counter, some physicists cited conduction, some cited convection, some cited radiation, and some cited the specific heat capacity of the materials involved. Many physicists also experienced difficulty coordinating their scientific knowledge of heat with their everyday experience of heat, as illustrated here:

RESEARCHER: Which would be a better wrapper for keeping a juice box cool, aluminum foil or wool?
PHYSICIST: I would guess wool, but I think that's probably wrong.

RESEARCHER: Why do you think it's wrong?

PHYSICIST: I don't know. It seems to me it ought to be wrong, but I don't know.

RESEARCHER: So, aluminum foil seems like it ought to be the right answer?

PHYSICIST: Yeah. Why? Because my mother puts stuff in the oven in aluminum foil, not in wool, but wool won't burn at that temperature. So, aluminum foil ought to be the answer, I would guess.

Wool is, in fact, a better insulator than aluminum, and the physicist recognized this fact, but he hesitated to endorse it, given his everyday experiences with wool and aluminum. Why would his mother have wrapped food in aluminum foil if aluminum was not a good insulator? And why isn't wool an integral part of kitchen equipment if wool is actually a better insulator?

This anecdote fits with a broader conclusion that has emerged from the study of professional scientists: they reason more accurately than do nonscientists, not because scientists have relinquished the nonscientists' misconceptions but because they have learned to inhibit those misconceptions. The misconceptions are still there, though, affecting scientists' ability to solve problems outside their immediate domain of expertise, like the problem described above. Even if scientists reason through the problem correctly, their brains still show evidence of grappling with misconceptions at an implicit level. We know this from studies that use functional magnetic resonance imaging (fMRI) to examine brain activity in the moment. fMRI measures how much blood is flowing to specific areas of the brain in relation to a specific task. The more active an area is, the more oxygen it requires, and thus the more blood it needs to provide that oxygen.

In recent years, researchers have monitored scientists' brains with fMRI as the scientists reason through two types of problems: problems that everyone (scientists and nonscientists alike) can answer correctly and problems that only the scientists can answer correctly. On the first type of problem, scientists show patterns of neural activity similar to those experienced by nonscientists, but on the second, they show more activity in areas of the brain associated with inhibition and conflict monitoring: the prefrontal cortex and the anterior cingulate cortex. Scientists can answer scientifically challenging problems—that's the benefit of their expertise—but to do so,

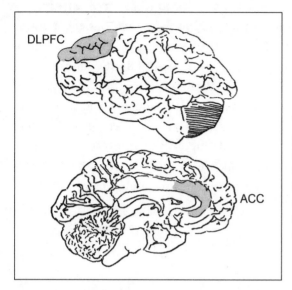

When viewing physically impossible circuits, physics experts show increased activity in their dorsolateral prefrontal cortex (DLPFC) and anterior cingulate cortex (ACC), areas of the brain associated with inhibition and conflict-monitoring.

they must inhibit ideas that conflict with their scientific knowledge of those problems. They must inhibit latent misconceptions.

Latent misconceptions about energy in particular have been documented with respect to how physicists think about electricity. In one fMRI study, physicists and nonphysicists were shown electric circuits that were either complete or incomplete and were asked to determine whether a lightbulb that was part of the circuit should be lit or unlit. Physicists know that a lightbulb can only be lit if it's connected with two wires, because two wires are needed to complete the circuit between a lightbulb and a battery. Nonphysicists, on the other hand, think that electricity flows down a wire in the same way that water flows down a pipe, so they think that a single wire is sufficient to transfer energy from a battery to a lightbulb.

As expected, the physicists perfectly distinguished correct electrical configurations (complete circuits with lit bulbs, incomplete circuits with unlit bulbs) from incorrect ones (complete circuits with unlit bulbs, incomplete circuits with lit bulbs), revealing no behavioral evidence of believing that a single wire is sufficient to light a bulb. In terms of brain activity, though, physicists showed more activity in their prefrontal cortex and anterior cingulate cortex (areas associated with inhibition and conflict monitoring) than nonphysicists did when evaluating scientifically incorrect circuits.

In other words, when physicists saw a lit bulb connected to a battery by a single wire, they correctly classified the circuit as wrong, but their brains showed signs of inhibiting a contradictory response. That contradictory response was presumably "a single wire is sufficient to light a bulb."

At an implicit level, then, even physicists view electricity as analogous to a liquid: "bottled" in a battery, "released" by a conductor, and sent "flowing" down a wire. The physical reality of electricity—as a system-wide, equilibrium-seeking, simultaneous, and ongoing process—is difficult to embrace even for physicists. Heat, sound, light, and electricity are all preferentially viewed as substances, and no amount of training can scrub these substance-based views from our brains.

4 | GRAVITY

Why Makes Something Heavy?
What Makes Something Fall?

WILLIAM JAMES, AMERICA'S FIRST EXPERIMENTAL PSYCHOLOGIST, speculated that infants perceive the world "as one great blooming, buzzing confusion." But James was wrong. Four decades of research using a preferential-looking paradigm (described in Chapter 2) have shown us that infants' perception of the world is much like our own. Infants perceive the objects in their environment as bounded, discrete entities that trace continuous paths through space and that move on contact with other objects. They perceive the people in their environment as agents of change, who act on objects to achieve specific goals and specific desires. And they perceive the environment itself as a three-dimensional space characterized by depth, color, surfaces, and textures.

There are, however, some marked differences between infants' perception of the world and our own. Consider the following situation. A table is placed on an empty stage, and a screen is placed in front of the table. A ball is held above the screen and then dropped so that it falls behind the screen, in line with the table. The screen is then lowered, revealing one of three outcomes: the ball has come to rest on the table's surface; the ball has come to rest on the ground beneath the table's surface, seemingly passing

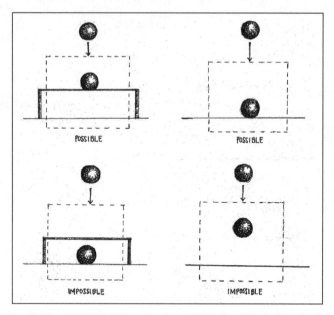

When a ball is dropped behind a screen (indicated by the dashed line), four-month-old infants are surprised if the ball appears to have passed through a solid table (bottom left) but are not surprised if the ball appears to float in the air (bottom right).

through it; or the ball has come to rest midway between the table and the release point, seemingly floating in the air.

Adults would be surprised to witness either of the latter two outcomes, but four-month-old infants are surprised only by the second. That is, they look longer when the ball appears to have passed through the table than when the ball has come to rest on top of the table, but they do not look longer when the ball appears to be suspended in midair. Four-month-olds thus seem to hold expectations about solidity but no expectations about gravity. Indeed, their expectations about gravity—or, more precisely, their expectations about *support*—develop gradually over the first few years of life.

Adults expect an object to fall if it is not adequately supported below its center of mass. This expectation seems simple on its face but is actually quite sophisticated. It entails a series of insights achieved in a regular developmental sequence, starting with the insight that objects fall if not in contact with other objects. Infants achieve this insight between four and six months of age, as shown by studies that measure infants' attentiveness to stationary objects that are either adequately supported or inadequately supported (and should thus fall).

In one study, infants were shown two boxes, one on top of the other. They watched a hand push the top box along the surface of the bottom box. The hand then stopped at one of two points: a point where the top box was still supported by the bottom box or a point where the top box had been pushed off the bottom box, appearing to float in midair. Five-month-old infants stared longer at the floating box than at the fully supported box, indicating that they had developed the expectation that floating objects should fall. Nevertheless, infants of this age showed no surprise when they watched a hand push the top box to the very edge of the bottom box so that the two boxes made contact only at their corners. Thus, infants attend to whether or not an object is in contact with another object before they attend to the type of contact. It takes another month or two for infants to realize that the only type of contact that provides support is contact from below.

Of course, contact from below is necessary but not sufficient for support. An object must be supported beneath its center of mass. For several months after they recognize the importance of support itself, infants do not attend to *how much* of an object is supported. Nine-month-olds, for instance, are not surprised to witness a triangular block remain perched atop a rectangular support even after the bulk of its mass has been pushed over the edge of that support. In fact, expectations about how much of an object requires support continue to be fine-tuned throughout childhood.

Young children, like older infants, recognize that the amount of contact between an object and its support is potentially important, but they do not heed the *location* of that contact. Children as old as six claim that an object will remain supported as long as half of its bottom surface is in contact with the support. They neglect to check whether at least half of its mass is located over the support. Young children are thus stumped by asymmetric objects, for these objects defy their amount-of-contact rule on two fronts: they can fall even if the majority of their bottom surface is supported (but the bulk of their mass is not), and they can remain aloft even if the majority of their bottom surface is not supported (but the bulk of their mass is).

Children thus progress through a series of ever-more-refined expectations about support, moving from the expectation that objects without contact fall, to the expectation that objects without contact from below fall,

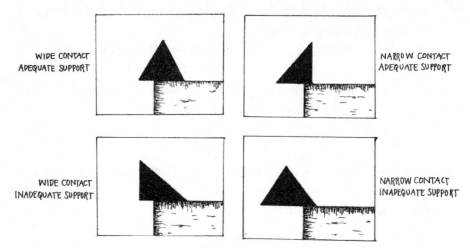

Young children judge whether an object will fall off a pedestal according to whether the object's bottom surface is supported, regardless of whether its center of mass is supported. So they would correctly judge that the bottom right block will fall and that the top left block will not, but they would incorrectly judge that the top right block will fall and that the bottom left will not.

to the expectation that objects without contact from below their center of mass fall. These expectations are evident not only from children's reactions to impossible configurations of objects but also from their interactions with objects themselves. In one study, infants were shown two toy pigs—one that was adequately supported from below and one that was not—and they were encouraged to reach for whichever pig they wanted. Half of the infants were given a choice between a fully supported pig and a pig that appeared to float in midair. The other half were given a choice between a fully supported pig and a partially supported pig—that is, a pig whose center of mass hovered beyond the support and should have fallen.

Which pig the infants reached for depended on how old they were. Five-month-old infants reached for the fully supported pig more than they did the floating pig, but they showed no preference for the fully supported pig over the partially supported pig. Seven-month-old infants, on the other hand, reached more for the fully supported pig in both conditions. Infants' reaching preferences thus accord with their looking preferences. As noted above, five-month-olds are surprised to witness an unsupported object remain aloft but are not surprised to witness a partially supported object remain aloft, whereas seven-month-olds are surprised to witness both. Whatever the age, infants are wary of the configurations that defy their current expectations.

Earlier, I noted that infants hold mature expectations about solidity long before they hold mature expectations about support. The same is true for expectations about continuity (that objects trace continuous paths as they move) and expectations about cohesion (that objects cohere as they move). Both expectations are in place several years before mature expectations about support. Why is support an outlier?

Perhaps the concept of support is more easily learned from experience than the other three concepts. Individuals born with innate knowledge of support may have fared no better, in the long run, than those left to acquire such knowledge on their own. Individuals born without knowledge of solidity, continuity, or cohesion, on the other hand, may not have fared as well. They would probably have encountered difficulties learning those principles from the "blooming, buzzing confusion" that results in their absence. Solidity, continuity, and cohesion define the very essence of what an object is. They allow us to parse an object from its background and track that object across changes in location and perspective—preconditions for answering the less essential question of whether an object has support.

This evolutionary speculation is consistent with what we know about nonhuman primates' conceptions of physical objects. Monkeys and apes, like human infants, hold strong expectations about solidity, continuity, and cohesion but only weak expectations about support. Indeed, adult chimpanzees' expectations about support are similar to those of a five-month-old human infant. Chimpanzees attend to whether an object is in contact with other objects, but they ignore whether that contact comes from below or from the side. They are surprised to see a banana floating in midair, for instance, but they are not surprised to see a banana floating next to a box, in contact with that box only at its edge. Evolution seems to have destined primates to learn about support from experience rather than instinct, but humans far outstrip other primates in what they end up learning.

✦ ✦ ✦

CHILDREN DEVELOP A relatively mature of understanding of support within their first few years of life, but understanding support is different from understanding gravity. The latter entails knowing not just when objects fall but where they fall and why. When objects fall, they often fall straight down. A spoon that has gone missing from your table is likely to be found on the floor next to the table, and a pencil that has gone missing from your desk is likely to be found on the floor next to the desk. There are, of course, exceptions to this rule. Objects in motion will hit the ground farther from where they fell, and objects whose path to the ground is obstructed will not hit the ground at all.

As it turns out, young children do not take either consideration into account. They fail to attend to whether a fallen object was moving as it fell (discussed in the next chapter) or whether the object's path was obstructed. They assume instead that the object can be found directly below where it was last seen. We know this from a task that psychologist Bruce Hood has dubbed the "tubes task." Since Piaget, psychologists have been interested in when and how children track objects across *invisible displacement*—namely, when and how they track objects occluded from view (as discussed in Chapter 2). Hood developed an invisible-displacement task in which the displaced object is a ball and the occluding surfaces are opaque tubes.

The tubes are affixed to a vertically oriented rectangular frame so that the ball can be dropped through them. At least three tubes are affixed to the frame, with each tube connected to a chimney at the top of the frame and a bucket at the bottom. The chimneys and buckets are aligned so that a ball dropped into a chimney at the top of the apparatus would fall into a bucket at the bottom if there were no tubes in the apparatus. The tubes, however, redirect the balls so that a ball dropped into the center chimney actually falls into the left bucket, a ball dropped into the left chimney actually falls into the right bucket, and a ball dropped into the right chimney actually falls into the center bucket.

Retrieving balls from this apparatus is trivial for anyone over the age of four. All you need to do is determine which bucket is connected to which chimney. Children younger than four, on the other hand, find this task surprisingly difficult. They tend to ignore the tubes and search in the bucket directly below the chimney where the ball was last seen—the left bucket, for instance, if the ball was dropped into the left chimney. They make what Hood calls a *gravity error*. These errors are not random guesses. Toddlers rarely search in the third bucket—the bucket that is neither connected to the chimney (the correct location) nor directly below the chimney (the gravity location). Likewise, toddlers rarely search in the

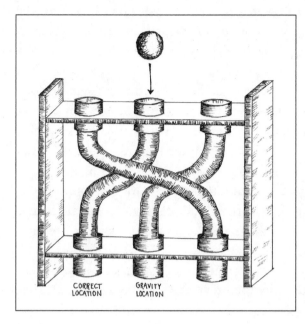

When a ball is dropped into the center chimney of this apparatus, toddlers typically search for the ball directly below its release point, ignoring the tube that would have redirected the ball to the left bucket.

bucket directly below the chimney if that bucket is not connected to any tubes, as toddlers realize they would have seen the ball fall through the air into the bucket.

Toddlers' performance on this task is not black-or-white. They do not make gravity errors 100 percent of the time or search in the correct location 100 percent of the time. Rather, they search in the correct location more and more, and the gravity-error location less and less, as they get older. Gravity errors thus seem to be the product of two conflicting beliefs: the belief that objects fall straight down and the belief that one solid object (the ball) cannot pass through another (the tube). Older children privilege the latter belief, recognizing that solidity always trumps gravity in this situation, but younger children are torn. The apparatus activates both beliefs, and they don't know how to prioritize them.

There are, of course, other explanations for why toddlers fail the tubes task. Perhaps toddlers are confused about the mechanics of opaque tubes, failing to realize that objects exit tubes only at their ends. Or perhaps they are making an *adjacency error* rather than a gravity error, searching for the ball in whatever bucket is closest to the chimney where they last saw it, regardless of their expectations about gravity.

Hood considered both of these explanations and showed that neither is correct. By laying the apparatus on its side and shuttling the balls from left to right rather than top to bottom, he showed that toddlers are not confused about the mechanics of opaque tubes. Under these conditions (which still involved balls and tubes), toddlers passed with flying colors. And by videotaping the task and reversing its motion, Hood showed that toddlers are making gravity errors rather than adjacency errors. In this setup, toddlers now watched the balls disappear from the bottom of the apparatus and reappear at the top, as if sucked up the tubes by a vacuum. Under these conditions, toddlers paid attention to the tubes and ignored the vertically adjacent bucket. The vertically adjacent bucket was no longer a preferred search location because gravity no longer drew their attention to that location.

The tubes task is not the only task where toddlers make gravity errors. Another task—the *shelf task*—pits solidity against gravity without the use of cumbersome tubes. Toddlers are shown a cabinet with two doors, one above the other. Behind each door is a shelf. The doors are opened, and toddlers are shown that the top shelf has no cover; it is open to the air. The doors are then closed, and the cabinet is hidden behind a screen. A ball is then dropped behind the screen, in line with the cabinet. The screen is removed, and toddlers are encouraged to retrieve the ball from within the cabinet. A solid plank of wood separates the top shelf from the bottom shelf, so the ball could only be on the top shelf, but most two-year-olds search for the ball on the bottom shelf instead. They ignore the solidity of the divider and focus their attention on the lowest point beneath where they last saw the ball.

In a variant on this task, toddlers search for a ball rolled down a ramp behind a screen. The screen has four doors placed at varying heights along the ramp, and a solid barrier (a block of wood) is placed on the ramp just behind one of the doors. The barrier is designed to protrude above the screen, remaining in view at all times. If the barrier were placed behind the third door, the ball would roll past the first door and the second door and come to stop at the third, prevented from going any further by the barrier. It would not roll to the fourth door, but that is where toddlers look for it. They ignore the barrier and presume that gravity pulled the ball all the way down the ramp.

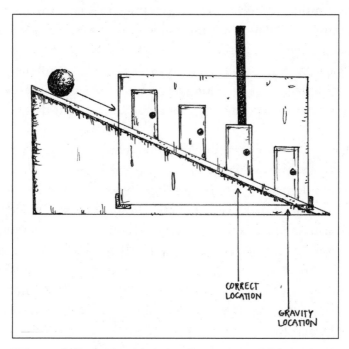

When a ball is released down this ramp, toddlers typically search for the ball behind the far-right door, ignoring the barrier that would have stopped the ball from rolling that far.

Watching an object fall causes toddlers to neglect the solidity of several objects: tubes, shelves, and barriers. We know that toddlers understand that one solid object cannot pass through another, because even four-month-old infants understand that principle. Infants look reliably longer at a ball that appears to have passed through a shelf than at a ball that has come to rest atop the shelf. (The task described at the beginning of the chapter is essentially the shelf task for infants.) Why does gravity trump solidity for the toddler but solidity trump gravity for the infant?

For infants, the shelf task is really only about solidity, as they have yet to acquire any knowledge of gravity (in the form of support). For toddlers, on the other hand, the shelf task is about both solidity and gravity, and gravity trumps solidity because the task primes a well-practiced procedure: retrieving fallen objects from the ground. Toddlers may know as much about solidity as infants, but that knowledge is overridden by a reflexive urge to search the ground. Indeed, if you track toddlers' gaze as they perform the tubes task, they follow the ball with their eyes, visually tracing its path through the tube into the correct bucket, but they then search in the vertically adjacent bucket. Their eyes reveal knowledge of solidity, but their hands reveal only knowledge of gravity, similar to how infants' eyes reveal knowledge of object permanence long before their hands do (as discussed in Chapter 2).

Toddlers' performance in hidden-displacement tasks—the tubes task, the shelf task, and the ramp task—is thus a battle between their knowledge of solidity and their knowledge of gravity. The likelihood that solidity will win the battle can be increased or decreased by changing the demands of the task. It can be increased by removing the chimneys from the apparatus and dropping balls directly into the tubes, thereby focusing toddlers' attention on the tubes themselves, and it can be decreased by asking toddlers to track two balls at once, thereby overloading their limited attention spans. The tubes task has not been used with adults, but researchers could certainly create a version that adults would find challenging. All they would have to do is increase the number of tubes and increase the number of balls. With enough tubes and enough balls, adults might even make gravity errors. Our belief that solid objects cannot pass through one another may be strong, but that belief is only as valuable as our ability to deploy it in real time.

+ + +

HUMAN TODDLERS ARE not the only creatures that fail the tubes task. Dogs, monkeys, and apes fail as well. These other animals cannot be tested in the human version of the task, but they can be tested in altered versions. When dogs are tested, the balls are replaced with dog treats and the buckets are replaced with boxes that the dogs can access with their snout. When monkeys or apes are tested, the balls are replaced with raisins or nuts, and the apparatus is shielded by a Plexiglas screen, to prevent them from tearing it apart. Despite these changes, the result are the same: nonhuman animals make gravity errors on their first attempts to retrieve fallen objects. They also make gravity errors on the shelf task and the ramp task.

The errors made by nonhuman animals are remarkably similar to those made by human toddlers. In one ambitious study, researchers at the Wolfgang Kohler Primate Research Center tested four species of apes—chimpanzees, bonobos, gorillas, and orangutans—on two versions of the shelf task, a vertical version and a horizontal version. In the vertical version, the apes were shown a table and two containers, one on top of the table and one below the table. The table was then covered by a screen, and the apes watched an experimenter drop a grape behind the screen, in line with the containers. The apes were then allowed to retrieve one, and only one, container from the display. Across several trials, they reached for the bottom container as often as they reached for the top container even though it was physically impossible for the grape to have fallen into the bottom container.

In the horizontal version of the task, the table was removed and the containers were tipped on their sides. They were aligned so that the right container blocked the opening of the left container. The containers were then covered by a screen and a grape was rolled behind the screen from the right. Now the apes reached almost exclusively to the correct container (the one on the right) and ignored the container where the grape could not have physically gone (the one on the left). All four species of apes performed this way. They made correct, solidity-based responses in the horizontal version of the task but vacillated between correct, solidity-based responses and incorrect, gravity-based responses in the vertical version. In follow-up studies, apes have also shown dissociations between where they look when tracking a fallen object and where they reach, similar to human toddlers. The apes' eyes reveal knowledge of solidity but their hands reveal only knowledge of gravity.

Searching for fallen objects is a task that any land-dwelling animal must perform, and humans are not the only animals that appear to have developed a simple heuristic for solving this task: search straight down. Only humans can learn to overcome this heuristic, however. When nonhuman animals perform the tubes task for several trials, they perform better on later trials than on earlier trials, but their overall improvement is modest and slow. Gravity errors on early trials often give way to random responding on later trials, as the animals have realized that the vertically adjacent bucket is never the correct location but have not realized that the tubes are the key to solving the problem. When nonhuman animals have practiced the task enough to solve it, they probably do so through pure association: they learn to associate each chimney at the top of the apparatus with a bucket at the bottom, paying no attention to the mechanism (the tubes) by which objects make their way from the chimneys to the buckets. Human toddlers can learn to pass the task by association, but they can also learn to pass the task by other means.

One way to help toddlers pass the task is to tell them where the fallen object has landed before they are allowed to search for it. This finding sounds trivial, but it's not. Other animals can watch each other solve problems and then mimic the solutions, but they cannot efficiently communicate those solution; nor do they try. In the tubes task, human toddlers readily heed the testimony of an adult, passing over the vertically adjacent bucket in favor of whatever bucket the adult has specified as the correct location. Toddlers are not pushovers, though. They cannot be talked into making a gravity error if they saw where the ball fell with their own eyes. Nor can they be talked into making a gravity error if they actually know how to solve the task (by paying attention to the tubes). Toddlers' use of testimony is thus nuanced and adaptive.

Another way to help toddlers pass the task is to encourage them to use their imagination—that is, to encourage them to imagine the ball as it falls through the tube. When toddlers make a gravity error, it's because they allow a practiced response (retrieving objects from the ground below) to overshadow any other thoughts they might have about where the ball fell. Encouraging toddlers to use their imagination doubles their accuracy; they become twice as likely to search in the correct location and half as likely to search in the gravity location. We humans thus have two capacities—the capacity to use our imagination and the capacity to learn from others—that allow us to transcend a bias so deep that it plagues the search behavior of other primates for their entire lives.

✦ ✦ ✦

Do you believe that humans have walked on the moon? Around 7 percent of the American public does not. The US National Aeronautics and Space Administration (NASA) has broadcast video footage of several moon landings, beginning with the first moon landing in 1969, but conspiracy theorists claim that the footage was staged. These naysayers acknowledge that the astronauts on film move around slower than they would on earth, but they deny that it's due to a reduction in gravity (from 9.81 meters per second squared [m/s^2] on the earth to 1.62 m/s^2 on the moon). Rather, they claim that NASA created the effect by filming astronauts on earth, in a sound studio or desert, and then slowing the film to 40 percent of its original speed.

But slowing the film would not alter how high or far the astronauts jumped, and they jump higher and farther than they ever could have done on earth. Some conspiracy theorists have posited invisible wires and hidden harnesses as an explanation for the jumps, but wires and harnesses cannot explain why every object the astronauts threw—from bags to hammers to metal plates—traveled farther and higher than they would on earth. Even the dust clouds kicked up by the astronauts' feet rose higher and farther than any dust cloud on earth, and no one could possibly believe the dust was rigged with wires.

Anyone who thinks that NASA's moon-landing footage is fake has to overlook the effects of a low-gravity environment on every object in every frame of that footage. But those effects are surprisingly easy to overlook. The conspiracy theorists overlooked them, and many of the people who have responded to the conspiracy theorists have overlooked them as well. Why argue about the plausibility of invisible wires and hidden harnesses when the dust is a dead giveaway?

Conspiracy theorist or not, we all find gravity's relation to mass difficult to understand. We learn *when* objects fall as infants and *where* they fall as children but we do not learn *why* they fall until we are formally instructed on the topic, if then. We know that gravity is responsible for falling, but we don't really think about falling in terms of gravity. We think about falling in terms of weight. If your groceries fell through the bottom of your grocery bag, you wouldn't blame the earth's gravity; you'd blame the weight of the groceries. Weight varies from object to object, but gravity is seemingly constant. So we ignore what's constant (gravity) and consider only what's not (weight).

But this habit of divorcing weight from gravity has conceptual consequences. We end up thinking of weight as an intrinsic property of objects rather than as a relation between an object and a gravitational field, and we find ourselves unable to answer basic questions about either weight or gravity. Why do objects weigh different amounts on different planets? Why do objects in outer space weigh nothing at all? Why do moons orbit planets rather than be pulled into them? Why do falling objects accelerate at the same rate regardless of their mass? Why does free fall produce a sensation of weightlessness? And at the most basic level, why don't objects on the other side of the earth fall off and float into space?

Children are particularly perplexed by this last question. If objects require support from below, how could the underside of the earth provide such support? Surely anyone who ventured to the underside of the earth would fall off like a mouse who has crawled to the other underside of a large ball. Researchers interested in how children come to integrate their beliefs about gravity with their beliefs about the earth have studied the process using thought experiments like these:

- Imagine that you have a new friend on the other side of the earth. Your friend is playing ball. If your friend throws her ball up, where will it go?
- Imagine that your friend also has a bottle of juice. Imagine that your friend puts their bottle on the ground with the top off. Will the juice stay in your friend's bottle?
- Imagine there is a well-hole in your garden that is very, very deep. So deep that it goes through the center of the earth to the other side. Imagine that you dropped a stone into the well-hole. What would happen to the stone?

What are your thoughts? Presumably you believe the ball in the first thought experiment will fall to the ground and the juice in the second thought experiment will stay in its bottle, but what about the stone in the third thought experiment? People have actually contemplated this thought experiment since the Middle Ages. Scholars at that time were split between two views of what would happen: (1) the stone would stop at the earth's center (a view championed by the scholar Gautier de Metz) or (2) the stone would oscillate back and forth like a pendulum (a view championed by Albert of Saxony). Today, physicists endorse the latter view, with the caveat that air resistance would prevent the stone from oscillating indefinitely. Air resistance would slow the stone with each pass through the earth's core so that it would eventually come to rest at the earth's center, but it wouldn't come to rest at the earth's center immediately.

For adults, only the third thought experiment is truly hypothetical; the other two have known outcomes. For preschoolers, on the other hand, all three thought experiments are hypothetical. Preschoolers tend not to know

During the Middle Ages, physicists debated what would happen to a stone dropped into a hole cut through the center of the earth. The thirteenth-century scholar Gautier de Metz argued that the stone would stop at the earth's center, as illustrated here.

(or believe) that people actually live on the other side of the earth. Accordingly, they claim that the objects in all three thought experiments would leave the earth and fly into space. Implicit in these responses is a "straight down" conception of gravity—the same conception that biases toddlers' performance in the tubes task.

Older children acknowledge that people do in fact live on the other side of the earth and that their balls drop to the ground the same as our balls do, but the children are less certain about the fate of a stone dropped through a hole in the earth. Most side with Gauthier de Metz, reporting that the stone would stop at the earth's center. This response signifies a new conception of gravity—a conception of gravity as inward-pulling rather than downward-pulling. The stone is thought to stop at the earth's most inward point because gravity is thought to emanate from that point.

It's not surprising that older children respond more accurately than younger children, but age is not the only predictor of how accurately children responded. Their knowledge of the earth is a strong predictor as well. The more children know about the earth's shape and its motion, the more accurately they respond to the thought experiments about gravity, regardless of their age. Apparently, conceiving of the earth as a rotating sphere helps children conceive of gravity as an inward-pulling force. And conceiving of gravity as an inward-pulling force helps them conceive of the earth as a rotating sphere. Gravity is not a concept that can be learned in isolation. It is inherently connected to several other concepts: support, free fall, weight, mass, acceleration, and planet. To develop a more sophisticated notion of gravity, children also have to develop more sophisticated notions of matter, motion, and cosmology.

The inherent connections between these notions raise a paradox: how do we revise any one notion if doing so requires revising several others at the same time? The philosopher Otto Neurath once likened this problem to building a ship in the middle of the ocean: "We cannot start from a *tabula rasa*. We have to make do with words and concepts that we find when our reflections begin. . . . We are like sailors who on the open sea must reconstruct their ship but are never able to start afresh from the bottom. Where a beam is taken away a new one must at once be put there, and for this the rest of the ship is used as support. In this way, by using old beams and driftwood, the ship can be shaped entirely anew, but only by gradual reconstruction."

Neurath was a philosopher, not a psychologist, but his metaphor rings true with what we know about learning scientific concepts. The process is slow and hard-won because we have no existing templates for these concepts. We must repeatedly replace one approximation of reality (e.g., "objects fall without contact from below") with another (e.g., "objects fall without contact from below their center of mass"). After many such revisions, our new theories look nothing like our old theories, but their lineage is unquestionable. Every astronomer starts out as a child who denies that people could live on the other side of the earth, and every physicist starts out as a toddler unable to track a ball as it falls through a set of tubes. What a mighty ship we build from such a humble skiff.

5 | MOTION

What Makes Objects Move?
What Paths Do Moving Objects Take?

M EDIEVAL PHYSICISTS, LIKE PHYSICISTS TODAY, ARGUED ABOUT THEIR theories. They agreed on some points of their theories but disagreed on others. They agreed that objects are set in motion by a force impressed into the objects—an "internal momentum" or *impetus*—and they agreed that objects remain in motion as long as their impetus has not been depleted, as noted in Chapter 1. But Medieval physicists disagreed about whether impetus can take multiple forms and how it interacts with other physical forces.

Some physicists believed that impetus dissipates on its own; others believed that impetus remains in an object until depleted by external forces, like friction or air resistance. There were also differing opinions about when gravity affects impetus: from the moment an object is set in motion or only after the object's impetus has dropped below a certain threshold. Some physicists theorized that carried objects acquire the impetus of their carriers, while others believed that carried objects acquire no impetus. Still other physicists debated whether impetus can induce curvilinear motion or only rectilinear motion.

These disagreements had no resolution, because impetus is not real. Arguing about whether impetus dissipates on its own is like arguing about whether gnomes wear hats. No experiment could ever settle the question, because the question was ill formed. The first person to recognize the futility of the question was Isaac Newton. In the *Principia*, Newton laid out three laws that forever changed our understanding of motion: (1) objects in motion stay in motion unless acted on by an external force; (2) a force acting on a mass produces acceleration; and (3) for every action there is an equal and opposite reaction.

These laws are no doubt familiar. Every physics student learns them, often in conjunction with canned illustrations: a ball rolling indefinitely on a frictionless surface (the first law), a block gaining speed as it slides down a ramp (the second law), two cars recoiling in opposite directions after a collision (the third law). But what do these laws mean? How do they render the notion of impetus obsolete? Many of us have memorized Newton's laws and their corresponding equations ($F = ma$, $p = mv$), but we still rely on impetus for predicting and explaining motion in everyday life. One way to understand Newton's laws is by considering how those laws paint a different picture of motion than the picture we intuit on our own.

Intuitively, we treat force and motion as inseparable: force implies motion, and motion implies force. The prototypical force is a push or a pull; either will set an object in motion. But what, then, keeps the object in motion? What maintains motion at a distance? Our intuition is that the force of our push or pull has been transferred to the object itself. Other factors, like gravity and friction, clearly affect an object's motion, but they appear to counteract motion rather than cause it—to redirect the object or to slow it down. We do not, therefore, think of gravity or friction as forces. We might call them forces, but we think of them more as anti-forces.

With Newton's theory, forces are reanalyzed from properties of objects themselves to interactions *between* objects. Forces can be applied to objects, but they cannot be imparted to objects. We intuitively connect force and motion, but Newton showed us that this connection is mistaken. Motion can exist in the absence of a force (e.g., a comet traveling indefinitely through space), and a force can exist in the absence of motion (e.g., a table pushing up on a plate, counteracting the force of gravity). Motion and force are dissociable because forces produce change in motion—where an object is going and how quickly—not motion itself. An object's velocity (speed and direction) is fundamentally different from its acceleration (change in speed or direction); only acceleration requires force.

As an illustration of the difference between our intuitive notion of force and a Newtonian notion, recall the thought experiment from Chapter 1. You imagined shooting a bullet parallel to the ground while dropping a second bullet from the same height. Most people think the dropped bullet will hit the ground before the shot bullet because they attribute an extra force to the shot bullet—the force of the gun, impressed into the bullet itself—and this force is thought to counteract gravity for an initial moment or two. In reality, the difference in horizontal velocity between the shot bullet and the dropped bullet is a red herring. That difference has no effect on gravity, which pulls both bullets to the ground with the same acceleration. The shot bullet would simply cover more distance as it fell.

By changing our understanding of force, Newton also changed our understanding of motion. We intuitively treat motion as distinct from rest. Motion is thought to require an explanation, but rest is not. And different types of motion—rising, falling, rotating, revolving—are thought to require different types of explanation. Newton, on the other hand, taught us that motion and rest are two sides of the same coin: *inertia*. Rest is just a way of describing a moving object whose motion has gone unnoticed. A book on a shelf may not be moving relative to us, but it is moving relative to the earth's axis (at 1,000 miles per hour) and relative to the sun (at 67,000 miles per hour). If motion requires explanation, then rest does too. But Newton showed us that motion does not require explanation; only changes in motion require explanation.

This point is well illustrated by the other thought experiment from Chapter 1 in which you imagined dropping a cannonball from the crow's nest of a speeding ship. Most people think the cannonball would land in the ship's wake rather than on the ship's deck, because we think the ship is in motion but the cannonball is at rest. We envision the cannonball falling straight down while the ship moves out from beneath it. But the cannonball is moving at the same speed as the ship, and it falls forward at the same speed as well.

If the cannonball example is not convincing, consider this real-world example, circulated on the internet in the form of a mock inspirational poster. The poster features an eighteen-wheeler truck whose cab has been crushed by its cargo: a giant stone that heaved forward when the truck came to a sudden stop. The poster's caption reads, "Inertia: Your truck has brakes. The massive hunk of stone doesn't."

+ + +

Nearly 350 years after Newton buried impetus theory in the graveyard of failed science, it remains alive and well in the minds of nonscientists. Impetus theory is the lens through which most of us interpret everyday instances of motion: marbles rolling off tables, carts rolling down hills, bombs dropped from planes, bullets shot from guns, balls kicked at goals, lassos flung at targets, coins tossed into the air. We use impetus theory to predict the trajectory of a moving object, to diagram the forces acting on a moving object, and even to interact with moving objects in real time. No matter the task or the context, impetus theory reigns supreme.

Take the task of drawing the predicted trajectory of a moving object. Many studies have used this task to diagnose whether our intuitive beliefs about motion align more closely with impetus theory or with reality. Participants are given a diagram of an object in motion—say, a marble rolling

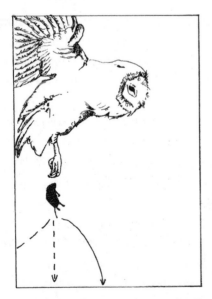 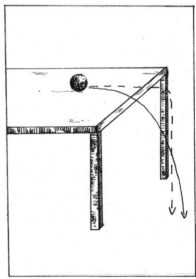

An object dropped by a moving carrier or rolled off a table will fall to the ground along a parabolic path (solid lines), but many people hold contrary ideas (dashed lines).

toward the end of a table—and are asked to complete the diagram by drawing what will happen next. In reality, a marble that rolls off a table will fall to the ground in a fully parabolic path—a path produced by the combination of its horizontal velocity and its downward acceleration due to gravity. Most participants, however, draw nonparabolic paths. They draw paths that are parallel to the ground at their beginning or perpendicular to the ground at their end. They appear to believe that the marble has acquired an impetus that will keep it aloft at the beginning of its fall (similar to the shot bullet) or that will be overcome by gravity at the end of its fall.

In another version of the task, participants are asked to draw the path of a bomb dropped from a moving plane. The bomb would follow a fully parabolic path in real life, just like the marble, but most participants predict the bomb would fall straight down. They appear to believe that the plane is in motion but the bomb is at rest, and they do not therefore grant it any horizontal velocity (similar to the dropped cannonball).

Perhaps the most blatant demonstration of a covert belief in impetus comes from tasks in which participants are asked to draw the expected trajectories of objects accelerated along curved paths, like a ball shot through a curved tube or a ball swung on a string like a lasso and then released. Such objects would travel in a straight path tangent to the curved path at the point of their release, but many participants predict that the objects will continue to travel in a curve. They appear to believe that objects accelerated along curved paths will maintain those paths even in the absence of external forces (the surface force of the tube or the tension force of the string).

The participants' drawings make sense only from the perspective of impetus theory because only an impetus could propel an object along a curved path in the absence of external forces. What's more, this inference flies in the face of everyday counterexamples, like water pouring from a coiled garden hose or bullets shot through a looped rifle barrel. In one study, participants were asked to draw those events, and they correctly surmised that water pumped through a coiled garden hose would exit in a straight line, as would bullets shot through a looped rifle barrel. But when participants were then asked to draw the path of a ball shot through a curved tube, they drew curved paths. Reminding participants of analogous, real-world situations had no effect on their impetus-based patterns of reasoning, which they deployed by default to the novel situation.

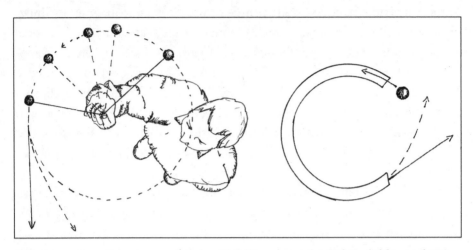

Objects moving along a curved path will follow a straight path (solid line) when released from external forces, but many people think those objects will follow a curved path instead (dashed line), imagining that the objects have now acquired a "curvilinear impetus."

In another task that reveals impetus-based patterns of reasoning, participants are shown a moving object and asked to draw the forces acting on that object, depicting them as arrows. Quite often, participants draw the impetus itself. When shown the trajectory of a coin toss, for instance, many participants draw two forces acting on the coin at all times: the downward force of gravity and an upward force described by participants as the "force of the coin" or the coin's "momentum"—pseudonyms for impetus. On the coin's ascent, the upward force is depicted as larger than the downward force. At the coin's apex, the two forces are depicted as equal. On the coin's descent, the upward force is depicted as smaller than the downward force. It is clear from such drawings that participants believe that an impetus is transferred to the coin when it is tossed into the air and that the impetus wanes over the course of its trajectory. The tipping point between impetus and gravity is the point at which the coin stops moving upward and starts moving downward. Our intuition that motion implies a force leads us to posit a force that doesn't actually exist. In reality, gravity is the only force that acts on the coin at all points in its trajectory; the speed of its ascent decreases until it has no upward velocity, at which point it begins to accelerate downward.

On the other hand, when it comes to drawing the forces acting on a stationary object, participants rarely draw a force that actually does exist: the upward force of a supporting surface, known to physicists as the *normal force*. Rest does not intuitively imply a force in the way that motion does, but a force must exist. Otherwise, the stationary object would be pulled through the supporting surface by gravity.

In studies where participants are asked to draw the trajectories of moving objects or the forces acting on those objects, researchers often ask participants to explain their drawings. The participants rarely refer to impetus in their explanations—at least not by name. Instead, they describe something that plays the role of impetus but is identified in more familiar terms: "momentum," "internal energy," "internal force," "force of motion." Consider the following explanations, all provided by college undergraduates in interviews about the source of an object's motion:

- "The momentum from the curve of the tube gives the ball an arc. The force that the ball picks up from the curve eventually dissipates and it will follow a normal straight line."
- "The force from the moving ball would be transferred to the stationary ball, so the force would move from the moving ball to the ball that wasn't moving."
- "This ball, now that it's travelling, has a certain amount of force. The moving object has the force of momentum and since there's no force to oppose that force it will continue on until it is opposed by something."

These explanations mirror those provided by Medieval physicists, as noted in Chapter 1. One such physicist, Jean Buridan, explained projectile motion as follows: "In moving, a moving body impresses in it a certain impetus or a certain force . . . in the direction toward which the mover was moving the body, either up or down, or laterally, or circularly. It is by that impetus that the stone is moved after the projector ceases to move [it]. But that impetus is continually decreased by the resisting air and by the gravity of the stone." Even Newton once explained projectile motion in terms of impetus. In a notebook dated 1664, a college-aged Newton wrote that "motion is not continued by a force impressed [from the outside] because the force must be communicated from the mover into the moved." Newton would eventually abandon the idea that a force "must be communicated from the mover into the moved," but it was the starting point for his studies of motion, as it is for all of us.

And lest you think that impetus theory is a trite idea—a mistaken belief with no obvious consequence—studies have also shown that impetus theory influences how we interact with real three-dimensional objects. In one study, participants were given a golf ball and asked to drop it on a target as they walked quickly past the target, like a plane dropping a bomb. Most participants released the ball directly over the target, neglecting the ball's horizontal velocity and thereby overshooting the target. They assumed the ball had no "impetus" of its own and would fall straight down. Only participants who released the ball *before* the target were actually successful. They hit the target because the ball fell forward in a parabolic arc similar to the path of a cannonball's when dropped from the crow's nest of a moving ship.

In another task, participants were given a hockey puck and asked to glide the puck through a curved tube. Many participants accelerated the puck along a curved path before releasing it, as if trying to impart a curved impetus. They missed. The only way to succeed at the task was to send the puck on a straight path tangent to the curve of the tube at its center.

Our interactions with physical objects are not always afflicted by impetus. An experienced hockey player, for instance, would never attempt to curve a puck by accelerating it along a curved path, because hockey players have learned how pucks actually move. Likewise, experienced baseball players would never position themselves under the apex of a fly ball, expecting the ball to fall straight down into their glove, and an experienced soccer player would never kick a passed ball perpendicular to the direction of the pass, expecting the force of the kick to "overpower" the ball's existing velocity. We can learn to interact with moving objects in optimal ways, but our first instincts are suboptimal, based on impetus rather than inertia.

✦ ✦ ✦

WHEN WE DRAW the path of a marble rolling off a table as momentarily parallel to the ground, we are drawing the path that Wile E. Coyote takes when chasing the Road Runner off a cliff in a Looney Tunes cartoon. Our expectation for the marble is bizarre, given that we are not fooled by the

While we often predict that projectiles will follow non-parabolic paths, we recognize immediately that those predictions are wrong when we see them play out before our eyes, as in cartoons.

cartoon. We know that Wile E. Coyote should fall the moment he steps off the cliff; that's why we find it amusing when he does not. Impetus-based trajectories are only plausible on paper. As soon as we watch them unfold before our eyes, we easily recognize them as unnatural and cartoonish. People who have had their brains monitored while they watch Wile E. Coyote–esque animations show evidence of detecting the unnatural motion within three hundred milliseconds of its occurrence. We detect unnatural motion even before we can reflect on what it is we saw.

Our perceptual expectations about motion turn out to be far more accurate than our conceptual expectations. For instance, if asked to indicate which of several paths a ball would take when shot through a curved tube, we correctly favor a straight path over a curved path if the potential paths are animated. But if those paths are presented as static drawings, we incorrectly favor a curved path over a straight path. Likewise, if asked which of several paths a ball would take when swung like a pendulum and released at its apex (where it has no velocity), we correctly favor a straight path over a curved path if the potential paths are animated and incorrectly favor a curved path over a straight path if the paths are presented as static drawings.

This dissociation between perceptual and conceptual expectations has been observed even in children. In one study, elementary-schoolers were asked to consider the path a ball would take if it were dropped from a hot-air balloon flying parallel to the ground. One group of children predicted whether the ball would fall forward, backward, or straight down. A second group of children watched the ball fall along each of those paths and judged which path was correct. Almost none of the children in the first group predicted that the ball would fall forward, but most children in the second group recognized that a forward-falling path is the correct path. Even two-year-olds show a dissociation between perceptual and conceptual expectations about motion. If two-year-olds are shown an animation of a ball falling straight down as it rolls off a table, they are surprised. They stare reliably longer at a ball that falls straight down than at a ball that falls in a parabolic path. Nevertheless, when children of this age are asked to predict where a ball will land after rolling off a table, they predict it will land directly below the table, even though they would be surprised to see the ball actually land there.

The fact that two-year-olds make impetus-based predictions implies that they construct an impetus theory of motion quite early in life—long before they've learned the words *motion* or *force*. And the fact that two-year-olds make these predictions despite their ability to recognize unnatural motion in animations implies that our conceptual expectations about motion are partitioned from our perceptual expectations from the very start.

One compelling demonstration of this partition comes from studies of motion-based memory. In one set of studies, college-aged participants watched a ball exit a curved tube along a straight path and were asked to draw what they just saw. Most participants misremembered having seen the ball exit the tube along a curved path. In another study, participants watched as two balls—one large and one small—were launched into the air at the same speed. The balls ascended and descended in unison, but participants misremembered having seen the small ball ascend quicker than the large one, as if the small ball was less affected by gravity. In these studies, it has also been found that the longer we hold the experience in memory, the more these illusions become etched in our minds; the additional time allows our conceptual expectations to more fully override our perceptual ones. We may recognize the veracity of Newton's laws when perceiving motion, but that recognition is as brief as sight itself.

✦ ✦ ✦

IMPETUS THEORY IS constructed early in life and persists despite our ability to perceive motion accurately in real time. Is there any way to move beyond impetus theory? Have educators devised successful strategies for imparting a more Newtonian view of motion? Most educators use problem sets to teach Newton's laws, but problem sets do not help students change their conceptions. One study makes this point crystal clear. Researchers recruited physics students who had received 4.5 hours of physics instruction per week per year for two years. The students had solved hundreds, if not thousands, of physics problems throughout their instruction. To determine whether solving all those problems was helpful, the researchers gave the students a test of their conceptual understanding of motion—a test designed to differentiate impetus-based reasoning from Newtonian reasoning—and compared their scores with the total number of physics problems they had solved. The results were disappointing: students who had solved three thousand problems were just as likely to deploy impetus-based reasoning as students who had solved only three hundred.

Solving thousands of physics problems may not increase your understanding of motion, but it does have one tangible benefit: it makes you better at solving physics problems. You learn how to map abstract equations to concrete situations—to recognize which equations apply to which situations. At no point, however, are you required to ponder the meaning of those equations. You just "plug and chug": plug the right numbers into the right equations, and chug through the math.

If problem sets are ineffective at improving our understanding of motion, what kinds of activities are effective? Many physics education researchers have suggested that *microworlds* are the answer. Microworlds are virtual environments in which students are taught the laws of physics through simulated interactions and simulated experiments. These activities have several attractive features from an educational point of view. They can instantiate any laws of physics, not just Newtonian laws. They can simulate any physical interaction, not just the kind that can be staged in a classroom. And they can measure any physical parameter, not just the kind that can be measured with a stopwatch or a ruler. The things that can be studied in a microworld far outstrip those that can be studied in the boring old real world.

Microworlds may be attractive, but are they effective? Researchers in one study looked at this question using the popular video game *Enigmo*.

In *Enigmo*, players redirect falling droplets of water from one part of the microworld to another by manipulating where they fall. The droplets conform to Newtonian principles, including the notoriously misunderstood principle that projectiles travel along parabolic paths. The participants in the study were middle-schoolers. Half played *Enigmo* for six hours over the course of a month, and the other half played a strategy game that did not involve any physics (*Railroad Tycoon*) for same amount of time. Both groups concluded the study by completing a thirty-minute tutorial on Newtonian principles. The researchers measured participants' conceptual understanding of motion at three times: before playing the video games, after playing the video games, and after completing the physics tutorial.

As predicted, those who played *Enigmo* increased their score from the first test to the second, but they did so by only 5 percent. The physics tutorial, on the other hand, boosted scores by 20 percent, and students who played *Railroad Tycoon* profited from the tutorial as much as did the students who played *Enigmo*. In other words, a thirty-minute tutorial on Newtonian principles proved several times more effective than a six-hour excursion into a microworld that instantiated those same principles. Similar results have been obtained using other kinds of microworlds. At best, microworlds are no better than standard instruction. At worst, they are a waste of time, yielding knowledge that cannot be generalized beyond the confines of the game.

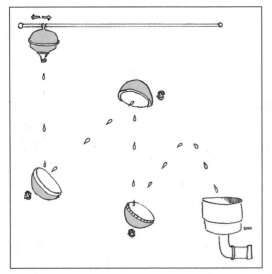

Exposure to Newtonian principles in the context of video games, such as in this game where players bounce water droplets off drums and into vesicles along parabolic paths, does little to help students learn and apply those principles outside the game environment.

In many ways, it's a blessing that we do not generalize the knowledge acquired in microworlds to real-world contexts, because the microworlds we are most familiar with—those contained in popular video games—rarely instantiate Newtonian principles. They instantiate whatever principles make the game most enjoyable for their players. Take Nintendo's *Super Mario Brothers*. Mario and his brother Luigi do not retain their horizontal velocity when they jump off moving platforms. They jump straight up, with the platforms moving out from underneath them. And when objects fall off moving platforms, they fall straight down. Some objects are subject to gravity, and some are not. And gravity, in general, works inconsistently, allowing Mario to jump twice his height but then causing him to fall eight times faster than he should, given the speed of his ascent. Of course, no one who plays *Super Mario Brothers* thinks that they can jump twice their height just because Mario can. We quarantine that knowledge, applying it to Mario's world only, just as students who play *Enigmo* quarantine whatever knowledge of Newtonian principles they happen to acquire from the game.

Perhaps microworlds have proven educationally ineffective because they provide students with virtual experiences, and such experiences are too indirect. Many educators believe that knowledge gained from indirect experiences—video games, documentaries, lectures, textbooks—pales in comparison to the knowledge gained from direct, hands-on experiences. Hands-on experiences have a tangible, authentic quality that many believe is critical for meaningful engagement and long-term retention. This belief has not been supported by research, however. Several studies have shown that hands-on experiences are no more effective than hands-off experiences (i.e., instruction) at teaching abstract ideas like Newtonian principles. The problem is that abstract ideas need to be *abstracted* before they can be learned, and hands-on experiences are not suited for that purpose.

Education researcher Maggie Renken conducted a study that nicely demonstrates the ineffectiveness of hands-on experiences. She and her colleagues compared hands-on and hands-off approaches to teaching that all objects fall at the same rate, regardless of their mass. The participants were two groups of middle-school students. One group conducted a series of experiments with balls and ramps. The students systematically manipulated the incline of the ramp and the mass of the ball to determine which variables affect the ball's speed as it rolls down a ramp. The other group read about those experiments—the methods, the results, the implications—but did not actually conduct any experiments themselves. At the conclusion of the study, only the latter group learned that objects fall at the same rate regardless of mass. Watching balls of different mass fall at the same rate (down a ramp) had no effect on students' prior belief that large objects fall faster than small ones. On the other hand, telling students that balls of different mass fall at the same rate did have an effect. Those students were able to recall and apply the principle not only the day it was taught but also three months later.

On first blush, these results are surprising. Why would students be more receptive to secondhand information about a physical principle than first-hand observation of that principle in action? On reflection, however, these results make a lot of sense. If exposure to physical principles was sufficient for learning those principles, then all of us would learn them on our own, before being introduced to the principles in school. But cognitive biases, like the belief that motion is distinct from rest or the belief that motion implies a force, lead us to overlook these principles in everyday life. And our biases lead us to overlook these principles when running hands-on experiments as well. From a historical point of view, it's ridiculous to think that students would discover the laws of motion for themselves in a thirty-minute experiment when it took physicists hundreds of years of observation and experimentation to discover them.

That said, hands-on experiences with physical objects are not worthless. Given the right instructional methods, they can serve as powerful inroads to learning. One such method has been devised by education researcher John Clement. The key to Clement's method is analogy. Rather than expose students to physical systems and merely hope they discover the principles that underlie those systems, Clement directs students' attention toward these principles through the use of structured comparisons or analogies.

Take Clement's method for teaching the counterintuitive idea that surfaces, like tables and counters, exert an upward force on the objects they support (the normal force). Most of us don't acknowledge that a table pushes up on a book, but most of us do acknowledge that a spring pushes up on a hand. Clement calls the latter an *anchoring intuition*, that is, a correct intuition to which an incorrect intuition can be compared and then revised. The knowledge that a spring pushes up on a hand does not, by itself, help a person understand how a table pushes up on a book. The conceptual gap between a hand on a spring and a book on a table is too great. But

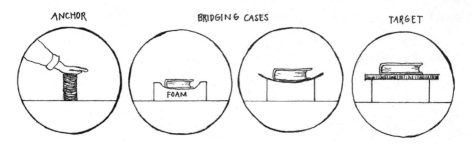

ANCHOR   BRIDGING CASES   TARGET

FOAM

An effective way to teach that surfaces exert an upward force on the objects they support (the *normal* force) is by bridging this idea to the more intuitive idea that a spring exerts an upward force on a hand.

that gap can be traversed with what Clement calls *bridging cases:* a book on a thick piece of foam, followed by a book on a flexible piece of plywood, followed ultimately by a book on a table. With each step—from spring to foam, foam to plywood, and plywood to table—we are willing to infer an upward force where we had been unwilling to infer one before. The bridging culminates in the inference that even tables must exert an upward force on the objects they support.

Bridging activities can be used to convey other counterintuitive ideas as well. To convey the idea that all surfaces exert friction—even smooth surfaces like ceramic or steel—we could start with the anchoring intuition of rubbing one piece of sandpaper against another and then move to bridging cases like rubbing one piece of corduroy against another or rubbing one piece of felt against another. To convey the idea that satellites orbit planets because their path is continuously curved by the planet's gravity, we could start with the anchoring intuition of a cannonball falling in an arc as it is shot horizontally from a tower and then move to bridging cases in which the cannonball is shot from higher and higher towers and thus falls in longer and longer arcs. With enough height (and enough speed), the cannonball would arc indefinitely, encircling the earth rather than falling to its surface.

Bridging analogies like this last one—first described by Newton in *A Treatise of the System of the World*—can be quite poetic. They render the counterintuitive intuitive and the imperceptible perceptible. Not surprisingly, then, they have proven highly effective. Clement has compared lessons with bridging analogies and those without them and has found that lessons with bridging analogies are nearly twice as effective at teaching counterintuitive physical principles as are those without them. By linking opaque manifestations of physical principles to more transparent ones, a bridging analogy allows us to glean from experience the principles we would otherwise overlook.

+ + +

THE SUCCESS OF Clement's bridging analogies raises questions about the nature of our preconceptions. Should preconceptions be viewed as obstacles to learning science or as resources for learning science? Clement's view is the latter. In a paper blatantly titled "Not All Preconceptions Are Misconceptions," he argues that the resource view and the obstacles view have different implications for how we should teach science. According to the resource view, preconceptions should be highlighted and used as bridges to more complex ideas. According to the obstacle view, they should be dismantled or sidestepped.

We have encountered examples of both types of strategies in previous chapters. In Chapter 3, we encountered a strategy for teaching students about heat that sidestepped their substance-based conceptions by introducing an alternative (emergent-process) framework for thinking about heat. In Chapter 2, on the other hand, we encountered a strategy for teaching students about matter that bridged their undifferentiated conceptions of weight and density to a scientific (per-unit) conception of those properties.

Is one strategy inherently better than the other? Education researchers are deeply divided on this question. Some are concerned mainly about what is effective in the classroom, whereas others are concerned about broader, epistemological issues as well. Education researcher Andrea DiSessa believes that labeling preconceptions "misconceptions" is uncharitable to the students who hold the preconceptions. In one paper, he notes that he has attended "too many talks where researchers deride or even ridicule students' knowledge, using deprecating terms such as 'pseudo-concepts' and comparing them to . . . ignorance or backwardness." This practice is wrong, he believes, because many naive ideas "actually become part of high quality technical competence. The rich naive cognitive ecology constitutes a generative pool of resources. Just as sub-conceptual elements can combine to create the impetus theory, better combinations of those or different elements are possible."

DiSessa's view may be charitable to novice learners, but it glosses over the reality of their preconceptions. Some preconceptions really are misconceptions. Heavy objects do not fall faster than lighter ones, projectiles are not subject to more forces than are objects at rest, objects dropped from moving vehicles do not fall straight down, and objects shot through curved tubes do not trace curved paths. What unites these misconceptions—across contexts, across people, across development, and across history—is that they are grounded in the belief that objects can acquire a fictitious force: impetus.

Impetus is not an inaccurate combination of otherwise accurate ideas. It is the root of our inaccurate ideas. Denying that impetus-based beliefs are misconceptions is tantamount to ignoring the empirical research on those beliefs. On the other hand, acknowledging that impetus-based beliefs are misconceptions is not tantamount to claiming that all preconceptions are misconceptions. Clement's bridging analogies are effective because they make use of preconceptions that clearly are not misconceptions—preconceptions that have avoided the taint of impetus, possibly because they defy an impetus-based interpretation.

Given the diversity of our preconceptions, the debate over whether preconceptions should be viewed as obstacles or as resources is a false start. Some of our preconceptions are accurate and some are not, and the question of which are accurate and which are inaccurate is an empirical one. We cannot know how accurate our preconceptions are unless we investigate how they influence our reasoning. Likewise, we cannot know how effective a particular instructional strategy is unless we put it to the test. Sometimes, sidestepping a preconception may be more effective, and sometimes, using it as a bridge may be more effective. It all depends on the preconception.

Sidestepping and bridging are not mutually exclusive strategies. Each achieves something different yet complementary. The bridging strategy renders counterintuitive scientific ideas (say, the normal force) intuitive but does not explain those ideas, either in terms of an underlying mechanism (molecular bonds) or an overarching framework (Newton's third law). The sidestepping strategy, on the other hand, provides a framework for explaining counterintuitive scientific ideas but does not render them intuitive. Educators might thus want to use both strategies in the same lesson, as Clement recommends they should. The world is a complex place, and acquiring an accurate understanding of that world is a complex process.

6 | COSMOS

What Is the Shape of Our World?
What Is Its Place in the Cosmos?

I F YOU SPENT YOUR ENTIRE LIFE WITHIN A DAY'S TRAVEL FROM HOME, AS many ancient peoples did, it would be natural to wonder what else is out there. What lies beyond the boundaries of our civilization? Where does our civilization lie within the world as a whole? What is the world's shape and size? Where did the world come from?

Questions like these inspired the creation of many unique cosmologies, each with its own method of completing the contours of an uncharted world. Ancient Egyptians posited a world in which people lived in the space between two gods locked in an eternal embrace, the god of the land and the god of the sky. Ancient Iroquois spoke of a world in which people lived on the back of a giant turtle afloat in a primordial sea. Ancient Norwegians believed that people lived in one of many realms lodged in a giant tree and encircled by a giant snake. And ancient Hebrews believed the world was a disc-shaped island inside a dome-shaped sky, surrounded on all sides by water.

Noticeably absent from these cosmologies was any notion of sphericity. It never dawned on ancient peoples that the earth was actually a sphere, but why should it have? The earth's curvature is not readily perceptible to the

Ancient Hebrews believed that the earth was flat, anchored in a vast ocean, and circumscribed by the dome of the sky.

naked eye; nor is it consistent with our experience of navigating the earth's seemingly flat surface. The idea that our flat ground belies a round world—that our Euclidean existence is a mere illusion of perspective—seems almost perverse. And then there's the problem of gravity. From infancy, we know that unsupported objects fall. It follows logically, then, that if the earth were round, anything on its "underside" would fall off (as discussed in Chapter 4).

Humans as a species have known the true shape of the earth since the second century BC, profiting from such clever observations as Aristotle's that constellations of stars visible from the equator are different from those visible further north and Eratosthenes's observation that sticks of the same height placed miles apart produce shadows of different lengths at the same time of day. But humans, as individuals, have not uniformly discovered this truth. Even today, millions of humans wander the earth oblivious to the fact that they are wandering atop the surface of a sphere. Most of them are children.

Like adults from ancient cultures, children walk on ground that has no obvious curvature, and they watch objects fall for no obvious reason other than lack of support. Today's children may be surrounded by artifacts that were unavailable to yesterday's adults—maps, globes, models of the solar system, cinematic depictions of extraterrestrial voyages, actual photographs of the earth from space—but do children interpret those artifacts accurately? Are they able to integrate their knowledge of maps and globes with their everyday experience of navigating a flat ground and feeling the downward pull of gravity?

No, they are not, at least not at first. Children readily memorize the fact that the earth is round, but their interpretation of that fact varies. *Round*, after all, can mean many things. Pizzas are round, donuts are round, racetracks are round, tree trunks are round—and none are round in the way the earth is round. "Round like a ball" is not children's first interpretation of the shape of the earth, as can be seen from their drawings. If you ask a preschooler to draw a picture of the earth, they will almost certainly begin with a circle. But as they embellish that picture—adding terrestrial objects, like people and houses, and extraterrestrial objects, like the sun and the moon—they make curious mistakes.

Some children place all additional objects at the top of their circle, depicting people residing on only the outermost edge of the earth and depicting the sun and the moon shining down on those people from directly above. In fact, children who place all their objects at the top of the circle often depict that part of the circle as flatter than the rest. Other children place the sun and the moon around the circle, not just at the top, but they then place people in an odd location: on a flat line below the circle. When asked to explain their drawing, these children note that the earth is round, like the sun and the moon, but claim that people do not live on the earth; they live on the *ground*. Still other children draw a flat line in the middle of their circle and place all the people on that line. They then place the sun and the moon above the line but within the circle. These children seem to have conceptualized the top of the circle as the edge of the sky, with people living on a flat plane inside a hollow earth rather than on the curved surface of its exterior.

Drawing pictures of the earth is a task that psychologist Stella Vosniadou and her colleagues have used in several studies of children's mental models of the earth. For decades, Vosniadou has been documenting the kinds of models children construct, as well as the consistency of those models. Of interest is whether children who fail to grasp the notion of a spherical earth have constructed alternative models of the earth—models that are mistaken but still cohesive, limited but still productive.

In this chapter, I will use the word *model* rather than *theory* to describe children's conceptions of the earth because models are inherently spatial whereas theories are not. Models still serve the same purpose as theories, though: to explain and predict everyday observations. And they share other features of intuitive theories as well, such as consistency across individuals, consistency across cultures, and resistance to being replaced by scientific models of the earth.

Terminological issues aside, what evidence do we have that children construct alternative models of the earth? Drawings, by themselves, are not great evidence. Many children simply can't draw, let alone depict three-dimensional forms in their drawings. More importantly, a single drawing cannot tell us whether children's mental models of the earth are internally consistent. What's needed to assess consistency are several measures of children's models, taken from different angles and requiring different kinds of responses. Accordingly, Vosniadou and her colleagues have studied children's models using as many tasks as a six-year-old child could be expected to sit through: drawings, thought experiments, truth judgments, and requests for explanation. In one task (a thought experiment), children were asked to consider where they would end up if they walked for many days in a straight line. This task prompted conversations like the following:

RESEARCHER: If you walked and walked for many days in a straight line, where would you end up?
CHILD: You would end up in a different town.
RESEARCHER: Well, what if you kept on walking and walking?
CHILD: In a bunch of different towns, states, and then, if you were here and you kept on walking, you walk right out of the earth.
RESEARCHER: You'd walk right out of the earth, huh?
CHILD: Yes, because you just go that way and you reach the edge and you gotta be kinda careful.
RESEARCHER: Could you fall off the edge of the earth?
CHILD: Yes, if you were playing on the edge of it.
RESEARCHER: Where would you fall?
CHILD: Down on other planets.

In another task (a request for explanation), children were shown a landscape photograph and asked to explain why the earth in that photograph looked flat even though the earth is actually round, something virtually all children believe to be true, despite being unclear on the proper meaning of *round*. Here's a sample conversation prompted by the landscape photograph:

RESEARCHER: So what is the real shape of the earth?
CHILD: Round.
RESEARCHER: Why does it look flat?
CHILD: Because you are inside the earth.
RESEARCHER: What do you mean inside?
CHILD: Down, like on the bottom.
RESEARCHER: Is the earth round like a ball or round like a thick pancake?
CHILD: Round like a ball.
RESEARCHER: When you say that people live inside the earth, do you mean they live inside the ball?
CHILD: Inside the ball. In the middle of it.

This child's remarks, on their surface, seem nonsensical, but that's only by comparison to a spherical model of the earth. Is there an alternative model with which it makes sense to claim that people live "inside the earth," "in the middle of it"?

Vosniadou thinks there is: a "hollow sphere" model, in which the earth is likened to a snow globe or fishbowl. With this model, the earth as a whole is spherical, but the upper half is hollow. The bottom of the hollow part is flat and constitutes the ground on which people live. Its sides are round and constitute the dome of the sky. Critically, children who claim that people live inside the earth are the same children who produce the third type of drawing described above, in which the sun and the moon are placed inside the boundaries of the earth itself. And they are the same children who deny that it's possible to walk off the edge of the earth because, in the words of one child, "you would probably bump into something . . . the end of the sky."

In addition to the hollow sphere, Vosniadou has identified two other nonspherical models popular among young children: the "flattened sphere" and the "dual earth." These models correspond, respectively, to the first and second types of drawings described above. Children who view the earth as a flattened sphere tend to draw the earth more as an ellipse than as a perfect circle. They view the flat parts of the earth as its only habitable parts, but they deny that a person could walk off the earth because its surface is thought to be continuous.

Children who hold a dual-earth model, on the other hand, draw a sharp distinction between the earth and the ground, viewing the earth as a distant

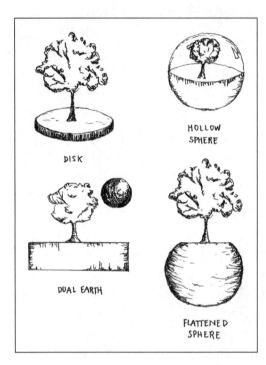

DISK

HOLLOW SPHERE

DUAL EARTH

FLATTENED SPHERE

Children who have not yet learned that the earth is a sphere often adopt alternative models of its shape—models that attempt to reconcile both their perception of the earth as flat and their acceptance of the culturally transmitted idea that the earth is round.

celestial object, similar to the sun or the moon, and the ground as the place where people live. When asked whether it's possible to walk off the earth, a dual-earth proponent might agree that it is but would add that it's okay because you would merely "fall down on the ground." One particularly telling anecdote of a dual-earth model was relayed to me by a parent of a preschooler. The mother had no idea that her son was confused about cosmological matters until, one starry evening, he pointed at the sky and announced, "Mommy, I think I see the earth!"

✦ ✦ ✦

CHILDREN'S NONSPHERICAL MODELS of the earth are quite remarkable both for their consistency and their coherence. Their consistency is remarkable because children devise these models on their own. No one ever instructs a preschooler to think of the earth as a cosmic fishbowl or a celestial object distinct from the ground on which we reside. And no one asks a preschooler to imagine where they would end up if they walked continuously in a straight line or why the earth looks round from space but flat from the ground. Yet, preschoolers still devise these untutored conceptions and are able to reason consistently on their basis. It's not remarkable that when children are asked to report the shape of the earth, they regurgitate the answer that's been fed to them many times before: "round." But it is remarkable that when children are asked questions about the earth they've never pondered before, they provide answers that consistently hint at the same underlying mental model.

Children's ideas are also remarkable for their coherence. In one unified model, they are able to resolve contradictions between the information they've acquired through culture and the information they've acquired through experience. That is, they can resolve contradictions between their secondhand knowledge that the earth is round and their firsthand knowledge of a flat ground and a downward-pulling gravity. Vosniadou labels children's hollow-sphere, flattened-sphere, and dual-earth models as "synthetic" to capture the sense in which those models synthesize seemingly incompatible pieces of knowledge. Synthetic models are a developmental achievement. They are more commonly held by older children (ages seven to nine) than by younger ones (ages four to six). Younger children tend to think the earth is just a large disc, flat and bounded like a pizza.

Some psychologists have challenged Vosniadou's conclusions. They find the idea that elementary-schoolers construct internally consistent and logically coherent models of the earth too far-fetched. We're talking about children who can barely read a clock or count money, after all. The critics argue that coherence lies not in the child's responses but in the experimenters' interpretation of those responses.

Recall that the children in these studies are asked several questions about several topics. The point of doing so is to triangulate on children's underlying beliefs—to determine, for each child, whether his or her collection of responses is consistent with a single mental model. Critics worry that some of this convergence may be an artifact of the interview itself. For instance, an experimenter who pegs a child as holding a hollow-sphere model of the earth may unintentionally change the nature of her questions midway through the interview, asking for clarification when the child provides responses that are inconsistent with a hollow sphere but failing to ask for clarification when the child's responses are only superficially consistent with that model.

One way to circumvent the messiness of open-ended interviews is to turn them into closed-ended, multiple-choice tests. As the critics would predict, children do exhibit less coherence on multiple-choice tests than in open-ended interviews. They select responses consistent with a spherical model of the earth on some questions but select responses consistent with a nonspherical model on others. This finding should not be a surprise, though. Children could easily provide correct answers to multiple-choice questions without understanding why those answers are correct. It's long been known that multiple-choice questions are easier than fill-in-the-blank questions because the correct answer to a multiple-choice question is provided as part of the question itself; one need only recognize it. And children are surrounded by the correct answers every day. Their classrooms are filled with globes, not hollow spheres, and their textbooks are filled with photographs of a round earth, not an elliptical earth. Multiple-choice tests measure children's memory for earth-related information but not their understanding of it.

Understanding that the earth is a sphere—beyond just knowing that it is—requires understanding how a person could live on the other side of the earth without falling off or how the earth could be spherical but the ground could appear flat. Vosniadou once conveyed to me a perfect example of this difference between knowing and understanding. In her studies of children's mental models of the earth, Vosniadou once interviewed her own daughter. Her daughter, who was around five at the time, revealed a flattened-sphere model of the earth. After completing the interview, the daughter sat quietly in the testing room while Vosniadou led an older girl through the same interview. The older girl revealed a spherical model of the earth.

After the older girl left, Vosniadou's daughter asked if she could do the interview again. This time, she proclaimed that the earth was round like a ball, and, when asked to depict the earth with clay, she rolled her clay into a perfect sphere. The daughter proudly showcased her newfound knowledge across several more questions until she hit a question she could not answer: if the earth is round, why does the ground in a landscape photo look flat? Unable to resolve the contradiction between what she had just learned (that the earth is a sphere) and what she knew to be true (that the ground is flat), she pressed her palm into the top of her clay ball, turning it into to a flattened sphere—the model she had revealed just moments prior.

Consistent with this anecdote, there is evidence from more formal studies that teaching children spherical models of the earth requires addressing the assumptions that lead them to create nonspherical models in the first place. In one such study, researchers created child-friendly tutorials that targeted two problematic assumptions: the assumption that the ground is flat and the assumption that gravity pulls things downward. The first was addressed with a tutorial on how our perspective of large objects changes as we move closer to them, and the second was addressed with a tutorial on how the earth's gravity functions like a magnet, pulling objects on its surface inward rather than downward. The researchers administered their tutorials to six-year-old children, who had not yet ascertained that the earth is a sphere. Some of the children received both tutorials, and some received only one.

Before instruction, children revealed the same nonspherical models of the earth as those revealed in Vosniadou's studies: hollow spheres, flattened spheres, and dual earths. After instruction, many children now revealed spherical models of the earth, but only if they had received both tutorials. Children who had received only one tutorial held fast to their original models. The tutorial on perspective may have shaken children's belief that the ground is truly flat, but it provided no answer (by itself) as to how people could live on the underside of a spherical earth without falling off. And the tutorial on gravity may have shaken children's belief that gravity pulls things downward, but it provided no answer (by itself) as to how a round earth could be perceived as flat. Both quandaries need to be addressed before children are willing to abandon their nonspherical models of the earth—models for which neither quandary arises.

✦ ✦ ✦

IMAGINE THAT YOU are floating in space, looking at the earth from outside its atmosphere. Very few humans have perceived the earth from this vantage point, yet we have no difficulty imagining what it might look like. Our imagination is aided by cultural artifacts like globes, photographs, drawings, and models. Those artifacts help us visualize things that we have not observed—and cannot observe—on our own, but they are not without bias. A veridical model of the solar system, for example, would be over a mile long if earth were represented as the size of a tennis ball (as it often is). Likewise, globes and maps almost always instantiate the arbitrary convention of depicting the Northern Hemisphere atop the Southern Hemisphere—that is, depicting north as "up" and south as "down." Did your own mental image honor this convention?

The convention is arbitrary not only because the earth is round but also because the earth is suspended in space. It has neither an internally determined axis of orientation (as a chair does) nor an externally determined axis of orientation (as a brick in a brick wall does), yet people around the world implicitly adopt the same orientation when imagining it or drawing it. The earth does spin on an axis, but that axis need not be thought of as oriented vertically, the way it is almost always oriented in maps and globes. Thus is the power of cultural artifacts. They shape our mental representations in subtle yet substantive ways, beginning with children's mental representations. Children everywhere experience the ground as flat and gravity as pulling downward, and those two experiences constrain the kinds of models they create, regardless of their culture. But children also experience culture-specific practices that introduce variation into those models—variation albeit on a common theme.

Take Indian children's mental models of the earth. Most adults in India know that the earth is a sphere, but elements of ancient Hindu cosmology continue to permeate Indian society, including the idea that the earth is supported by a mystical ocean divided into layers of water, milk, and nectar. When researchers interviewed elementary-schoolers in Hyderabad about the shape of the earth, they found that these children, like American children, had constructed hollow-sphere and flattened-sphere models of the earth. The nature of those models, however, was slightly different. Whereas American children envisioned their hollow spheres and flattened spheres floating in space, Indian children often envisioned them floating in water, cradled from below by some kind of ocean.

Other cultural variations have been discovered in Native American communities and in Samoa. Native American children from the Lakota tribe hold almost exclusively hollow-sphere models, consistent with the Lakotan creation myth of an ancient god whose body became a giant rock disc (the earth) and whose powers became a giant blue dome (the sky). Samoan children, on the other hand, hold a model not observed in any other culture: a ring-shaped earth. Rings are an important feature of Samoan architecture.

Many children growing up in Samoa initially conceive of the earth as a ring, similar to how their houses, markets, and villages are constructed.

The living space in a Samoan house is arrayed in a ring around an interior courtyard, the stalls in a Samoan market are arrayed in a ring around a central forum, and the buildings in a Samoan village are arrayed in a ring around an open plaza. Accordingly, Samoan children project this structure, ubiquitous in their built environment, onto the earth itself.

Cross-cultural diversity can also affect how quickly children acquire correct spherical models of the earth, as documented in a comparison of English and Australian children's mental models. England and Australia have very similar cultures—England, after all, colonized Australia—but they diverge in one key respect relevant to learning the shape of the earth: they are located on opposite sides of the equator, and Australian children are keenly aware that they live on the earth's "underside." Their country is depicted on the bottom of a standard globe; their flag contains an image of the southern cross constellation, visible only from the Southern Hemisphere; and their homeland is colloquially referred to as "the land down under."

The question of how people could live on the underside of a round earth without falling off is thus highly salient to Australian children. They either dismiss the question, since they themselves live on the underside of the earth and have not fallen off, or they become keenly motivated to answer it. As a consequence, Australian children acquire spherical models of the earth two to three years earlier than do their English counterparts. The arbitrary convention of representing north as up and south as down actually serves to spur their conceptual development.

✦ ✦ ✦

FIGURING OUT THAT the earth is a sphere is only the first step in coming to understand the cosmos and our place within it. Other cosmological phenomena in need of explanation are the day-night cycle, the seasons, the tides, the changing constellations, and the phases of the moon. We have witnessed these phenomena for millennia, but our perceptions of them, like our perceptions of the earth, are inherently biased. The twentieth-century philosopher Ludwig Wittgenstein once asked a colleague about the curious nature of such perceptions: "Why do people say that it was natural to think that the sun went round the earth rather than that the earth turned on its axis?"

The colleague replied, "I suppose, because it *looked as if* the sun went round the earth."

To which Wittgenstein replied, "Well, what would it have looked like if it had looked as if the earth turned on its axis?"

Our perception of the day-night cycle is open to multiple interpretations, and the particular interpretation we adopt turns out to be constrained by our mental model of the earth's shape. Children who hold a hollow-sphere model, for instance, believe that the sun and the moon are contained within the dome of the sky. For this reason, they often think that day occurs when the moon is occluded by something within the dome—say, clouds or mountains—and night occurs when the sun is occluded by those objects. Children who hold a flattened-sphere model, on the other hand, construe the earth as separate from the sun and the moon, so they explain day as the sun rising above the flat plane where people live and night as the moon rising above this plane. Things get more complicated on a spherical model of the earth because day is now explainable in terms of either the sun's motion relative to the earth or the earth's motion relative to the sun. And the nature of that motion is up for grabs as well, as it could be anything from rotation to revolution to oscillation.

When my son Teddy was seven, I was curious to see whether he understood, first, that the earth is spherical and, second, that the day-night cycle is caused by the rotation of the earth. I thus prompted the following conversation:

ME: What shape is the earth?
TEDDY: It's a sphere. I used to think it was flat, and then I thought it was round like a circle, and now I know it's actually a sphere.
ME: If we live on the top part of the earth, are there any people who live on the bottom?
TEDDY: Yes.
ME: Why don't they fall off?
TEDDY: Because if you were where they are, the ground would be underneath you.
ME: So why doesn't gravity pull them off the earth?
TEDDY: Because gravity isn't something on the earth; it's inside the earth.

Convinced that Teddy understood that the earth is a sphere, I then asked about the day-night cycle:

ME: What do you think causes day and night?
TEDDY: The sun and the moon.
ME: How does that work?
TEDDY: Well, the earth goes around the sun and when it gets close to the sun, then it's day.
ME: What about night?
TEDDY: The moon gets close to earth at night.
ME: Where is the moon when it's not night?
TEDDY: In its regular position.
ME: Which is where?
TEDDY: I don't know. Not by California.

Teddy knew that the earth's motion (not the sun's) was responsible for the day-night cycle, but he had not yet pegged rotation as the appropriate form of motion, postulating revolution instead.

Such ideas are typical of children who have just discovered that the earth is a sphere. Prior to that discovery, they progress through two prior levels of explanation. First, they explain day and night in terms of simple occlusion: day occurs when the moon is hidden by objects within the earth's

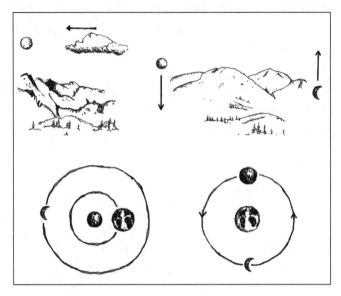

Before learning that the earth rotates on an axis, children devise alternative explanations for the day-night cycle—explanations that are constrained by whether they conceive of the earth as a plane (top) or as a sphere (bottom).

atmosphere (clouds or mountains) and the sun is left to shine alone, and night occurs when the sun is hidden and the moon is left to shine alone. Next, they shift to the idea that the sun and the moon are occluded by the earth itself, with the sun rising above the earth's surface while the moon drops below that surface, and vice versa. Once children realize the earth is a sphere, they begin to postulate more sophisticated relations between the earth, sun, and moon. They first postulate either that the sun revolves around the earth or that the earth revolves around the sun. The latter is, of course, correct, but children do not initially realize that this type of motion accounts for our experience of a year rather than our experience of a day. The idea that the earth rotates, as well as revolves, is not usually grasped until early adolescence.

This progression in children's understanding of the day-night cycle is apparent simply by asking, "What *is* a day?" Researchers who have posed this question to children in grades one through eight have found that elementary-schoolers typically define a day in terms of the activities that occur during daylight hours, for example, "a day is when you are awake" or "a day is when you go to school and play." At this age, there is seemingly no connection between the human experience of a day and the motion of celestial bodies. Middle-schoolers, on the other hand, are more likely to make that connection, defining a day in terms of the causal processes that give rise to a day. As one thirteen-year-old explained, "A day is a full rotation of the earth, like a 360 degree turn. A day lasts 24 hours. A year is 365 days. A year is when the earth goes completely around the sun."

The ability of an adolescent to provide such a definition is, from a historical point of view, quite remarkable. It took humans thousands of years to discover that the earth is spherical and then hundreds more to discover that the earth is in motion. Today, most children acquire this knowledge within the first decade of life. The speed at which such knowledge is acquired should not, however, undermine its complexity.

To understand why the sun rises and sets or why there are 365 days in a year, a child must make three fundamental discoveries. The child must first realize that the earth is fundamentally different from the ground—specifically, that the earth is a sphere, not a plane. Next, the child must realize that the earth's motion is fundamentally different from our experience of that motion. In other words, he or she must learn that the earth is perpetually rotating and revolving and is not at rest. Finally, the child must realize that the earth's relation to the sun is fundamentally different from the earth's relation to the moon: the moon orbits the earth but the earth orbits the sun. These realizations are hard-won accomplishments, much harder than learning state capitals or multiplication tables. They require insight, not just memory.

✦ ✦ ✦

Now that you've learned about children's cosmological misconceptions, you may feel smug about your own cosmological knowledge. But can you explain any cosmological phenomena other than the day-night cycle—say, the tides? Yes, the moon exerts a gravitational pull on the earth's oceans, but how does that really explain the tides? Why, for instance, are there two tidal cycles per day when it takes the moon nearly a month to revolve around the earth just once? And do you know why the moon's shape appears to change over the course of a month? (Hint: it's not because the moon becomes more or less occluded by the earth's shadow.) Or why the earth changes seasons?

(Hint: it's not because the earth is closer to the sun during summer than during winter.)

Even if you think you know the correct answers, I'd still recommend checking them on the internet. The seasons, in particular, are something most of us think we understand but few of us actually do. In one study, over 90 percent of recent Harvard graduates claimed that the seasons are caused by the earth's proximity to the sun. In reality, they are caused by the earth's 23.4-degree axial tilt, which changes how much sunlight falls on the Northern Hemisphere relative to the Southern Hemisphere during the earth's solar revolution (which also explains why summer in the Northern Hemisphere is accompanied by winter in the Southern Hemisphere, and vice versa). The earth's proximity to the sun does change throughout a year, but does so by less than 4 percent and thus has little bearing on the earth's average daily temperature.

Proximity-based explanations for the seasons are pervasive, and they are also quite robust. In one study, researchers attempted to correct this misconception by teaching Dartmouth undergraduates a tilt-based explanation instead. The researchers used animated videos as their instructional materials—videos created by NASA for children. Before instruction, 8 percent of Dartmouth undergraduates gave a tilt-based explanation for the seasons, and 92 percent gave a proximity-based explanation. After instruction, 10 percent gave a tilt-based explanation, and 90 percent gave a proximity-based explanation. The videos had virtually no effect. While participants learned a fair amount of factual information from the videos—the precise shape of earth's orbit and the precise angle of the earth's tilt—they learned no conceptual information from them.

Perhaps the NASA videos were not particularly good and the Dartmouth undergraduates were not given a fair chance to learn. Still, there are other reasons to think that adults' cosmological misconceptions run deep. One study found that adults may not even truly appreciate that the earth is a sphere. In this study, college-aged adults were asked to estimate all pairwise distances between six international cities: Berlin, Rio de Janeiro, Cape Town, Sydney, Tokyo, and Los Angeles. Each city is located on a different continent so the paths between them cover the entire globe. Participants' distance estimates were then fed to an algorithm that extracted a measure of the earth's radius implicit in those estimates.

A participant who chronically underestimated the distances at hand would be assigned a model whose radius was smaller than the earth's actual radius (of 3,960 miles), whereas a participant who chronically overestimated those distances would be assigned a model whose radius was larger than the earth's radius. As it turned out, the model that best fit most participants' estimates was one with an infinite radius—infinite because those estimates could not be mapped to a spherical model of any size. From a geometric point of view, a sphere with an infinite radius is just a plane. In other words, implicit in participants' estimates of the distances between international cities was a perfectly flat model of the earth, similar to children's early models of the earth. A critic of these results could fault our familiarity with two-dimensional maps as an explanation for our poor distance estimates, but that's part of the point: we treat the distortions inherent in a two-dimensional projection of a spherical space as true representations of Euclidean distance.

For me, those distortions first became salient in a conversation I had with a fellow American while traveling abroad in Switzerland. I had flown to Zurich from Los Angeles, and she had flown to Zurich from Alaska. Learning of her travel, I expressed sympathy that her flight was surely much longer than mine. Not so, I was told; her flight was actually two hours shorter. Her plane had flown over the Arctic circle and not, as I had imagined, across the lower forty-eight states.

My mistake was simple but disconcerting nonetheless. It hadn't occurred to me that the shortest distance between Switzerland and Alaska might be a path over the top of the globe. Was my knowledge of geography as disconnected from my knowledge of astronomy as preschoolers' knowledge of the day-night cycle is disconnected from their knowledge of celestial motion? Probably so. The true nature of a celestial system is not easily grasped. If it were, we would all balk at representations of the solar system in which the earth is depicted as half as large as the sun (it's actually less than 1 percent as large) or representations in which the distance between the earth and the moon is depicted as half as long as the distance between the earth and the sun (it's actually less than 1 percent as long).

Not only do we fail to balk at such representations, but we don't even register them as errors. Conceiving of the solar system in geometrically (and mechanically) accurate terms does not come for free with our theoretical knowledge of its size and structure. Nor does it come for free with our experience navigating the earth itself. That experience easily fails us—children and adults alike—because astronomical phenomena cannot be fully appreciated from our limited vantage point. My favorite example of such a failing was a comment posted on NASA's Facebook page below a photograph of a Martian sunrise: "I never knew that Mars had a sun." The comment surely set Copernicus rolling in his grave.

7 | EARTH

Why Do Continents Drift?
Why Do Climates Change?

NOTHING FEELS MORE SOLID OR MORE PERMANENT THAN THE GROUND beneath our feet. But this feeling is an illusion. The ground beneath our feet has not always been there; nor will it always be there. It started out as molten rock, and it will someday return to molten rock, recycled deep within the earth. Far from our everyday experience of the earth as inert and eternal, the earth is forever moving and forever changing.

When the earth first formed, four and a half billion years ago, there was no ground. The entire planet was molten. Only later, as the earth cooled, did its surface harden into solid rock. This rock then broke into several massive plates, which geologists call *tectonic plates*. Tectonic plates glide along a layer of hot, viscous material and are continually breaking, fusing, and colliding, reshaping the earth's surface in the process. Even today, these plates—and the continents embedded within—continue to move under our feet, though this motion is so gradual that we need laser-equipped satellites to measure it directly.

The first person to hypothesize that the continents move—or had at least once moved—was the cartographer Abraham Ortelius. In the sixteenth century, he noted that the east coast of the Americas seemed oddly similar to the west coast of Africa and Europe. Others echoed this observation in the centuries that followed, but it wasn't paid any heed until the early twentieth century, when geophysicist Alfred Wegener marshaled the observation as one of several pieces of evidence in support of continental drift. Wegener's theory of continental drift is a quintessential example of the triumph of evidence over intuition. The prevailing intuition of a historically uniform earth was strong, but Wegener's evidence was vast and varied.

First, the geological record indicated that coastal rock formations are often more similar across contents than within continents. Rock formations along the eastern coast of South America, for instance, are more similar to those along the western coast of Africa than to those along the other coasts of South America. This pattern holds not only for rock formations but also for coal deposits, mineral deposits, and mountain ranges. Geological features that stop when they hit an ocean seemingly reappear thousands of miles away.

Second, the paleontological record indicated that areas now characterized by tropical or subtropical climates (South Africa, India, Australia) were once covered by glaciers, but at the same time in geological history, there were no glaciers covering regions of the world now characterized by artic or subarctic climates (Canada, Siberia). If proximity to the earth's poles determines climate, then these regions would seem to have swapped places.

Third, much as Ortelius had suggested centuries earlier, a geometric analysis of the continents indicated that they would interlock if pushed together. Africa would form the center of this global jigsaw puzzle, bordered by Eurasia to its east, South America to its west, North America to its north, and Antarctica and Australia to its south.

In addition to these geological data, Wegener also gathered some compelling data from biology. By the early twentieth century, zoologists had documented several instances of the same animals living on geographically isolated landmasses. Lemurs, for instance, are found today only on the island of Madagascar, an island located off the eastern coast of Africa, yet lemur fossils have been discovered in India, which is separated from Madagascar by over three thousand miles of ocean. To explain how lemurs migrated from India to Madagascar, one zoologist postulated that India and Madagascar were once connected by a now-sunken continent—a continent he dubbed "Lemuria."

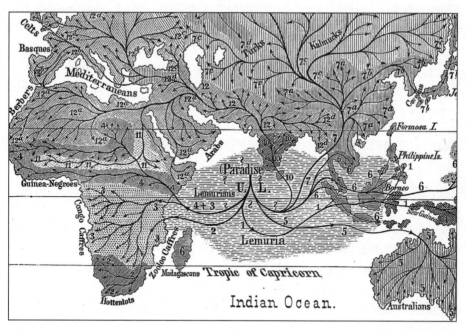

Nineteenth-century biologists postulated ancient land bridges to explain migration patterns across continents now separated by ocean. One such land bridge, postulated to connect Africa and Asia, was named Lemuria in honor of the lemurs that were thought to cross it.

The name Lemuria sounds almost too fanciful to be taken seriously, but postulating lost continents, or land bridges, was serious business in nineteenth-century zoology. Without continental drift, land bridges were needed to explain how animals of the same genus, or even the same species, came to live in places as distant as North Africa and the West Indies (beetles), South Africa and South America (earthworms), and South America and Australia (opossums). The land-bridge theory was also needed to explain how extinct species—Cambrian trilobites, Permian ferns, Triassic lizards—left behind fossils on opposite sides of vast, uncrossable oceans.

Wegner's argument was, in essence, an exercise in pattern matching. He showed that despite the scattered locations of the earth's continents, their geological patterns, paleontological patterns, and zoological patterns matched when brought together. Wegener stressed the importance of these data with a metaphor: "It is just as if we were to refit the torn pieces of a newspaper by matching their edges and then check whether the lines of print ran smoothly across. If they do, there is nothing left but to conclude that the pieces were in fact joined in this way." The geophysicist further argued that the preponderance of evidence—and diversity of evidence—was too great to be coincidental: "If only one line [of the newspaper] was available for the test, we would still have found a high probability for the accuracy of the fit, but if we have n lines, this probability is raised to the nth power."

Despite the evidence, Wegener's theory was never accepted within his lifetime. Geologists were skeptical of the theory not because they were convinced that the earth was unchanging. They already knew that the earth had begun its existence in a molten state, that its interior was still hotter and more fluid than its exterior, that its landmasses eroded and deformed over time, that its oceans had once covered more land than they currently cover, and that its mountains now stand where no mountains had stood before. Rather, they were skeptical of Wegener's theory because they were unable to reconcile the theory with its implications.

Geologists of the early twentieth century were willing to concede that the earth's crust could wrinkle, crack, or fold, but they were unwilling to concede that it could rearrange itself into radically new configurations. By what mechanism could entire continents plough their way through the solid seafloor?

Around the time that Wegener first unveiled his theory, one of his contemporaries, Bailey Willis, summarized the state of the field as follows: "The great ocean basins are permanent features of the earth's surface and they have existed, where they now are, with moderate changes of outline, since the waters first gathered." In that same paper, published in the preeminent journal *Science*, Willis entirely dismissed the importance of the zoological record: "When we find a German fauna in New York or a Russian fauna in western North America . . . what do [such findings] signify? Simply that the surviving species of a fauna have remained unchanged during a longer or a shorter period, either at home or during migration, or that variations have developed similarly in two provinces from an ancestral stock similarly conditioned." In short, they signify nothing that geologists need pay attention to.

Another geologist of the time, Rollin T. Chamberlin, dismissed Wegener's hypothesis as "foot-loose," saying the hypothesis took "considerable liberty with our globe" and was not "bound by restrictions or tied down by awkward, ugly facts." According to Chamberlin, "If we are to believe Wegener's hypothesis we must forget everything which has been learned in the last seventy years and start over again."

But start over they did. Wegener's theory brought to light phenomena that geologists of the time were unable to explain and thus investigated over the following decades. Those investigations rendered Wegener's incredible hypothesis credible—first, through the discovery of mid-ocean ridges, which indicate that ocean basins are not a "permanent feature of the earth's surface" but are malleable surfaces that spread and contract, and, second, through the discovery of magnetic stripes on the ocean's floor, which indicate that currents of molten rock deep within the earth's interior have changed the magnetic properties of the earth's crust as that crust forms anew at the boundaries of tectonics plates. In just forty years, Wegener's theory went from foot-loose folly to paradigmatic truth—at least for scientists. For nonscientists, Wegener's theory remains confusing to this day. The idea that we live on drifting, deforming plates is even less believable than the idea, covered in Chapter 6, that we live on an orbiting, rotating sphere.

✢ ✢ ✢

THE PROFESSIONAL GEOLOGISTS of Wegener's time knew a great deal about geological processes and geological history. If they were reluctant to accept continental drift, then it's easy to see why nongeologists are even more reluctant. Our naive conceptions of the earth are much less dynamic than the those of Wegener's contemporaries. We see the earth as essentially an inert chunk of rock, solid and eternal. To accept continental drift, we must reconceptualize the earth from a static object characterized by small and infrequent change (e.g., shifting coastlines, eroding mountains) to a dynamic system characterized by large and continual change (e.g., sinking landmasses, colliding continents).

Over the past few decades, it has become apparent that students in geoscience classes do not leave these classes with a modern, tectonic understanding of the earth but rather maintain their naive, static understanding of the earth from the beginning of their classes to the end. One wide-scale study found that geoscience education has virtually no effect on geoscience misconceptions. The study involved twenty-five hundred students enrolled in one of forty-three different courses in thirty-two colleges. Each student was administered a test of his or her understanding of geologic time, plate tectonics, and the earth's interior both before instruction and after.

Before instruction, students answered an average of eight questions correctly out of nineteen. After instruction, they answered an average of nine questions correctly. The results were the same, regardless of whether the students were enrolled in a community college, a four-year public university, or a four-year private university and whether they were enrolled in a course on physical geology, a course on historical geology, or a more specialized course like Geology for Engineers. Frustratingly, the strongest predictor of students' final performance was not their major, their school, or their course but how well they had performed on the pretest. It was as though they had hardly taken a class at all.

Part of the problem in understanding a geological process like continental drift is that the phenomena explained by this process are not observable to the naked eye; nor are they even known to the average person. Few people know that fossils of the same species have been unearthed on distant continents or that rock formations on distant continents have been found to match in size and structure. And when we become aware of such phenomena, they do not cry out for explanation in the same way that other, more salient phenomena do (e.g., freezing, falling, boiling, or burning, as discussed in earlier chapters). Geological ideas are treated more as curiosities than as explanations; we assimilate them without connecting them to the phenomena they are meant to explain.

Take, for example, common misconceptions about plate tectonics. Although plate tectonics explain several kinds of large-scale changes to the earth's crust, many students fail to connect the ideas of plates and crust. They assume instead that plates are located in the earth's interior, stacked in layers or arrayed as a shield around the earth's molten core. If students do accept that the earth's plates are contiguous with its surface, they often fail to accept that the plates move laterally, assuming instead that they move vertically (rising and falling, as experienced in an earthquake) or circularly (spinning around a fixed axis at the plate's center).

Contrast this with geological phenomena that we can experience, like earthquakes, volcanos, tsunamis, and geysers. These phenomena are not quaint curiosities; they are dramatic and potentially deadly, and we want to know why they occur. But the explanations for these phenomena are not

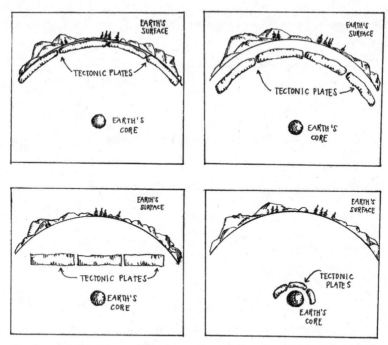

Geology students have difficulty understanding that the earth's surface is composed of tectonic plates (upper left). They assume instead that tectonic plates lie somewhere deep inside the earth (remaining images).

simple. They involve a series of causal interactions, many of which are far removed from the event itself, both in time and in space.

Consider (from a safe distance) the eruption of a typical volcano. At least eight steps are involved: (1) the earth's tectonic plates move; (2) this motion causes one plate to be pushed beneath another; (3) friction and pressure build between the colliding plates, causing heat; (4) rock within the plates begins to melt; (5) the melted rock, or *magma*, has a lower density than that of the surrounding rock and thus rises within the earth's crust; (6) rising magma then pools in subterranean chambers; (7) the rock surrounding these chambers weakens and cracks; and (8) pressure builds within the magma chambers until the magma is pushed through the cracks into the atmosphere. Integrating this series of events into a complete causal sequence is not easy. In one study, researchers taught a group of college students this sequence of events and then asked them to recount the sequence in a follow-up essay on why Mount Saint Helens erupted. On average, students could recount only three of the eight events.

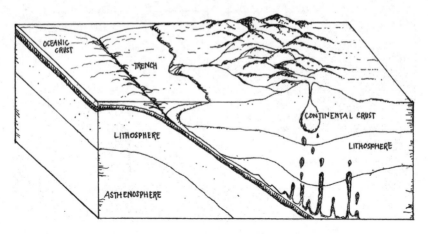

The eruption of a volcano involves several unfamiliar and imperceptible processes, and geoscience students have difficulty integrating those processes into a single sequence of events.

There were, however, substantial differences in the number of events recounted by individual students. Some students recounted as few as one, and others recounted as many as six. Those differences were not random. Students with strong visuospatial skills recalled more of the causal chain than those with weak visuospatial skills. That is, students who performed well on an independent measure of visuospatial ability (a dynamic object-tracking task) also integrated more geophysical events into their understanding of volcanic eruptions. This association held even when the instructional materials included illustrations, which eliminated the need to construct mental images. Understanding geophysical processes requires more than just envisioning those processes; it requires integrating them into a series of interactions. Geophysical systems are highly dynamic, and learning those systems requires dynamic thinking.

✦ ✦ ✦

ANOTHER ASPECT OF geoscience that makes geophysical systems difficult to understand is the immense amounts of time involved. We can look at rocks on a beach and understand that they will eventually be beaten into sand, but it's difficult to appreciate this idea viscerally. Geologists call the time implicit in geological events *deep time*, to differentiate it from our lived experience of time. Deep time and lived time are as different from one another as galaxies are from atoms, but the difference is often lost on us.

Ask yourself, Is dirt from the dinosaur period the same dirt that we find today? No, not even close, but the question may have given you pause. If our dirt is not the same as the dinosaurs' dirt, where did the dinosaurs' dirt go? And where did our dirt come from?

Our intuition is that dirt is dirt, as eternal as the earth itself. It's an intuition we share with children. As one fifth-grader explained in an interview with a geoscientist, "It's possible for dirt to live that long, because . . . [people] will get killed and stuff, and they might just die. And plants, anybody could smoosh them, or a tree could be cut down. But dirt's so small, nobody would really want to do anything to it. And if they do anything, nothing would really happen. You can't kill dirt. It's just there forever."

Surprisingly, dirt is not there forever. It is eroded by wind and rain; washed away by floods; scraped away by glaciers; covered by inorganic matter (silt, sand, dust), covered by organic matter (rotting animals, decomposing plants), heaved upward in earthquakes, buried in landslides, and recycled into the earth itself. Dinosaurs went extinct sixty-five million years ago, and that's a lot of time for dirt to change. But we rarely see any of those changes unfold before our eyes. The timescale of a human life is exponentially shorter than the timescale of most geological events, and we find it difficult to connect the geological features around us—dirt, mountains, islands, canyons—to the historically ancient processes that gave rise to those features.

Charles Darwin was one of the first people to note the difficulty of understanding such processes. In the *Origin of Species*, he wrote: "We are always slow in admitting any great change of which we do not see the intermediate steps. The difficulty is the same as that felt by so many geologists, when [Charles] Lyell first insisted that long lines of inland cliffs had been formed, and great valleys excavated, by the slow action of the coast-waves. The mind cannot possibly grasp the full meaning of the term of a hundred million years; it cannot add up and perceive the full effects of many slight variations, accumulated during an almost infinite number of generations." Darwin's focus was on changes in the biological world, which unfold over vast periods of unseen time just like changes in the geological world. Consider the following milestones in the evolution of life. Can you order them from most ancient to least ancient?

- First appearance of hominids
- First appearance of life
- First appearance of mammals
- First appearance of primates
- First appearance of vertebrates

These events are not too difficult to order. Their sequence is inherent in their content. Life had to emerge before life with backbones (vertebrates); vertebrates had to emerge before warm-blooded vertebrates (mammals); mammals had to emerge before prehensile, tree-dwelling mammals (primates); and primates had to emerge before upright, bipedal primates (hominids). Now for a much tougher question: which of these events occurred approximately 200 million years ago?

If you're like most people, you picked either the appearance of vertebrates or the appearance of life itself. But those events actually occurred much earlier—525 million years ago and 3.8 billion years ago, respectively. The event that occurred 200 million year ago was the appearance of mammals, which most people estimate as having occurred only 10 million years ago. Our estimates are off by a whole order of magnitude, as are our estimates for many other ancient events: the formation of the earth, the formation of the moon, the appearance of fish, the appearance of trees, the extinction of woolly mammoths, and the extinction of dinosaurs.

This last event—the extinction of dinosaurs—is particularly vexing. The amount of time that has passed between the extinction of dinosaurs (65 million years ago) and the appearance of modern humans (200 thousand years ago) is equivalent to 912,000 human lifespans, yet millions of Americans believe that humans and dinosaurs once coexisted. This belief is fueled, in part, by popular depictions of human-dinosaur coexistence in books (*The Lost World, Danny the Dinosaur*), cartoons (*The Flintstones, Denver the Last Dinosaur*) and movies (*One Million Years BC, The Good Dinosaur*). Humans and dinosaurs could coexist in the future—if we clone them, as depicted in the movie *Jurassic Park*—but we never coexisted with dinosaurs in the past.

Some of the strongest proponents of the myth that humans and dinosaurs once coexisted are creationists, or those who believe that God created humans and all other organisms in their current form—no evolution required. The Creationist Museum in Petersburg, Kentucky, actually contains a saddled *Triceratops* that children are encouraged to ride. Creationists

Dinosaurs went extinct nearly sixty-five million years before the appearance of humans, yet many instances of popular culture depict humans and dinosaurs as coexisting.

advocate for human and dinosaur coexistence because this idea allows them to explain how dinosaurs left fossils in a world ostensibly populated by humans since its creation (or, more precisely, since its sixth day of creation).

Religion has imposed many constraints on geology—constraints on how old the earth is, where the earth came from, and where it is located in the cosmos at large. But the constraint that humans coexisted with dinosaurs is perhaps the strangest. It would be simpler to deny the existence of dinosaurs flat out, as creationists did when dinosaur fossils were first discovered, but doing so nowadays would be a death knell for the movement. Dinosaurs and their fossils are too ingrained in popular culture for even the most religious individuals to deny their existence. Dinosaurs must be embraced—embraced and reinterpreted. One such reinterpretation has made waves on the internet. It's a page from a coloring book, presumably for children. The page depicts Jesus riding a *Tyrannosaurus rex* and is captioned, "Even though we know dinosaurs survived the Flood (on Noah's Ark), we don't know if Jesus ever rode them. But he probably did!" The idea that Jesus rode a *T. rex* may be too preposterous to believe, but so should be the idea that ancient people rode *Triceratops*.

✦ ✦ ✦

CONCEPTUALIZING THE EARTH as a dynamic system changing over deep time is critical not only for understanding its geology and its ecology but also for understanding its climate. It is now abundantly clear that the earth's climate is changing because of human activity, and the pathways involved in the change are complex and interlinked. Humans are releasing carbon dioxide and other greenhouse gases into the atmosphere at unprecedented rates through the burning of carbon-rich fossil fuels—coal, oil, and natural gas. The additional carbon dioxide slows the release of heat from the atmosphere by trapping infrared radiation (a low-energy form of light), thereby increasing the earth's temperature.

Higher temperatures then set in motion a cascade of meteorological events. Polar ice caps melt, raising sea levels and altering ocean currents. Altered ocean currents change regional weather patterns, rendering polar regions colder and equatorial regions hotter. Changing weather patterns also affect how much rain falls and where it falls, leading to droughts in some regions and floods in others. Coastal regions are particularly likely to flood, because of the combined effects of higher sea levels and more powerful tropical storms. In short, climate change affects all atmospheric systems: oceans, glaciers, currents, winds, sea levels, air pressure, precipitation.

Things are much simpler from a layperson's point of view. Climate is considered synonymous with weather, and climate change synonymous with hotter weather. This conflation of climate and weather was notoriously illustrated by Republican Senator James Inhofe, who brought a snowball onto the Senate floor in an attempt to show that global warming is a hoax. "We keep hearing that 2014 has been the warmest year on record," he announced. "[But] you know what this is? It's a snowball, from outside here. So it's very, very cold out." The argument implicit in this stunt was that if today's weather is not unusually warm, then the earth's climate cannot be heating up, either.

Senator Inhofe is not alone in conflating weather and climate. Public acceptance of climate change has been shown to fluctuate with the weather, with more people accepting climate change on hot days than on cold days. In one study, researchers asked people to rate how certain they were that global warming is happening and how much they personally worried about global warming. The researchers then compared those ratings to weather reports from the day each participant completed the survey, calculating deviations between daily temperatures and historical averages. Participants who completed the survey on days that were warmer than usual expressed more certainty about global warming and more concern about global warming than did participants who completed the survey on days that were cooler than usual. Participants were also asked to donate some of their payment for completing the survey to a nonprofit dedicated to reducing global warming (Clean Air–Cool Planet), and the size of those donations tracked the weather as well. The warmer the day, the more the participants donated.

The same findings have been observed outside the lab, on a much larger scale. US polling agencies like Gallup, Harris, the ABC/Woods Institute, and the Pew Center have been measuring public acceptance of climate change for nearly twenty years. Public acceptance has increased in general, but it still fluctuates by sizable margins from one poll to the next. Those fluctuations turn out to be related to the weather. Polls taken within a year of unusually warm weather reveal greater public acceptance of climate change than did polls taken within a year of unusually cool weather. Media coverage of climate change follows the same pattern. Climate-related editorial and opinion pieces published in major US newspapers within a year of unusually warm weather expressed greater concern over climate change than those published within a year of unusually cool weather. Fluctuations in weather are only tenuously connected to climate change, but they are a driving force behind people's concern over climate change nonetheless.

In some ways, our conflation of weather and climate doesn't really matter in the long run, given that unusually hot days are increasingly outnumbering unusually cold days, which should raise concerns about climate change across the board. Still, naive conceptions of climate change are problematic because they breed equally naive solutions. For starters, many people refuse to believe that humans are causing climate change and thus refuse to take part in the solution—a misapprehension we will revisit later in the chapter. Others accept that humans are causing climate change but fail to understand how. Humans' relationship with the environment is often reduced to an overly simplistic dichotomy between activities labeled as environmentally friendly, or "green," and activities labeled as environmentally harmful, or "brown." Commonly cited green activities include recycling, planting trees, turning off lights, picking up litter, and commuting by bicycle; commonly cited brown activities include driving cars, taking long showers, using pesticides, dumping chemicals into the ocean, and spraying aerosol cans.

All activities with environmental consequences are seen as related to climate change, though some activities, such as picking up litter, using pesticides, or spraying aerosol cans, are not related, at least not directly. And among activities actually related to climate change, some have larger consequences than others, yet we don't care much about the difference. Transportation, for instance, is estimated to contribute 14 percent of our carbon emissions, whereas waste is estimated to contribute only 4 percent. But we are significantly more inclined to tackle the problem of waste (buying less or recycling more) than to tackle the problem of transportation (using public transportation or minimizing air travel) even when we explicitly acknowledge that the former is less consequential than the latter.

The sacrifices entailed by adjusting our transportation habits are too unpalatable to take on, so we delude ourselves into thinking that separating our recyclables from our trash will save the planet. But it won't—not on its own. The behavioral changes needed to reduce global warming are as life-altering as the consequence of not making those changes. We know this fact implicitly but have yet to embrace it explicitly, opting instead to deny that climate change is serious or even to deny that climate change is occurring.

✦ ✦ ✦

IN CASE YOU haven't noticed, America is deeply divided over climate change. About 16 percent of Americans are alarmed about climate change, 29 percent are concerned, 25 percent are cautious, 9 percent are disengaged, 13 percent are doubtful, and 8 percent are dismissive. The climate science community calls these groups "global warming's six Americas." The size of each group has remained roughly the same from 2008 to the present, despite dramatic increases in the evidence for global warming and the publicity surrounding that evidence.

Global warming's six Americas differ not just in their attitudes toward climate change but also in their climate-related beliefs and behaviors. Those on the "alarmed" side of the spectrum are more likely than those on the "dismissive" side to agree (1) that global warming is happening, (2) that most scientists think that global warming is happening, (3) that global warming is caused by human activity, (4) that it is worrisome, (5) that it is harmful, (6) that it will impact future generations, and (7) that it can be reduced if we take the right actions. Demographically, global warming's six Americas are quite similar. They vary little by age, income, race, or gender. A young, high-income Latino man is just as likely to deny global warming as is an old, low-income Caucasian woman. But what does separate the six Americas is religion and politics. Those on the "alarmed" side of the spectrum are more liberal in their religious and political views, whereas those on the "dismissive" side are more conservative.

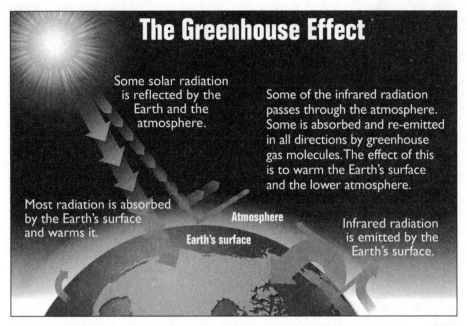

Teaching people the mechanisms behind global warming, which few people actually know, increases their acceptance of global warming.

Clearly, there are sociological factors at play in the rejection of climate change—factors that are deep-rooted and far-reaching—but are there also conceptual factors? Do those who dismiss climate change understand what climate change actually is? Studies by psychologist Michael Ranney and his colleagues suggest that these people do not. When Ranney and colleagues asked hundreds of Americans to explain the causes of global warming, very few people could do so. Only 15 percent even mentioned greenhouse gases in their explanations. Ranney then provided the participants with a four-hundred-word description of the chemical and physical mechanisms behind climate change and measured how that information affected people's climate-related beliefs and attitudes. The full description can be found at HowGlobalWarmingWorks.org, but Ranney summarizes it as follows: "Earth transforms sunlight's visible light energy into infrared light energy, which leaves Earth slowly because it is absorbed by greenhouse gases. When people produce greenhouse gases, energy leaves Earth even more slowly, raising Earth's temperature."

Providing people with this information has two effects. First, it leads to more accurate beliefs about the nature of global warming—beliefs they retain for at least several weeks later. Second, it leads to increased acceptance of global warming, regardless of a person's politics. Even politically conservative individuals are more inclined to accept the reality of global warming after learning about the causes of global warming (though not by a lot—political blinders are hard to remove).

Another type of information that increases acceptance of global warming, and climate change more generally, is information about the scientific consensus surrounding these issues. When asked to estimate the percentage of scientists who agree that human-induced carbon emissions cause climate change, people typically estimate between 60 percent and 70 percent, which is far below the true value of 97 percent. Nevertheless, when told flat out that 97 percent of scientists agree that human carbon emissions cause climate change, we immediately revise our beliefs, endorsing the statement "human carbon emissions cause climate change" significantly more than if told nothing about the current scientific consensus.

The reason that consensus information has such a powerful effect on our acceptance of climate change is the same reason that our clothing preferences are shaped by what other people are wearing and our eating preferences are shaped by what other people are eating: peer pressure. Humans are social animals; we care deeply about the beliefs and attitudes of other humans and whether our beliefs and attitudes align with theirs. We are particularly sensitive to consensus information about empirical matters because we construe consensus as a proxy for truth. The more widespread a belief is perceived to be, the more we are inclined to hold that belief ourselves.

Consensus information influences not only our acceptance of climate change but also our commitment to reducing climate change. In one study, participants were asked to indicate which of several organizations should be doing more to address global warming, including local government, state government, national government, and corporate industry. They were also asked to indicate whether they support several climate-related policies, including regulating carbon dioxide as a pollutant, requiring electric companies to utilize renewable energy sources, providing tax rebates for purchasing energy-efficient vehicles, and increasing taxes on gasoline. The more participants believed (correctly) that global warming is scientifically uncontroversial, the more they believed that public organizations should take action against it and that public policies should be implemented to further those actions. And the more participants believed (correctly) that global warming is caused by human activity, the more they believed that global warming is a serious and immediate problem and that it can be reduced if humans take collective action.

Psychologists have thus identified two routes to increasing public acceptance of climate change: the cognitive route of teaching the causal mechanisms behind climate change and the social route of emphasizing the scientific consensus surrounding climate change. Both routes are effective, yet we often take neither when attempting to raise public concern over climate change. Our default strategy is to guilt trip—to cloak discussions of climate change in a rhetoric of harm and injustice. The earth is cast as a victim, in need of protection from exploitation, and humans are cast as the transgressors, in need of more self-restraint. A prime example of this rhetoric can be seen in President Obama's address to the nation during the week of Earth Day 2015. "Wednesday is Earth Day," he announced, "a day to appreciate and protect this precious planet we call home. . . . This is the only planet we've got. And years from now, I want to be able to look our children and grandchildren in the eye and tell them that we did everything we could to protect it."

This rhetoric may resonate at an emotional level, but it is unlikely to resonate at a conceptual level, because we don't really think of the earth as something that needs protection. How can we harm an object that is seemingly eternal? And why should concerns over harming an eternal object take precedence over the harm we do to ourselves by denying our energy-related needs and desires? A more conceptually effective rhetoric—in addition to emphasizing mechanism information or consensus information—embraces our perception of the earth as eternal and thereby emphasizes the earth's indifference to humans rather than its dependence on humans. Geological systems have operated for billions of years before the appearance of humans and will continue to operate under new conditions, such as higher levels of atmospheric carbon and higher global temperatures, regardless of how those conditions affect our preferred manner of existence.

This more realistic rhetoric is nicely captured by a cartoon that circulated on the internet around the same time that President Obama made his speech. In it, a human apologizes to Mother Gaia—a personification of the earth—for humankind's harmful actions:

HUMAN: Mother Gaia, I come on behalf of all humans to apologize for destroying nature and beg for forgiveness.

GAIA: Oh, my beloved self-centered humans. Nature is adaptable. No matter what you do to it, it will simply change and take on new forms. It has survived worse things than you. You are, however, in the process of changing it so much that you can't live in it. You're not killing nature; you're killing yourself.

HUMAN: What?

GAIA: You're [screwing] yourself over, and you won't be missed.

+ + +

THIS CHAPTER MARKS the conclusion of our discussion of intuitive theories of the physical world. The next six chapters are devoted to intuitive theories of the biological world. To recap, we covered the following physical theories:

1. An intuitive theory of matter, where material substances are viewed as holistic and discrete rather than particulate and divisible

2. An intuitive theory of energy, where heat, light, and sound are viewed as material substances rather than emergent properties of a system's microscopic components

3. An intuitive theory of gravity, where weight is viewed as an intrinsic property of objects rather than a relation between mass and a gravitational field

4. An intuitive theory of motion, where force is viewed as something transferred between objects—an internal state that causes motion rather than an external factor that changes an object's motion

5. An intuitive theory of the cosmos, where the earth is viewed as a motionless plane orbited by the sun rather than a rotating sphere in orbit around the sun

6. An intuitive theory of the earth, where geological features like continents and mountains are viewed as eternal and unchanging rather than transient and dynamic

We form these theories because we are built to perceive the environment in ways that are useful for daily living, but these ways do not map onto the true workings of nature. We perceive matter in terms of heft and bulk, not weight and size. We perceive thermal energy in terms of warmth and coldness, not heat and temperature. We perceive gravity as pulling us down, not pulling us toward the earth. We perceive velocity as a product of force, not a consequence of inertia. We perceive the earth as a flat plane, not a giant sphere. And we perceive geological systems in terms of discrete events, not continuous processes. These biased perceptions lead us down the wrong path when we theorize about the causes of physical phenomena, pushing us to draw distinctions that are empirically meaningless and to overlook distinctions that are empirically meaningful. Only scientific theories draw the right distinctions and thus only scientific theories can furnish us with beliefs that are consistently accurate and broadly applicable.

PART 2 | Intuitive Theories of the Biological World

8 | LIFE

What Makes Us Alive?
What Causes Us to Die?

To a child, mortality is not an obvious property of life. Children get sick and they get hurt, but they don't relate those experiences to physical health. They know them only as psychological discomforts. The firsthand experience of being alive provides few hints about the physiological processes that underlie that experience. Children go about their day blissfully unaware of the vital functions supporting their activities or the possibility that those functions might someday fail. They are, in their own minds, immortal.

Introspection alone will not break the illusion of immortality. Children must discover mortality as a feature of the external environment—first as something true of others, then as something true of themselves. As the poet Edna St. Vincent Millay elegantly described the situation, "Childhood is the kingdom where nobody dies."

I remember quite well the day my son Teddy discovered death. He was four and half, and I had taken him to see Mummies of the World, an exhibit at the California Science Center. The advertisements for the exhibit featured sarcophagi and other Egyptian artifacts, so I thought the exhibit would be mainly about Egyptian burial practices and that the mummies we would encounter would be wrapped in linens.

Not so. Mummies of the World was truly about mummies *of the world*: ancient Incans left in mummifying caves, ancient Celts thrown into mummifying peat bogs, ancient Peruvians buried under mummifying sands, ancient Hungarians laid to rest in mummifying crypts. The mummies' bodies were displayed in their full, desiccated glory. Some were human and some were nonhuman (dogs and monkeys), some were adults and some were children. There were even mummified infants on display.

Teddy was clearly confused by what he saw. His notion of a mummy was limited to the Halloween type—a bandaged figure who chased Scooby Doo through haunted mansions but who was essentially a living person underneath. One of the first mummies we encountered was a mummified child, and he asked what it was. I explained that it was a child who had died in a climate so dry that it preserved his skin and his hair. Teddy looked confused, so I explained that people normally turn into skeletons when they die but that the mummies on display died under special conditions where that didn't happen.

As my explanation sunk in, Teddy's eyes grew wide. "Am I going to die and become a mummy?!" he yelled. I assured him that he wouldn't become a mummy and then ushered him out of the exhibit, past a crowd of chuckling observers who had also witnessed Teddy's epiphany.

For the next several months, Teddy regularly brought up the topic of death. He wanted to know what caused a person to die, whether a person could avoid death, and where a person went after they died. At the age of six, a full year and a half after the mummy encounter, we had the following conversation:

TEDDY: What does Grandma's grandma look like?
ME: I don't know. You'd have to ask Grandma.
TEDDY: Is Grandma's grandma dead?
ME: Yes.
TEDDY: Oh. That's sad.
ME: Well, if she were still alive, she'd be like a hundred and thirty years old. Everyone dies eventually.
TEDDY: Everyone?! Why?

ME: That's just the way it is.
TEDDY: Is Heaven where people die?
ME: No, Heaven is where people go after they die. At least that's what some people believe.
TEDDY: Am I going to die?
ME: [Pause] Not for a very long time.

As a parent, I wanted to tell Teddy that he would never die, that he was special and different from all other human beings. But as an educator, I didn't want to lie to an inquisitive child. If Teddy had asked whether the earth's continents are moving or whether the earth's climates are changing, I would certainly tell him they are. Why should I lie about death?

Death, and other biological phenomena—aging, illness, reproduction, evolution—have an emotional salience that physical phenomena do not. This salience has competing effects when it comes to learning about those phenomena. On one hand, parents and other educators are more reluctant to provide children with facts about biology than to provide them with facts about physics. But on the other hand, children are more inclined to seek out biological facts on their own. In one study, five-year-olds proved twice as likely to ask questions about biological phenomena than to ask questions about physical phenomena.

Children are eager to know why grandma died or where their baby sister came from, and they ask their parents for answers. If their parents are not forthcoming, children then invent their own answers—answers grounded in the domain that children know best: psychology. All biological activities, after all, have psychological components. We eat to refuel our bodies, but we also eat because we are hungry. We drink to hydrate our bodies, but we also drink because we are thirsty. We sleep to replenish our energy, but we also sleep because we are tired. Death is a harder case. Children have no phenomenological experience of death and thus no means of assimilating it to a feeling or desire. They do, however, know of two seemingly related experiences: sleep and travel.

Sleep, like death, is a motionless and sensationless state, and travel, like death, removes people from our lives. Moreover, adults talk about death as if it were a kind of sleep ("eternal slumber," "sleeping with the fishes," "dirt nap," "rest in peace") or a kind of travel ("moved on," "passed away,"

Euphemizing death as rest or sleep may be comforting to adults but is confusing to children, as children have yet to grasp the biological reality of death.

"gone to a better place," "departed this world"), using such euphemisms to cloak death's grimmer reality. Who can blame a child for being confused about death when we describe it as such? Sometimes it takes an encounter with a mummy to cut through the euphemisms and confront death face-to-face.

✦ ✦ ✦

To UNDERSTAND DEATH, we must first understand life, as death is the cessation of life. But what is life? Biologists tell us that life is essentially a metabolic state. Living things extract energy from their environment, and they then use that energy to undertake activities that further their own existence: moving, growing, and reproducing. These activities are universal across the biological world, uniting entities as diverse as algae, aloe, alligators, and antelopes under the heading *alive*.

But organisms from different biological kingdoms instantiate the same metabolic activities in very different ways. They extract energy from the environment in different ways (photosynthesis, eating plants, eating animals), they grow in different ways (sprouting, expanding, segregating), and they reproduce in different ways (releasing seeds, laying eggs, bearing live young). Such diverse manifestations of the same activities make it difficult

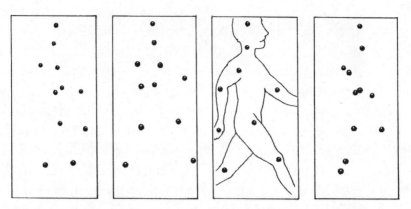

When shown displays of moving dots, infants are more attentive to displays whose motion connotes a walking figure (depicted here) than displays whose motion is random.

for children to see the activities as filling the same life-sustaining roles. So children focus on a more superficial manifestation of life: self-directed motion. Entities that move on their own are considered alive, and entities that do not are considered not alive.

Children's attentiveness to self-directed motion begins in infancy. Infants not only prefer moving objects to stationary objects but also prefer objects that move organically (the way animals move) to objects that move mechanically (the way vehicles move) or chaotically (the way a swarm of bees moves). We learned of these preferences from experiments in which infants are shown two videos of moving objects, side by side, and are monitored for their preferences. In one video, a cluster of white dots moves across a black background as if those dots were attached to the joints of a walking person. In the other video, the same cluster of dots moves across the same background but in no coherent pattern.

Both videos were designed to contain the same amount of motion from a physical standpoint, but infants consistently prefer the video that connotes a walking person, and they show this preference as early as three days old. Thus, even before infants have observed much walking, let alone walked themselves, they are instinctively drawn to this biologically specific pattern of motion. This instinct makes sense from an evolutionary point of view because objects that can walk (humans and other animals) are also objects that can interact with us. They can carry us, feed us, clean us, or bite us, so the earlier we attend to those objects, the better.

Our innate sensitivity to biological motion leads young children to treat the word *alive* as synonymous with "can move on its own." Preschoolers claim that birds, mammals, and fish are alive but deny that flowers, mushrooms, or trees are alive, as none of the latter move on their own. Preschoolers also sometimes attribute life to entities that move on their own but are not biological in nature: clouds, rivers, flames, the sun. This pattern of life attributions has been documented among children in both Western and Eastern cultures and in both industrialized and developing societies. Four-year-olds the world over will typically claim that the sun is alive but that a sunflower is not.

Four-year-olds are also confused about which entities in the world engage in biological activities like eating, breathing, growing, or reproducing. Children know that humans engage in these activities, but they often deny that other organisms do as well. Part of the problem is that biological activities can take vastly different forms in different organisms, as noted above, but another part is that children are unaware of any principled reason for extending these activities to other organisms. Their understanding of life is grounded in animacy, or the ability to move on one's own, and their understanding of biological processes is grounded in psychology.

Take the biological activity of eating. Children know from experience that humans eat, and they know from observation that several other animals eat. But what about the animals they have never seen eat? Do jellyfish eat? Do butterflies eat? Do worms eat? For a child, the question of whether worms eat is not a question about whether worms need energy but a question about whether worms get hungry. Likewise, the question of whether worms reproduce is not a question about whether worms are self-replicating but a question about whether there is such a thing as a baby worm—a small, helpless worm coddled by its parents. One four-year-old, when asked whether worms have babies in a psychology study, denied that they do, asserting instead that "worms have *short* worms." Likewise, when my daughter Lucy was three, she insisted that people have stomachs but birds do not. When I asked her where the birds' food goes, she looked puzzled, asserting "it just goes down."

Lucy's reluctance to attribute stomachs to birds is typical of how most preschoolers attribute biological properties to nonhuman organisms. They do so only if they can imagine how those properties might apply in the same way the properties apply to humans. The more similar an organism is to a human, the more likely preschoolers will attribute biological properties to it. Mammals are thus attributed more biological properties than birds or fish, birds and fish are attributed more biological properties than worms or insects, and worms and insects are attributed more biological properties than flowers or trees. Viruses and bacteria are not even considered candidates for biological properties—a finding we will revisit in Chapter 11.

This graded pattern of attributions, from more humanlike creatures to less humanlike creatures, is observed even when children are asked to attribute properties they know nothing about. If you tell a preschooler that people have Golgi in their bodies and then ask what other things might have Golgi in their bodies, the child is more likely to agree that dogs have Golgi than to agree that worms have Golgi. (Golgi, by the way, are cellular structures involved in protein transport.)

This pattern changes, however, if children are told that the novel property is true of a nonhuman organism—for example, that dogs have Golgi in their bodies. Children now refrain from attributing that property to other organisms, particularly humans. They quarantine the information, treating it as applicable only to dogs. In other words, children are willing to generalize biological information about humans to dogs, but they are unwilling to generalize biological information about dogs to humans, treating humans as if they were royalty in the biological world. Facts that children learn about humans are occasionally assumed to be true of other organisms, but facts that children learn about other organisms are rarely assumed to be true of humans.

Asymmetries of this nature lessen as children grow older, but even some ten-year-olds are disinclined to make biological attributions to, and from, plants. Plants are a sticking point in the transition from an animistic understanding of life to a metabolic understanding. Self-moving yet nonliving entities, like the wind and the sun, are also sticking points. When my son Teddy was on the cusp of turning seven, he surprised me by declaring that cactuses are not alive. I reassured him that cactuses are alive and then quizzed him on the life status of several other entities:

ME: Is a flower alive?
TEDDY: Yes.
ME: Is a mushroom alive?
TEDDY: Yes.
ME: Is the sun alive?

TEDDY: [Pause] No. Am I right?

ME: Yes, you're right. Is a computer alive?

TEDDY: No! That's silly.

ME: Is a robot alive?

TEDDY: Yes.

ME: It is?

TEDDY: Yes, because it can walk and talk. And it can steal your brain.

ME: What makes something alive?

TEDDY: I don't know. What?

ME: Well, things that are alive need energy. And they need water. And they make waste. And they reproduce.

TEDDY: What does reproduce mean?

ME: It means they make babies.

TEDDY: Oh. [Pause] Things that are alive also grow old.

ME: That's right. So do you still think a robot is alive?

TEDDY: No, because robots don't grow old. And they don't have lungs or a heart. And they can't move very much.

Notice how Teddy, in response to my description of what makes something alive, spontaneously contributed other properties: growing old, having lungs, and having a heart. But also notice that his final thought was about motion, as if the fact that a robot is not alive means that it shouldn't be able to move on its own either.

Around the time Teddy and I had this conversation, Teddy had developed an interest in riddles. One of his favorites was Gollum's fourth riddle to Bilbo Baggins in *The Hobbit*: "Alive without breath / As cold as death / Clad in mail never clinking / Never thirsty, ever drinking." The answer is a fish. Teddy was captivated by this riddle because it was so counterintuitive. Fish instantiate the properties of life in very different ways than humans do. They extract oxygen from water, not air; they stay hydrated through osmosis, not drinking; and their body temperature is variable, not constant. Gollum's riddle exemplified Teddy's ongoing struggle to decipher the properties of life. If Teddy had encountered the riddle before this struggle, I doubt it would have resonated with him, as it would not have made much sense.

The transition from an animistic understanding of life to a metabolic one was difficult for Teddy, as it is for all children, because it requires two interrelated insights: not all animate entities are alive and not all living en-

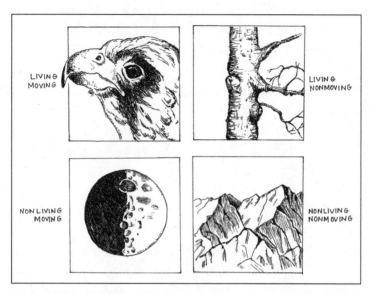

Young children identify life with animacy, or the ability to move on one's own. So they would correctly judge that birds are alive and that mountains are not, but they would incorrectly judge that the moon is alive and that trees are not.

tities are animate, at least not to the naked eye. (Plants move on their own, but they move very slowly.) Exposure to more instances of living, yet seemingly inanimate, entities might have helped Teddy differentiate animacy from life, but Teddy, like many modern children, was largely isolated from the biological world. He lived in a city, and city living does not lend itself well to exploring nature.

Indeed, urban children's understanding of the biological world develops slower than that of rural children. Urban children treat humans as biologically special for longer than rural children do, generalizing biological information learned about humans to nonhumans but refraining to generalize biological information learned about nonhumans to humans. Urban children also reason about biological properties in less sophisticated ways, claiming that diseases are more likely to spread between organisms within the same taxonomic family living in diverse environments (e.g., from polar bears to panda bears) than to spread between organisms within the same environment belonging to diverse taxonomic families (e.g., from polar bears to polar foxes). Sound ecological reasoning seems to require firsthand experience actually exploring an environment.

One notable exception to this pattern is urban children who own pets. These children are more likely than their pet-less counterparts to attribute biological properties to nonhuman organisms. They are also more likely to treat humans as biologically ordinary—that is, to treat humans as subject to the same biological constraints as other organisms. Pets are the urban child's answer to how they can live apart from nature but still remain connected to it. Urban families may sometimes treat their pets like humans—cooking them meals or taking them to spas—but those pets serve as valuable reminders that even humans are animals too.

+ + +

As CHILDREN REFINE their view of what is alive, they also refine their view of what can die and what causes those things to die. They move from conceiving of death as a kind of behavior (sleep or travel) to conceiving of death as a biological terminus—the universal destination for all living things. As one friend soberly summarized the situation, "The best news a doctor can give you is that you'll die of something else."

For several decades, researchers have charted children's ideas of death by assessing their understanding of five biological principles: (1) that death is inevitable, (2) that death is irreversible, (3) that death applies only to living things, (4) that death brings an end to all biological activity, and (5) that death is caused by a breakdown of the body and consequent loss of vital functions.

Knowledge of the first principle (death is inevitable) is assessed by asking children to name things that are alive and whether those things must also die. Of interest is whether children mention people. Older children tend to mention people, but younger children do not. Knowledge of the second principle (death is irreversible) is assessed by posing the thought experiment "If a person dies and they haven't been buried in their grave for very long, can they become a live person again?" Older children claim they can't, but younger children sometimes claim they can.

Knowledge of the third principle (only living things die) is assessed by asking children to name things that do *not* die. Older children mention only nonliving things (furniture, clothing, tools), but younger children sometimes mention both living things and nonliving things. Knowledge of the fourth principle (biological activity ceases upon death) is assessed by asking children whether dead people need food, water, or air; move around; have dreams; or use the bathroom. Older children say dead people do not, but younger children sometimes say they do.

Finally, knowledge of the fifth principle (death is caused by a loss of vital functions) is assessed by asking children to name some things that cause a person to die and to explain why those things cause a person to die. Younger children typically name lethal instruments—knives, guns, poison—but provide no explanation for why those instruments are lethal. Older children, on the other hand, provide such explanations (e.g., "knives cut your body and all your blood comes out"), and they cite causes of death other than violence, like cancer or heart disease.

Children do not come to understand all five principles at once. Rather, they understand that death is inevitable (principle 1) and that death is irreversible (principle 2) one to two years before they understand that death applies only to living things (principle 3) and that death brings an end to all biological activity (principle 4). And they understand that death is caused by a loss of vital functions (principle 5) several years later.

This pattern makes sense when you consider what children need to know to grasp each principle. To grasp the first two principles, they need to know that death is endless and unavoidable, akin to an endless sleep or an unavoidable trip, but they need not know anything genuinely biological about death. To grasp the next two principles, children need to know more about biology. They need to know what kinds of things are alive and what kinds of processes sustain life, but they need not know anything specific about biological processes. To grasp the last principle, on the other hand, children need to know the details. They need to know what kinds of processes sustain life, how they are interrelated, and how they are instantiated in real, flesh-and-blood bodies.

Most children come to hold a biologically mature concept of death by age ten, but this age can vary depending on how frequently the adults in the child's community talk about death. Children in modern, industrialized societies tend not to hear much talk about death. They do not regularly encounter death—either human death or animal death. Nor do they encounter much discussion of death in child-directed speech or child-directed media. When children do encounter such discussions, the material tends to focus more on grieving than on dying. For instance, children's books on death typically discuss the sadness, anger, or longing felt by the deceased's loved ones but rarely discuss the biological process of death itself.

Further complicating matters is religion. Most adults do not actually believe that humans cease to exist on death; they believe that at least some component of a person's identity survives the death of their physical body. Thus, when discussing death with children, adults tend to cloak the discussion in spiritual or religious terms, claiming that, in contrast to death principle 4, human activity does not cease with death but is instead altered by death. The deceased are described as continuing to think, feel, and move but in a different form (e.g., as an angel) and in a different place (e.g., Heaven). This way of thinking about death is well summarized by the meme, "We are not human beings having a spiritual experience; we are spiritual beings having a human experience."

Studies show that this kind of testimony is positively confusing to young children. If young children are primed to think about death in religious terms—by, for example, listening to a story about a priest visiting a dying person on the person's deathbed—they become significantly less likely to claim that biological activity ceases upon death, claiming instead that a dead person's eyes continue to see or that a dead person's heart continues to beat. The partition between life and death, which young children must actively work to understand, breaks down when they hear religious testimony about death.

And religious testimony about death is incredibly common. Most adults in most cultures think of death as both a biological terminus and a spiritual transformation, and they convey this dual conception to their children. But the dual conception relies on a distinction that children have yet to make: the distinction between a material component of human existence (the body) and an immaterial component (the soul).

Young children cannot make this distinction, because they have yet to grasp the concept of a body. They know what a body is from a physical point of view—they have one, after all—but they are ignorant of what it is from a biological point of view: a machine whose internal parts work in concert to support the functioning of the machine as a whole. Adults may conceive of the soul as "the ghost in the machine," but children have no conception of the machine and thus no way to distinguish it from the ghost.

✦ ✦ ✦

THE CONCEPT OF a body is the glue between the concept of life and the concept of death. All living things have bodies, and all bodies eventually break down. These bodies may be as simple as a single cell or as complex as trillions of cells organized into distinct tissues and organs, but bodies share the common property of having internal parts that subserve the functioning of the whole.

Thinking about organisms in terms of bodies provides children with a framework for making sense of biological facts. It allows children to recognize the following:

1. Only entities with bodies are alive (hence, the sun and the wind are not alive).
2. All entities with bodies are alive (hence, flowers and trees are alive).
3. External biological functions subserve internal biological functions (hence, we eat because our bodies need energy and we breathe because our bodies need oxygen).
4. Death results from the breakdown of the body (hence, the cessation of biological activity upon death).
5. Bodies can break down in different ways (hence, the possibility of a nonviolent death).
6. All bodies eventually break down (hence, the inevitability and irreversibility of death).

In support of this idea, children who know the names, functions, and locations of the human body's internal organs also tend to know several other biological facts. They know that flowers and trees are alive, that the wind and the sun are not alive, that biological activities have metabolic functions, that biological activities cease upon death, and that death is caused by a loss of vital functions. These correlations might be an artifact of general knowledge—that is, children who know a lot about the body happen to know a lot about many other things, including life and death—but other studies suggest not.

In one such study, psychologist Virginia Slaughter and her colleagues visited local preschools and assessed the children's understanding of life, death, and the body. The researchers then taught the children biological facts about the body. Slaughter's group predicted that the more the children knew about the body, the better they would understand life and death. The

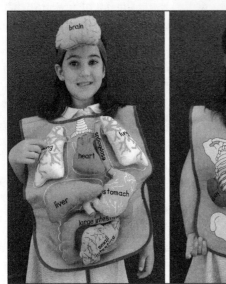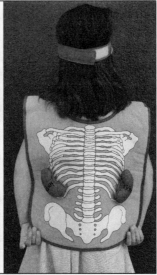

Teaching children the locations and functions of internal organs helps them grasp the higher-order concepts of life and death.

researchers taught the children biological facts about the body using an *anatomy apron*, or a cloth apron on which were attached physical models of the body's organs. Children were encouraged to detach and reattach each organ, learning in the process where the organs are located, what they do, and how they are interrelated.

Before instruction, the children exhibited a minimal understanding of death, as assessed by the five-principle "death interview," and a moderate understanding of life, as assessed by their ability to articulate the life-sustaining functions of biological properties (e.g., "we breathe because our bodies need oxygen"). After instruction, they exhibited a significantly more sophisticated understanding of both life and death. On the death interview, for instance, they went from claiming that dead people continue to eat and breathe to claiming that all biological activity ceases upon death and from claiming that death is caused only by guns or poison to claiming that death occurs whenever vital organs fail. They progressed in their understanding of death despite being taught nothing specifically about death. Their new-found knowledge of the body was sufficient.

One might wonder how the parents of the children in Slaughter's study felt about the study's outcome—that their children went to school to learn about the human body and came home with a nuanced appreciation of their own mortality. The study is reminiscent of one described in a fake news epi-

sode from the *Onion*. In the episode, a reporter visits the lab of two researchers who taught Quigley, a Western lowland gorilla, the concept of mortality:

RESEARCHER: The first thing we did was teach him patterns, like "red block,"
"blue block," "green block" over and over. Then it became a pattern of "gorilla born," "gorilla grow," "gorilla die" over and over.
REPORTER: The researchers then showed Quigley photographs of dead and
dying gorillas, while communicating the phrases "you someday" and "no
choice."
RESEARCHER: It took thousands of repetitions, but Quigley finally became
cognizant of the correlation between himself and the decomposing pile of
hair and flesh in the photo.
REPORTER: The researchers say that, at first, Quigley could only communicate rudimentary fears about his own death, but he soon moved on to
expressing more complex emotions, like indifference and self-hatred. And,
just two days ago, they even witnessed what they believe to have been a
panic attack in Quigley.
RESEARCHER: He was letting out these anguished cries and banging his head
against the wall, and I just thought, "We did it!"

Does teaching children about death increase their fear of death, as it
did for Quigley? Slaughter and her colleagues investigated this question as
well. In a follow-up study, they administered the five-principle death interview to children between the ages of four and eight, along with measures
of how strongly the children feared death-related words, like *dead*, *dying*,
funeral, and *coffin*. Children's scores on the death interview were correlated
with their fear ratings, but the correlation ran in the opposite direction of
what you might think: the better the children understood death, the less
they feared it.

Understanding death turns out to be helpful—not harmful—to a child's
emotional well-being. This finding is consistent with what clinicians have
long believed from their personal experience counseling grieving children.
Clinicians almost always advise parents to tackle death head-on, talking
with their children about death in clear, concrete terms rather than skirt-
ing the issue or cloaking it in euphemisms. The biological explanation for
death may be disconcerting, but a disconcerting explanation is better than
no explanation at all.

Children know of death long before they understand it, initially conceiving of death as an altered form of life. How frightening it must be for them to think that we bury people who still need food and water or that we cremate people who still think and feel pain. And how sad it must be for children to think that a loved one has left home but is still living on somewhere else. Understanding death in biological terms quells those unfounded fears—fears never entertained by a gorilla but certainly entertained by human children.

✦ ✦ ✦

WE ADULTS MAY understand death better than children do, but we still feel conflicted about it. A great example is the Pentagon's decision to exhume the remains of nearly four hundred sailors and marines who died in the Japanese attack on Pearl Harbor over seventy years ago. The remains rest in a series of comingled graves in Honolulu and will be exhumed and submitted to DNA analysis in an attempt to identify them. The identified remains will then be returned to the individuals' families, though the Pentagon estimates that it will be able to identify the remains of only half the interred sailors and marines.

The cost of this endeavor will be high—tens of millions of dollars—and it's debatable whether its benefits exceed its costs. The goal is to help the families of the deceased achieve closure, but there is no doubt that these men are dead. And most of the sailors' immediate family members are dead now as well. How would moving bones from one burial plot to another change anyone's knowledge of the deceased or their emotional relationship with that person?

On one level, we may recognize that bones are just bones, but on another, we see them as signifying something more: a part of our being that transcends the breakdown of our body. Most of us never fully commit to the idea that death brings an end to all human activities, especially psychological activities, even though we have no direct evidence to the contrary. Our reluctance to accept death as a biological terminus must stem, in large part, from our emotional reaction to the idea of nonexistence, but it may also stem from confusion about the very nature of life and death. We may no longer wear this confusion on our sleeves, as children do, but we still wear it under our sleeves, so to speak.

Consider adults' understanding of the life status of plants. Plants are alive on even the most restrictive definitions of life (as opposed to, say, viruses or individual organs), yet we don't talk about plants as if they were alive, and we don't reason about plants as if they were alive either. In conversations about plants, we use the terms *life* and *alive* one-fifth as often as we do in conversations about animals, which is no more often than children do. We know far less about plants than we know about animals; we can rattle off the names of hundreds of mammals but can recall the names of only a handful of trees. And when asked explicitly about the properties of plants, we tend to deny that they exhibit any goal-directed behaviors, like sensing their environment, communicating with one another, or moving on their own.

My favorite example of our impoverished knowledge of plants comes from a college-level ecology course. On the first day of class, the instructor gave her students a questionnaire to gauge their pre-instructional knowledge of ecology. The first question was to list five ways that animals interact with each other, and the second was to list five ways that plants interact with each other. In response to the first prompt, one student wrote "eat each other," "fight each other," "talk to each other," "chase each other," and "mate with each other." In response to the second, he wrote, "they DON'T."

Perhaps the most striking demonstration of our conceptual ambivalence toward plants comes from a study of biology professors' classification of plants as living things. In this study, the professors were shown a series of labels on a computer screen and asked to decide, as quickly as possible, whether each of those labels named something alive. The list included animals (parakeet, walrus), plants (petunia, willow), animate artifacts (clock, rocket), inanimate artifacts (pencil, teaspoon), animate natural objects (geyser, tsunami), and inanimate natural objects (pebble, shell).

Biology professors spend their entire careers studying the properties of life, so if anyone should be good at discerning what is and is not alive, it's a biology professor. Nevertheless, under time pressure, biology professors experienced difficulty classifying plants as alive, making more errors for plants than for animals. They also had difficulty classifying the natural objects as not alive if those objects were animate, making more errors for animate objects (like geysers and tsunamis) than for inanimate ones (like pebbles and shells). Even when their classifications were correct, biology professors were significantly slower at classifying plants than they were at classifying animals. The professors were also significantly slower at classifying animate objects than they were at classifying inanimate ones.

Children's motion-based conceptions of life apparently stick with us as we acquire a more refined understanding of the biological world, even an expert understanding. We tuck those conceptions away but never discard them completely, similar to how we tuck away rather than discard our childhood conceptions of matter (Chapter 2), heat (Chapter 3), and the shape of the earth (Chapter 6). They reemerge when we are rushed or burdened. They also reemerge when we are afflicted by cognitive impairments, like the impairments in memory and reasoning wrought by Alzheimer's disease.

Researchers have long observed that people with Alzheimer's disease lose certain aspects of their biological knowledge: the names of common animals, where those animals live, and what those animals do. Scientists used to think that this loss entailed merely factual information, but we now know that people with Alzheimer's lose their *conceptual* understanding of biology as well. When these people are administered the kinds of biological reasoning tasks described throughout this chapter, they perform just like preschoolers.

Asked what it means to be alive, people with Alzheimer's disease rarely mention metabolic functions (e.g., eating, breathing, growing) but often mention the capacity for motion. Asked to name examples of living things, people with Alzheimer's disease almost always mention animals but rarely mention plants. Asked whether specific entities are alive, people with Alzheimer's disease rarely classify flowers or trees as alive but often classify rain, wind, and fire as alive. These results are not attributable to the fact that Alzheimer's disease typically afflicts the old, and older people are generally more forgetful. Adults of the same age who do not have the disease provide biologically accurate responses.

Alzheimer's disease thus appears to strip away the metabolic understanding of life that we attain around age ten, returning people who have the disease to the naive state at which they began their exploration of the biological world. This development may well have emotional consequences for how people with Alzheimer's disease view death. They may be frightened if the disease erases their biological understanding of death, since confusion about death breeds fear of death, but they could also be comforted, if the disease erases their knowledge of death altogether. If nature is kind, a person with Alzheimer's disease experiences the latter, joining the youngest of children in the kingdom where nobody dies.

9 | GROWTH

Why Do We Grow Bigger?
Why Do We Grow Older?

B IRTHDAY PARTIES MEAN A LOT TO YOUNG CHILDREN. FOR WEEKS beforehand, they talk about who they are going to invite, where they are going to hold their party, and what they are going to do. And for good reason: birthday parties are a confluence of many important events in a child's life. They are an opportunity for social recognition and esteem. They are an opportunity for special foods (cake!) and material rewards (presents!). They mark a change in status among a child's peers. And, of course, they mark a change in age.

This last event is the most mysterious. Birthdays are a commemoration of the day we were born, but children have no recollection of that day; nor do they understand the meaning of birth as a biological origin. For all they know, they've always existed as an independent being, and they have no idea that their age reflects the number of years that have passed since a time when they didn't exist as an independent being.

Children know that four-year-olds are bigger, smarter, and more capable than three-year-olds and that three-year-olds are bigger, smarter, and more capable than two-year-olds, but the numerical meaning of those labels is lost on them. To a child, an age is just a social identifier, like a name or an address. When my son Teddy turned four, it took him a couple of months to remember that he was no longer three. When prompted for his age, he would say "Three," and I would remind him that he was now four. Once, when prompted for his age, he turned to me and said, "Daddy, I forget. What's my numbers name?"

Age, at its core, is a biological concept—a numerical index of growth—and children must come to understand how and why people grow before they can understand how and why people age. Accordingly, the birthday party and its age-changing repercussions are topics of much curiosity among preschoolers. Many preschoolers associate the party itself with the process of aging. They think that if you miss a birthday party, you'll miss the opportunity to age.

Researchers have explored children's beliefs on the matter with this thought experiment: "Suppose there was a boy whose mother got sick and could not give him a birthday party. The following year, she decided to give him a birthday party not only once, like everybody else has, but rather again and again until he is older than everybody else. One birthday for age five, like his friends, and then quickly another birthday for age six, and then a few days later, one for age seven. What do you think? Is that a good idea?" When this thought experiment was proposed to children between the ages of four and seven, few of the oldest children thought it would work, but nearly all of the youngest children thought it would.

Children who claim that missing a birthday party will delay aging or that having an extra birthday party will hasten aging lack what psychologists term a *vitalistic* theory of biology. Vitalism is the idea that living things possess an internal energy, or life force, that allows those things to move and to grow. This life force is depleted through daily activity but can be replenished by eating, drinking, or sleeping.

From a scientific point of view, vitalism seems to be nothing more than a gloss for metabolic functioning—our life force is our biochemical supply of energy—but vitalism can stand on its own with no understanding of the tissues or organs that instantiate metabolic functions. In the history of biology, vitalism predated materialistic (or mechanistic) conceptions of life by thousands of years. The notion of a life force has gone by different names in different cultures—*élan vital*, *spiritus animus*, *chakra*, *chi*, *the soul*, *the humors*—but its purpose is always the same: to explain the seemingly unexplainable

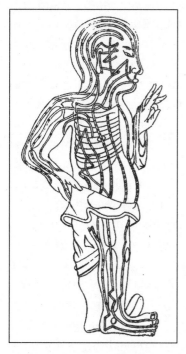

Ancient Chinese medicine was predicated on the belief that all bodily functions derive from an internal life force, or *qi* (chi).

processes of health, locomotion, intention, perception, growth, and development.

Vitalism, in its strongest formulation, is incompatible with a biochemical view of life because it implies that life cannot be reduced to mere matter. But in weaker formulations, it implies only that external activities depend on some kind of internal energy and is thus compatible with a biochemical view of life. Vitalism provides the outline for how living systems function, and biochemistry fills in the details.

From a developmental point of view, vitalism is a stepping-stone to more complex conceptions of life, like the mechanistic conceptions discussed in Chapter 8. Many years before children endorse mechanistic explanations for biological phenomena, they endorse vitalistic ones. Given a choice between a vitalistic explanation for why we eat food ("because our stomach takes in energy from the food") and a mechanistic explanation ("because we take the food into our body after the food is changed in our stomach"), preschoolers and young elementary-schoolers prefer the vitalistic explanation to the mechanistic one.

The same goes for other bodily functions. Asked why we have hearts, young children prefer the vitalistic explanation "because our heart works hard to send out energy with our blood" to the mechanistic explanation "because the heart works like a pump and pushes our blood around." Asked why we breathe air, young children prefer the vitalistic explanation "because our chest takes in energy from the air" to the mechanistic explanation "because our lungs take in oxygen and change it into carbon dioxide." Older children and adults, on the other hand, prefer mechanistic explanations to vitalistic ones. The vitalistic ones strike us as shallow.

Another sign that children develop vitalistic conceptions of life before mechanistic ones is that their beliefs about vital functions don't align with their beliefs about what is alive and what is not. Consider these entities: humans, bears, squirrels, birds, fish, beetles, worms, trees, bushes, dandelions, rocks, water, wind, the sun, bicycles, scissors, and pencils. Which of them grow? Which of them are alive? To adults, both questions merit the same answer. We know that everything on that list that grows is alive and everything that is alive grows. But to preschoolers and young elementary schoolers, the two questions merit different answers. They recognize that the first ten entities (humans through dandelions) grow and that the last seven (rocks through pencils) do not, but they also think that trees, bushes, and dandelions are not alive and that the wind and the sun are alive. Not until age nine do children recognize that life and growth are intimately related.

The same is true for needing water, needing nutrients, and getting sick. Several years before children recognize that plants are alive, they recognize that these three properties nevertheless apply to plants. Recognizing that something is alive requires a mechanistic conception of life, whereas recognizing that something eats, drinks, grows, or gets sick requires only a vitalistic conception of life. A child recognizes that plants possess vital powers, long before he or she recognizes *where* and *how* those vital powers are physically instantiated.

This dissociation between vitalistic (energy-based) notions of life and mechanistic (body-based) notions of life has consequences for how children learn biological concepts. For instance, it's common practice in kindergarten classrooms to grow plants as a foray into basic physiology, but doing so hardly convinces children that plants are alive. By kindergarten, children know that plants grow and develop and that plants need water and nutrients, just like animals. But observing those processes firsthand does not help a child see that plants are similar to animals at a more fundamental level—that their vital powers are both instantiated by internal tissues and organs. For children of this age, vital powers are not distinctly biological.

Consider again the concept of growth. Young children understand that growth entails change in shape and size, but they do not understand that growth entails change in life status. Their idea of growth is akin to how crystals grow or how clouds grow. Crystals and clouds do indeed grow—the term applies literally, not just metaphorically—but their growth is the by-product of nonbiological processes and thus has different implications. Crystals and clouds grow bigger but not more complex, and their growth has no functional consequences for the entity as a whole. When children claim that plants grow, they mean simply that plants get bigger.

Vitalism may set the stage for relating growth to life, but growth is not seen as a consequence of life until life is seen as a consequence of the inner workings of the body. Growth can be observed, but it cannot be interpreted. Children must posit an extra, unobservable layer to reality: the layer of the body and all its hidden organs.

+ + +

ONE LITMUS TEST for whether children hold a vitalistic theory of life, aside from their beliefs about plants, is whether they understand the nutritional value of food. Food is integral to growth and health, but it's also integral to social customs and social norms.

What we eat is dictated as much by social considerations as by biological ones: daily routines (cereal is eaten for breakfast but not dinner; hamburgers are eaten for dinner but not breakfast), cultural taboos (Americans eat curdled milk, in the form of cheese, but not fermented cabbage; Koreans eat fermented cabbage, in the form of kimchi, but not curdled milk), religious taboos (Muslims eat beef but not pork; Hindus eat pork but not beef), and dietary restrictions (vegetarians eat dairy products but not meat; people with lactose intolerance eat meat but not dairy products).

Layered on top of these social considerations are food-related buzzwords: *carbs, gluten, antioxidants, additives, preservatives, processed, probiotic, organic, free-range, whole-grain.* These words have technical definitions, but they've also picked up moral connotations—connotations of inherent goodness or inherent badness. This morass of sociomoral information makes it difficult for children to determine the causal properties of food, let alone what they should and should not eat.

When my daughter Lucy was four and a half, she was particularly fixated on one property of food: protein. We saw her fixation manifest itself in unexpected ways, as in the following conversation about a bad dream:

LUCY: I had a bad dream. I was being chased by pirates.
ME: Try to think about something else, something happy.
LUCY: I want to think about happy things, like mermaids and dolphins, but my brain won't let me.

ME: You control your brain. Tell your brain to think about mermaids and dolphins.

LUCY: I can't. I didn't eat enough protein.

Lucy had glommed on to protein as critical for bodily functions because her teachers at school had advised her to eat her lunch foods protein-first (e.g., pepperoni before pretzels). At age four, Lucy frequently let us know what on her plate was a protein and what was not, and much of the time, she was wrong. Her analysis was biased by what she wanted to eat ("donuts have protein") and what she did not ("eggs don't have any protein").

Four-year-olds, in general, are surprisingly bad at discerning the nutritional value of food. They have yet to disentangle the biological dimensions of eating (what we should eat) from either its social dimensions (what we see others eat) or its psychological dimensions (what we want to eat). In one study, researchers asked four-year-olds to classify the following foods as healthy or unhealthy: bacon, beans, broccoli, cake, carrots, celery, Cheetos, corn, doughnuts, fudge, potato chips, and red pepper. Half the list consisted of vegetables, and half consisted of junk food, but four-year-olds were largely oblivious to the difference. They classified vegetables as healthy only 70 percent of time, and they classified junk food as healthy 47 percent of the time. Apparently, many four-year-olds think that bacon and potato chips are as healthy as celery and red pepper.

I once stumbled on similar misconceptions in my own children. My son was seven and my daughter was three, and we were at the pediatrician's office for a wellness visit. The pediatrician asked my daughter what her favorite vegetable was, and she yelled, "Watermelon!"

"That's not a vegetable," corrected the pediatrician. "That's a fruit." The pediatrician then turned to my son and asked him the same question.

"Macaroni," he said.

"Oh my!" the pediatrician exclaimed. "This doesn't reflect well on your parents."

Fortunately for us parents, children's food-based misconceptions are correctable. In a follow-up study to the one described above, researchers exposed four-year-olds to one of two tutorials on healthy eating: a prescriptive tutorial and a vitalistic tutorial. The prescriptive tutorial advised children on what they should and should not eat. For example, "Healthy foods give your body what it needs. There are many healthy foods you should eat a lot of. Vegetables are healthy foods. Examples of vegetables are beans, celery, carrots, broccoli, and corn. You should eat vegetables every day."

The vitalistic tutorial provided the same information but couched it in an explicitly vitalistic framework (denoted here with italics): "Healthy foods give your body what it needs *because they have many vitamins. Vitamins are inside of healthy foods. Vitamins help you grow, give you long-lasting energy, and keep you from getting sick.* There are many healthy foods you should eat a lot of. For example, vegetables are healthy foods *because they have many vitamins inside of them.* Examples of vegetables *that have many vitamins inside* are beans, celery, carrots, broccoli, and corn. *These foods help you grow, give you long-lasting energy, and keep you from getting sick.* You should eat vegetables every day." The tutorials also covered unhealthy foods, either in a prescriptive context ("you should not eat foods with a lot of fat every day") or in a vitalistic context ("high-fat foods do not have vitamins that help you grow").

Both tutorials took the same amount of time to complete, and both provided children with a basis for deciding whether a food is healthy or unhealthy. Only the vitalistic tutorial, however, proved effective. Children who received this tutorial made significantly better healthy-versus-unhealthy judgments after the tutorial than before. And it proved effective both immediately after the tutorial and five months later. Emphasizing the vitalistic properties of food allowed children to reconceptualize food from a source of pleasure (or displeasure) to a source of nutrition (or lack thereof).

The food industry also seems to have recognized the effectiveness of vitalistic arguments, as it has increasingly emphasized nutritional information in its marketing of healthy foods to adults. Adults know, in the abstract, that vegetables are healthier than junk food, but companies like Whole Foods and Trader Joe's have found it useful—and profitable—to remind adults of the health consequences of the foods they sell. Kale, seaweed, and acai have thus been elevated from bland plant matter to "superfoods." Twinkies, Big Macs, and orange soda, on the other hand, have been degraded from tasty treats to "silent killers."

Human foods aside, an even stronger test of whether children hold a vitalistic theory of life is whether they recognize that food can take different forms across the biological world and that substances that humans do not consume can still have nutritional value for other organisms. Humans consume only a small slice of the organic world, after all. Food options that humans are not equipped to utilize include wood (consumed by termites and beetles), plankton (consumed by whales and jellyfish), and dung (consumed by flies and fungi).

The idea that something inedible to humans may be edible to other organisms makes sense only if food is understood as a source of nutrition. When my son Teddy was three and a half, he had yet to acquire such an understanding, as illustrated in this conversation about mosquitos:

TEDDY: What does a mosquito bite look like?
ME: It's round and red and itchy.
TEDDY: Do mosquitoes have big teeth?
ME: No, they have pokey little things they use to suck your blood.
TEDDY: Why do they suck my blood?
ME: Because that's what mosquitoes eat for food.
TEDDY: Blood isn't food! Chicken is food.
ME: You eat chicken but mosquitoes eat blood.
TEDDY: Will a mosquito bite my transformer?
ME: No, your transformer doesn't have any blood.

Teddy's conception of food was grounded in taste, not sustenance. He would eventually learn to identify food with sustenance, but doing so required adopting a vitalistic framework for reasoning about biological processes in general.

Acquiring this framework is not a given. Individuals with intellectual disabilities sometimes never do. We know this from studies of a particular form of intellectual disability: Williams syndrome. This syndrome is a rare genetic disorder resulting in low intelligence but normal language skills. Adults with Williams syndrome lack much of the knowledge acquired by other adults during childhood, but because they have normal language skills, they can converse about their knowledge in ways that individuals with other forms of cognitive disabilities cannot.

Intrigued by this unusual combination of abilities, psychologist Susan Johnson and her colleagues sought to determine whether adults with Williams syndrome ever acquire a vitalistic conception of biology. Accordingly, they interviewed a sample of adults with Williams syndrome on their understanding of several biological concepts, including life, death, growth, metabolism, reproduction, and inheritance.

During the interviews, Johnson and her colleagues discovered that one of their participants, a twenty-one-year-old woman with a below-average IQ but average verbal ability was fascinated by the mythology of vampires. She had read several vampire novels and was eager to share her knowledge of vampires with the researchers. The researchers, in turn, were eager to hear what she had to say, as vampires defy the very biological principles targeted by their interviews.

"What exactly is a vampire?" they asked.

"Oooh," she replied, "a vampire is a man who climbs into ladies' bedrooms in the middle of the night and sinks his teeth into their necks."

The researchers then asked why vampires do this, and the woman was visibly taken aback.

"I've never thought about that," she said. After a long pause, she offered an explanation: "Vampires must have an inordinate fondness for necks."

Despite a long-standing interest in vampire lore, this woman had not constructed a vitalistic interpretation of vampires' chief activity, drinking blood. Nor was she able to construct one when prompted to do so. Instead, she defaulted to a psychological interpretation of the activity, surmising that vampires drink blood because they *want* to drink blood, not because they *need* to drink blood.

On the whole, Johnson observed that adults with Williams syndrome rarely construct vitalistic interpretations of biological phenomena—all biological phenomena, not just those related to vampires. Adults who have Williams syndrome know the names of dozens of animals and the activities they engage in, but they show little understanding of why animals engage in these activities—why they eat, why they grow, why they die. In fact, these adults' understanding of biological activities is more similar to a four-year-old's understanding than it is to a nine-year-old's, let alone to a fellow adult's.

Knowing a lot of biological facts does not guarantee an understanding of those facts, either a vitalistic understanding or a more detailed, mechanistic understanding. Both types of understanding must be actively constructed, and adults with Williams syndrome appear to lack the cognitive resources needed to undertake that construction.

✦ ✦ ✦

As we have seen, our theories of biology shape our beliefs about food: what constitutes food, why we eat food, and how food promotes growth and health. Our theories of biology also shape our decisions about which foods to eat—and which to avoid—beginning in childhood. Children are notoriously picky eaters. They reject foods high in vitamins and minerals (vegetables) and focus instead on foods high in sugars (breads) or fats (dairy). Getting children to eat their vegetables is a perennial challenge. But children can be convinced to eat vegetables, on their own accord, if they are taught the vitalistic rationale behind doing so.

Psychologist Sarah Gripshover and her colleagues made this discovery in a study comparing preschoolers' food choices with their understanding of the nutritional value of food. Preschoolers who participated in the study were taught five vitalistic principles: (1) that people need to eat a variety of foods, not just one type; (2) that foods of the same type can take a variety of forms; (3) that food contains microscopic elements known as nutrients; (4) that nutrients are extracted from food by our stomachs and then carried to other parts of the body by our blood; and (5) that nutrients are required for all biological activities, from high-octane activities like running and climbing to low-octane activities like thinking and writing.

When children learned these principles, they changed their eating habits as well. At snack time, they voluntarily selected nine pieces of vegetables—twice as many as those selected by children who had not received the vitalism tutorial. In fact, children who received the vitalism tutorial added more vegetables to their plate than even children who received a nutrition tutorial created by the US Department of Agriculture (USDA). Unlike Gripshover's tutorial, the USDA tutorial did not emphasize the biological benefits of healthy eating. Instead, it emphasized the enjoyment of healthy eating—a message the children simply didn't buy.

Connections between healthy eating and beliefs about nutrition have been documented in adults as well. Adults may bemoan how children choose fatty foods and sugary foods over vegetables, but most adults—particularly American adults—are equally guilty of overindulging their appetite for such foods. American adults weigh more today than ever before. For decades, we have been consuming more calories than we need (overeating) and burning fewer calories than we should (underexercising). Both overeating and underexercising contribute to weight gain, but ask yourself, which is the primary cause?

Medical experts cite overeating as the primary cause. Exercise, by itself, has only marginal effects on weight if overeating is not addressed as well. Nevertheless, many people hold the opposite view, and this view has significant consequences for their health. Those who cite underexercising as the primary cause of weight gain have a 9 percent higher body mass index (BMI) than those who cite overeating as the primary cause.

This result has been obtained in several countries—the United States, France, China, South Korea—and it has been shown to be independent of other factors known to influence a person's BMI, including gender, level of education, hours of sleep per night, chronic stress, preexisting medical conditions, current socioeconomic status, childhood socioeconomic status, pregnancy status, employment status, self-reported health, interest in nutrition, tobacco use, and self-esteem. Even after controlling for all these factors, individuals who cite exercise as more consequential than diet still have higher BMIs than those who cite diet as more consequential than exercise.

Researchers have actually observed the detrimental effects of an exercise-based theory of weight gain firsthand. In one study, they asked participants to complete a questionnaire on weight-related beliefs and weight-related behaviors while given the opportunity to snack on chocolate. Each participant was given a cup of individually wrapped chocolates, and those who overvalued exercise relative to diet, as revealed by their questionnaires, ate more chocolates than those who did not. In other words, overweight adults, while completing a questionnaire about their weight gain, engaged in the very behavior that led to that weight gain. Clearly an intervention is in order.

✦ ✦ ✦

So far, our discussion of growth has focused on beliefs about what promotes growth (and health more generally), but our intuitive theories of growth have a second dimension as well: beliefs about what changes because of growth. These beliefs are shaped not by vitalism but by a different cognitive bias known as *essentialism*.

Essentialism is the idea that an organism's outward appearance and behavior are products of its inner nature, or "essence." As the organism grows, its appearance and behavior may change, but its essence stays the same. In fact, the essence is what drives the change in appearance and behavior. According to this line of thinking, an organism inherits its essence from its parents, thereby inheriting the potential to develop species-typical traits. Cows and pigs, for instance, are thought to inherit fundamentally different essences. The cow's essence propels it to develop horns, udders, and an appetite for grass, whereas the pig's essence propels it to develop pink skin, a curly tail, and an appetite for slop.

We don't use the term *essence* in everyday parlance, but the idea pervades our thinking about growth and development anyway. Consider all the familiar stories in which the protagonist's true nature is masked by an unfortunate or unusual turn of events, only to shine through in the end: *The Ugly Duckling, The Frog Prince, The Fox and the Hound, Cinderella, Beauty and the Beast, The Sword and the Stone, The Princess and the Pea*. Most of these stories are about people, not animals, but their plots are essentialist, all the same. The protagonists, at their core, are different from what the other characters perceive them to be, but they are destined to defy those perceptions. Some ducklings are destined to become swans, and some peasants are destined to become princesses.

Because essentialist tales are enjoyed by children and adults alike, it would appear that children do not have to be taught to think in essentialist terms—that essentialism develops on its own without any special experience or instruction. Psychologists have looked into the matter, and their studies support this idea. Children are essentialists from the moment they first ponder how and why organisms change with growth.

The psychologist who pioneered the study of essentialism in young children was Susan Gelman. She and her colleagues have probed children's essentialist intuitions in several ways, but the most straightforward is with a thought experiment similar to the story of the Ugly Duckling: "I'm going to tell you about a cow named Edith. Right after Edith was born, when she was just a tiny baby cow, she was taken to a farm that had pigs—lots of pigs. The pigs took care of Edith. Edith grew up on the farm with all the pigs, and she never saw another cow. When Edith got to be a grown-up, what did her tail look like? Was it straight or was it curly? When Edith got to be a grown-up, what sound did she make? Did she say *moo* or did she say *oink*?"

This thought experiment pits an organism's upbringing against its parentage as the source of species-specific growth, and children typically

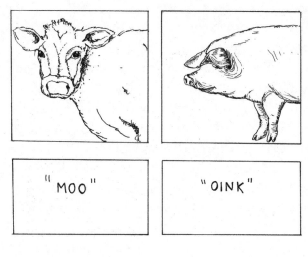

Children told of an animal born to a cow but raised by a pig predict that the animal will grow to possess the traits of a cow, not a pig, including both anatomical traits (e.g., whether it grows to be white or pink) and behavioral traits (e.g., whether it grows to say *moo* or *oink*).

side with parentage. By age four, they claim that Edith will grow to have a straight tail and say *moo*. And if the story was reversed—if children were told that Edith was born to pigs but raised by cows—they claim that Edith will grow to have a curly tail and say *oink*.

The particular animals and the particular traits included in the story do not matter. Four-year-olds claim that a kangaroo raised by goats will grow to be good at hopping, not climbing; that a tiger raised by horses will grow to have striped fur, not plain fur; and that a rabbit raised by monkeys will grow to eat carrots, not bananas. Four-year-olds even recognize that a seed from a lemon planted in an orange orchard will grow to yield lemons not oranges, which is impressive considering that children of this age do not even think that plants are alive.

Researchers have posed thought experiments about cross-species adoption to Brazilian children, Israeli children, Mayan children (from Mexico), Vezo children (from Madagascar), and Menominee children (from Wisconsin), and all agree that adopted animals will grow to exhibit the traits of their birth parents, not their adopted parents. Essentialist beliefs about growth thus appear to be universal. In fact, these beliefs are so commonplace that they crop up in contexts where an essentialist analysis is patently inappropriate.

One such context is human sociology. Social categories like race, ethnicity, occupation, religion, and socioeconomic class have little biological coherence, if any, but many of us essentialize these categories nonetheless, treating them as stable, discrete, uniform, and psychologically informative.

Children, in particular, are prone to essentialize social categories. They think the members of distinct social categories are as different from one another as are the members of distinct species.

When seven-year-olds are asked to rate the similarity between members of different social categories—say, Arabs and Jews or rich people and poor people—they rate them only slightly more similar than they rate two animals of different species. They claim, for instance, that rich people and poor people differ in their preferences, appearance, behavior, and physiology as much as elephants differ from lions along those same dimensions. Children thus treat social categories similarly to biological categories, imbuing the members of those categories with different innate potentials.

Another context in which essentialist notions of growth are misapplied is organ donation. Organs are attributed essences just like full organisms are; they are attributed the essence of the person within whom the organ resides. As an illustration, imagine the following scenario. Doctors have discovered that you have a defective heart and that it needs to be replaced to prevent serious health consequences down the line. Someone else's heart will need to be transplanted into your body. Unfortunately, the list of heart donors is limited, and the only available donor is a serial killer. Would you accept the serial killer's heart? How about the heart of a schizophrenic patient? Or the heart of a pig?

Most people are reluctant to accept hearts from any of those donors, because they conceive of the heart as imbued with the donors' essence. When asked to imagine how they might change after such a transplant, most people think that their personality and behavior would change significantly, becoming more similar to those of the donor. Such perceptions are not limited to heart transplants. Blood transfusions and gene therapies are also thought to alter one's personality and behavior. A middle-aged woman who received a heart and lung transplant from an eighteen-year-old man who loved beer and motorcycles wrote an entire memoir about how her personality and interests become aligned with his. She named her memoir, quite aptly, "A Change of Heart."

From a scientific point of view, beliefs about transferring an essence from one person to another, or from one species to another, are preposterous. But essentialism is not scientific. It is a prescientific notion of inheritance in the same way that vitalism is a prescientific notion of metabolism.

It wreaks havoc not only on our notions of growth and development but also on three other biological notions, discussed in later chapters: genetics (Chapter 10), evolutionary adaptation (Chapter 12), and the origin of species (Chapter 13).

✦ ✦ ✦

ESSENTIALISM, FOR ALL its trouble, allows us to map different physical states to the same organism across development: from calf to cow, piglet to pig, gosling to goose. We can even map vastly different physical states to the same organism: from caterpillar to pupa to butterfly, egg to tadpole to frog, seed to sapling to tree. We recognize not only that an organism retains its species identity as it grows but also how its identity unfolds over time, affecting its appearance and behavior.

Oddly, we have much less trouble tracking species identity over time, particularly our own identity. From a preschooler's point of view, people never change—at least not that much. Some people appear to have been placed on the earth as children, and others as adults. The idea that children grow into adults is not as intuitive as it might seem. Take, for example, the following conversation between the psychologist Susan Carey and her daughter Eliza when Eliza was three and a half:

DAUGHTER: When I grow up, there won't be a little girl named Eliza around here anymore.
MOTHER: That's right.
DAUGHTER: Will you go out and buy another one?
MOTHER: Oh no, we love the Eliza we have, and we won't need to. What do you think will happen to you when you grow up?
DAUGHTER: I'll be a teacher.
MOTHER: But what will your name be?
DAUGHTER: Satu [the name of her favorite preschool teacher].

Carey and her daughter had conversations like this for several weeks, as her daughter tried to make sense of how she could remain the same person as she transitioned from a child to an adult. Carey knew that her daughter had finally made sense of the conundrum when she announced, "Mommy, you were a little girl once, and your name was Susan."

I remember going through a similar episode with my son Teddy. It started when he was four and a half, and we were playing a card-sequencing game. The objective of the game was to put four cards in chronological order from the beginning of a causal sequence to the end. So, given cards depicting an apple pie, apples on a tree, sliced apples, and apples in a bushel, the objective was to recognize that they were the steps to making an apple pie and that they should be sequenced accordingly (apples on a tree, apples in a bushel, sliced apples, apple pie).

The game is trivial for adults but challenging for preschoolers. For Teddy, one set of cards was particularly challenging: baby, child, young man, old man. He couldn't discern that the underlying causal relationship was growth, and when I sequenced the cards for him, he looked astonished. "Why is that the right order?" he asked. Then, after staring intently at the cards, he blurted out, "Am I going to become an old man?!"

The game sparked several angst-ridden conversations about growth and aging over the next month. In one conversation, at bedtime, I became aware of the source of Teddy's angst:

ME: Go to sleep. You need to get lots of sleep so you can grow.
TEDDY: I'm going to grow bigger and bigger and then . . . Am I going to grow into an old man?
ME: Not for a long, long time. You have to grow into a big boy and then a teenager and then a young man and then a daddy.
TEDDY: But when I'm an old man, how will I get back to my real self?
ME: Your real self?
TEDDY: How will I get my arms back? And my legs back?

Teddy couldn't fathom how his physical body would come to resemble that of an old man. Where would his current body go? The gradual and continuous nature of aging was lost on him, as he hadn't observed much aging in his four short years. For all he knew, the old people in his life had always been old. What cruel trick of nature turns young people into old people?

My daughter Lucy, at age five, exhibited a different but equally compelling misconception about growth. At a science museum, she was prompted to draw a picture of herself in the future. She actually drew three, which she labeled "I am rich," "I am rich and old," and "I am dead." In each picture,

Aging is continuous, but we perceive it in stages. Children, in particular, have difficulty discerning the continuity between their current life stage, their past life stage (infancy), and their future life stage (adulthood).

she drew her entire family—we were all in caskets in the "I am dead" picture—and in each depiction of her family, she depicted herself as half the size of her parents. That is, she depicted herself as a child. She knew that she would someday get old and die, but she had not yet discerned what that meant biologically. She also had not discerned that her parents were likely to die long before she did.

Children's confusion about aging is tied up with their confusion about biological processes in general, as they have yet to connect aging and growth. We come to make that connection in the early years of schooling, but we may never fully grasp the ramifications of such a connection. Even as adults, we have trouble accepting the inevitable changes wrought by age, both physical changes (gray hair, sagging skin, expanding waistlines) and psychological changes (new attitudes, new values, new interests). Indeed, psychologists have found that we are particularly oblivious to the latter.

If you ask twenty-year-olds how much their preferences have changed over the last decade—their preferred music, foods, hobbies, and friends—they claim that those preferences have changed a lot (an average of 40 percent). If you then ask those twenty-year-olds how much they expect their current preferences to change over the next decade, they claim that those preferences will change much less (an average of 25 percent). In other words, they recognize that they didn't always prefer Taylor Swift to other musicians, sushi to other foods, and yoga to other hobbies, but they think that they will continue to prefer Taylor Swift, sushi, and yoga over the next decade.

Perhaps twenty-year-olds' reflections on the increased stability of their preferences are correct. The teenage years, after all, are a time of rapid growth, and the preferences that emerge by the end of that period may be more stable than those held before. The problem with this interpretation is that thirty-year-olds report the same expectation as twenty-year-olds: that their preferences will change less over the next decade than they changed over the past decade. And forty-year-olds report the same expectation as thirty-year-olds, and fifty-year-olds report the same set of expectation as forty-year-olds.

People of all ages, it turns out, rate their current preferences as more stable than their past preferences. We are convinced that the last decade of our life was more identity-forming than the next decade will be, and we hold this conviction for many aspects of our identity, including our personality (e.g., our degree of openness, conscientiousness, extraversion, agreeableness, and neuroticism) and our core values (e.g., the value we place on achievement, hedonism, self-direction, benevolence, tradition, conformity, security, and power).

Thus, even adults hold misapprehensions about the extent to which our personal identities change over time. We adults have observed many such changes firsthand, but we still chronically underestimate the changes in store for our future. At any given moment, we think we've arrived at the final phase of identity formation, the culmination of our character development. So while we may be more adept than children at recognizing the possibility of physical change with age, we're not particularly adept at recognizing the possibility of psychological change with age. Our current self is always our "real self," our once and future identity.

10 | INHERITANCE

Why Do We Resemble Our Parents?
Where Did We Get Our Traits?

F YOU SEARCH THE INTERNET FOR IMAGES RELATED TO "CLONE," YOU'LL uncover all sorts of horrors: two-headed cows, six-legged dogs, one-eyed kittens, human cyborgs, human babies in vats. Likewise, if you search for images related to "genetic engineering," you'll uncover another set of horrors: phosphorescent cats, fanged strawberries, blood-filled apples, chipmunk-tarantula hybrids. These images actually have nothing to do with cloning or genetic engineering. They have either been doctored (e.g., the fanged strawberry) or taken from situations involving naturally occurring deformities (e.g., the two-headed cow).

Cloning and genetic engineering are much scarier in the popular imagination than they are in reality. Clones are nothing more than genetically identical organisms, and they have existed for as long as organisms have been reproducing. Every marbled crayfish is a clone of its mother, as is every Brahminy blind snake, every mourning gecko, and every New Mexico whiptail lizard. These species reproduce asexually—that is, without the contribution of a second parent's genetic material—so every member of the species is a clone of its ancestors. And every identical twin is a clone of its sibling, whether those twins are cows, kittens, or (gasp!) humans.

The practice of labeling the rare food item that does not come from living organisms (e.g., salt, baking soda, water) as "Non GMO" is a sign of widespread genetic illiteracy.

Genetic engineering has also been in practice for millennia. Humans have only recently invented the technology that allows us to splice genes directly from one genome (say, a fish genome) into another (say, a tomato genome), but we have been mucking with the genomes of other species for millennia. Corn would not exist if humans had not selectively bred wild grasses to produce plumper, more nutritious kernels. The same is true of apples, oranges, strawberries, almonds, pigs, chickens, horses, and dogs. Most of the organisms we raise for food, labor, or companionship have been genetically engineered through selective breeding. No one ever found a poodle wandering around the wilderness in search of an owner; we genetically engineered poodles from wolves.

Some of the most controversial technologies in modern society involve genetics: cloning, genetic screening of job applicants, genetic screening of fetuses, genetic exploration of personal ancestry, genetic modification of bacteria for use in industry, genetic modification of crops, genetic modification of livestock, and the sale of genetically modified foods. Most people are wary of these technologies, both in the United States and abroad. Yet few people actually understand what genes are or what genes do.

In one recent survey, 82 percent of Americans supported mandatory labels on foods produced with genetic engineering, but nearly the same percent (80 percent) also supported mandatory labels on "foods containing DNA." If 80 percent of the American public doesn't know that virtually all food contains DNA—as virtually all food comes from plants or animals—then what credence should be given to their opinions regarding genetically modified foods?

To be fair, genetics is a difficult topic, and many adults never received adequate instruction on genetics in school. As a test of your own genetics knowledge, try to decide whether each of the following statements is true or false:

- Identical twins have exactly the same genes at birth.
- On average, a person has half their genes in common with their siblings.
- Two people from the same race will always be more genetically similar to each other than two people from different races.
- Two women will always be more genetically similar to each other than a man and a woman.
- There are different types of genes in different parts of the body.
- Single genes directly control specific human behaviors.

Most people judge all six statements to be true. In reality, only the first two are true; the rest are false.

The relationship between genes and physical traits is significantly more complicated than we think it is. Humans have approximately twenty thousand genes, and those genes are expressed through a cascade of interdependent biochemical reactions. There is no single gene that determines race or even gender, and the genes that two people of the same race or gender do have in common are dwarfed by the hundreds they do not. In fact, the genetic variation among people of the same race is typically just as large as the genetic variation among people of different races. For this reason, most scientists consider race a social construct.

One reason people lack knowledge of genetics is poor education, but another is the human predisposition toward essentialism. As discussed in the previous chapter, essentialism is the idea that an organism's observable traits are determined by something unobservable at its core: its essence. Essences are thought to be immutable (once a tiger, always a tiger), homogenous (all tigers are fundamentally the same), discrete (tigers are fundamentally different from other animals), and inherent (tiger-hood is conferred at birth).

Children believe that an organism's growth and development are constrained by its essence, but they don't know which part of the organism constitutes its essence beyond something internal. Adults, on the other hand, associate essences with genes. We know that an organism's traits are determined by its genes, so its genes must be the seat of its essence. But this association is problematic, as most of our beliefs about essences do not apply to genes.

Genes are not immutable; they mutate in the presence of carcinogens or because of copying errors. Nor are genes homogenous; they are involved in the expression of multiple potentially diverse traits. Genes are not discrete; they work in concert with several other genes. And genes are not inherent; they change over an organism's lifespan in terms of how they are methylated (chemically modified) and thus how they are expressed.

This link between genes and essences leads to many maladaptive attitudes and behaviors. We overvalue the role that genes play in traits we see as highly heritable (e.g., intelligence, impulsivity, mental illness), construing those traits as inflexible and deterministic. We overemphasize the dissimilarity between members of different social categories when those categories are seen as genetically predetermined (e.g., race, gender, sexual orientation). We underemphasize the moral culpability of individuals who engage in criminal behaviors when the behaviors are seen as grounded in genetics (e.g., substance abuse, domestic violence, rape). And we are loath to eat foods produced through transgenic modification—the splicing of genes from one species' genome into another—even though these foods have proven safe for consumption.

Essentialist construals of genetic information are neither accurate nor productive, but they are an enduring obstacle to how we interpret such information because essentialism is our universal starting point for thinking about inheritance. Even geneticists were once preschoolers intent on imbuing the biological world with discrete, immutable essences.

+ + +

ESSENTIALISM IS NOT all bad. It allows us to track an organism's identity across changes in appearance and environment, and it allows us to make predictions about the development of species-typical traits, as discussed in Chapter 9. But essentialism has nothing to say about the transmission of those traits from parent to offspring. Children know that parents produce offspring of the same species and that those offspring will develop species-typical traits, but they don't know why—that is, why some organisms inherit the innate potential to become a duck and others inherit the innate potential to become a swan.

Put differently, essentialism provides children with an intuitive theory of growth but not an intuitive theory of inheritance. And without a theory of inheritance, they come to hold several misconceptions about the topic, including (1) the belief that mental traits are as heritable as physical traits, (2) the belief that kinship terms refer to social relations rather than reproductive relations, and (3) the belief that an organism can change species if its physiology is sufficiently altered.

With respect to the first misconception, recall that preschoolers expect baby animals to develop the traits of their birth parents even if those babies were raised by animals of another species. So if told of a piglet raised by cows, they expect the piglet to develop a curly tail and say *oink*, and if told of a calf raised by pigs, they expect the calf to develop a straight tail and say *moo*. In making these judgments, four-year-olds the world over privilege birth parents over adopted parents, but they don't understand why birth parents matter. That is, they don't understand that the birth parents' traits are programmed into its physical being and that this program is passed from parents to offspring by mechanisms that operate before the offspring's birth.

It's difficult to query preschoolers' understanding of trait transmission directly, but they can be asked indirectly with thought experiments. Here, the relevant thought experiment is about traits *not* programmed into an organism's physical being and thus *not* passed from parent to child before birth. Mental traits fit this description. Although they are heritable—children usually come to hold the beliefs, values, and customs of their parents—mental traits are inherited through instruction rather than conception, through nurture rather than nature. If children understand trait transmission in a biologically mature way, then they should recognize that physical traits are fixed at birth but mental traits are mediated by upbringing.

Psychologist Gregg Solomon and his colleagues investigated this possibility by presenting children between the ages of four and seven with adoption scenarios similar to the cow-pig scenario but involving humans. Here's an example: "Once upon a time, there was a king. The king could not have children, but he wanted a child very much. So he went out into his kingdom where he met a shepherd who had many children. The king told the shepherd that he wanted to adopt the shepherd's baby boy and raise him as his own son and that the baby would then grow up to be the prince. The shepherd agreed that this was a good idea so the king adopted the baby boy and took him to the palace. The king loved the baby and the baby loved the king. The baby grew up in the palace with the king and became a prince."

After this backstory, Solomon asked children whether the full-grown prince was more likely to resemble the king or the shepherd across several traits, some physical and some mental. Children were told, for instance, that the king has green eyes and that the shepherd has brown eyes and were asked whether the prince, now grown up, has green eyes like the king or brown eyes like the shepherd. The physical traits included hair texture (curly or straight), voice type (high or low), and height (tall or short), and the mental traits included beliefs about what an aardvark eats (plants or meat), beliefs about what a red traffic light means (stop or go), and beliefs about what oil does in water (floats or sinks).

Children over the age of seven provided a differentiated pattern of judgments, claiming the prince would come to have the physical traits of the shepherd (his birth father) but the mental traits of the king (his adopted father). Children younger than seven, on the other hand, provided a mixed pattern of judgments, siding with the birth father on some traits and the adopted father on others but not consistently pairing the birth father with physical traits and the adopted father with mental traits.

In short, children younger than seven showed no evidence of understanding why children resemble their parents. Their beliefs about innate potential were no help in this situation, as both the birth father and the adopted father were of the same species and both the physical traits and the mental traits were species-typical.

In a follow-up study, Solomon provided even stronger evidence that children's earliest expectations about inheritance are not distinctly biological. Rather than contrast physical traits with mental traits, Solomon contrasted physical traits with a completely arbitrary trait: shirt color. The adoption scenario was as follows: "These two people, Mr. and Mrs. Smith, had a baby girl. That means that the baby came out of Mrs. Smith's tummy. Right after it came out of her tummy, the baby went to live with these people, Mr. and Mrs. Jones. The baby lived with them, and Mr. and Mrs. Jones took care of her. They fed her, bought her clothes, and hugged her and kissed her when she was sad. They loved her very much and she loved them. They called her 'Daughter' and she called them 'Mommy' and

Young children's view of inheritance is similar to the view illustrated here, as young children do not differentiate traits transmitted by physical means (e.g., skin color) from traits transmitted by social means (e.g., shirt color).

'Daddy.' Now, this baby has grown into a little girl. Here are two pictures of girls. Can you tell me which is a picture of that girl?"

In one version of the story, the Smiths were depicted as having white skin and the Joneses as having black skin, and the children had to decide whether the girl who was born to the Smiths but raised by the Joneses had white skin or black skin. In another version, the Smiths and the Joneses were depicted as having the same color skin, but the Smiths wore red shirts and the Joneses were blue shirts. In this scenario, children had to decide whether the girl who was born to the Smiths but raised by the Jones wore a red shirt or a blue shirt. Technically, there's no correct answer to the second question, but the preschoolers in Solomon's study did not see it that way. They sided with the birth parents (the Smiths) in both cases, seemingly believing that the color of one's shirt is as heritable as the color of one's skin.

In light of young children's beliefs about the heritability of shirt color, it would be inappropriate to grant them a biological understanding of the heritability of skin color, or any other physical trait, for that matter. They draw no distinction between traits acquired through biological means and traits acquired through social means.

This is true regardless of how much experience children have with socially acquired traits. For instance, children who learn a new language as toddlers—because they move to a new country or because they attend a language-immersion program—have firsthand experience with a socially acquired trait (language) and might therefore develop a precocious understanding of the difference between socially acquired and physically acquired traits. But even these children fail to differentiate the two types of traits in an adoption task.

These sequential-bilingual children (who learned one language first, then another) fail the adoption task just as their monolingual peers do, but they fail in a unique way. Rather than side with the birth parents for both physically acquired traits and socially acquired traits (as some children do) or vacillate between birth parents and adopted parents inconsistently (as other children do), they side mainly with the adopted parents. Their knowledge of the social origins of language apparently leads them to believe that *all* traits are acquired through social means, including the color of their eyes and the texture of their hair. They take cultural relativism to new extremes.

✦ ✦ ✦

ANOTHER CONTEXT IN which young children have been shown to lack a biological theory of inheritance is kinship. Kinship titles are inherited just as physical traits are. The title of *son* is a birthright, not a developmental achievement. A baby boy inherits that title the moment he is born, and possibly other kinship titles as well (e.g., *cousin*, *nephew*, *brother*).

These titles are inherently biological. They are a map of the reproductive relationships between members of the same family. They denote who gave birth to whom, who is descended from whom, and who shares common ancestors with whom. But this is not how children initially interpret kinship terms. They interpret them only as referring to social relations.

Of course, the social aspects of kinship are more salient than the reproductive aspects. Not many children witness the birth of their younger siblings or their younger cousins, at least not in societies where birth takes place in a hospital. And no child has ever witnessed the birth of older siblings or older cousins, let alone the child's parents or grandparents. Children are thus surrounded by people labeled *brother*, *uncle*, or *cousin* with no explanation as to what those labels mean, so they devise social explanations for those labels. An uncle is explained as a male friend around the same age as one's parents, and a brother is explained as a male friend around the same age as one's self. Two brothers are assumed to share the same house, whereas an uncle is assumed to live in a different house. Two brothers are assumed to share the same interests, whereas an uncle is assumed to have different interests. And so forth.

When my son Teddy had just turned four, we noticed that he started calling his closest friends "brother." He didn't have any siblings at the time, but he desperately wanted one, particularly a brother, and he wasn't willing to wait for his parents to "find" him one. He was particularly keen on appropriating his cousins as his brothers. Teddy has three cousins—Matt and Charlie, who are a few years older than he is, and Kevin, who is a few years younger—and I noticed that he only referred to Matt and Charlie as his brothers. So I asked why:

ME: Do you have any brothers?
TEDDY: Yes, Matt and Charlie.
ME: Aren't Matt and Charlie your cousins?
TEDDY: No, they're my brothers.
ME: What about Kevin?
TEDDY: He's a baby!
ME: So babies can't be brothers?
TEDDY: No, they can't.
ME: Why not?
TEDDY: Because they just drink bottles and play with baby toys.
ME: So if Kevin is not your brother, what is he?
TEDDY: [Pause] He can be my cousin.

Around the same time that Teddy decided *brother* means "boy who is a close friend," he overheard a conversation about brothers that challenged this definition. We were at a family function, and one of his great-uncles referred to another great-uncle as "brother." Teddy then investigated:

TEDDY: *Who* is your brother?
UNCLE: Uncle Dan is my brother. And your Grandpa Steve is my brother too. We're all brothers.
TEDDY: [Eyes widening] How did you discover that?!

With Teddy's definition of *brother*, it was not possible for three adult men to be brothers, because they were the wrong age. Somehow, these men must have detected a secret bond between them—a bond that united them in the same way he felt united with his own brothers (who, in point of fact, were his cousins).

Of course, kinship terms are not always used in a biological sense. Adults use them to refer to social relations as well: band of brothers, fraternity brother, sorority sister, soul sister, reverend father, Father Christmas, Dutch uncle, Uncle Sam. But adults ultimately recognize that social uses of kinship terms are metaphorical. Children do not.

This point is nicely demonstrated by a study in which children aged five to ten were asked to entertain the possibility of noncanonical kin, like an uncle who is only two years old or a twin sister who lives with another family. More specifically, they were told about two people: one who embodied the social features of a kinship role but not its biological features and one who embodied the biological features of a kinship role but not its social features. They were then asked whether each of those people could, in fact, be kin. For example, children were told about the following two hypothetical uncles: "This man who is your daddy's age loves you and your parents, and he loves to visit and bring presents, but he's not related to your parents at all. He's not your mommy or daddy's brother or anything like that. Could he be an uncle? Now suppose your mommy has all sorts of brothers, some very old and some very, very young. One of your mommy's brothers is so young he's only two years old. Could he be an uncle?"

The youngest children in the study adamantly denied that a baby could be an uncle but agreed that an unrelated friend of the family could be one. In fact, even nine-year-olds were more inclined to label the unrelated friend of the family as an uncle than to label their mother's baby brother as an uncle. Their reasoning behind these judgments was clearly nonbiological:

RESEARCHER: Could [the baby] be an uncle?
CHILD: No . . . because he's little and 2 years old.
RESEARCHER: How old does an uncle have to be?
CHILD: About 24 or 25.
RESEARCHER: If he's 2 years old can he be an uncle?
CHILD: No . . . he can be a cousin.

Cousins are apparently children's catch-all category for kin. If a family member doesn't fit the social mold of an uncle or a brother, then he must be a cousin. There's actually some truth to this belief. From a biological point of view, we're all cousins. All our family trees converge if we trace them back far enough. We may have to trace them back several generations to find a common ancestor with someone seemingly unrelated, but that ancestor most certainly exists. Reader, even you and I are cousins. We may be thirtieth cousins twice removed, but we're still cousins. It's a fact of kinship that even adults with mature, biologically informed theories of kinship often overlook.

✢ ✢ ✢

THE THIRD CONTEXT in which young children have been shown to lack a biological theory of inheritance is a situation ripped from the pages of H. G. Wells's *Island of Doctor Moreau*: cross-species transformation. In Wells's book, a doctor attempts to turn nonhuman animals into humans by surgically altering their anatomy and physiology—shaving away their fur, removing their tails and claws, reshaping their paws and faces, retraining their gestures and instincts.

But the doctor's attempts ultimately fail because, although he alters the animals' external features, he is unable to alter their inner nature—their essence. A visitor to Dr. Moreau's island observes the doctor's results and describes them as follows: "Each of these creatures, despite its human form, had woven into it, into its movements, into the expression of its countenance, into its whole presence, some now irresistible suggestion of a hog, a swinish taint, the unmistakable mark of the beast."

The premise behind Wells's dystopian tale—that an animal's species-specific nature is fixed and enduring—rings true with adults but not with children. Children actually think that species-hood, though heritable, is alterable. From their point of view, a baby born to a pig will develop the traits of a pig as long as nothing changes the pig's species. Being raised by cows is not viewed as sufficient to change the pig's species (as discussed earlier), but surgery is.

Children have never seen anyone surgically transform an animal from one species into another, but they have intuitions about what would happen if you tried. We know this from the work of psychologist Frank Keil, who asked children between the ages of five and ten to contemplate Doctor

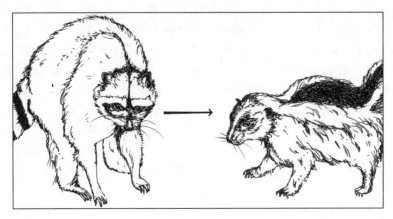

Young children who are told a story about how a raccoon was transformed into a skunk believe that the animal is still a raccoon if the transformation is achieved with a costume. But they believe that the animal has become a skunk if the transformation is achieved with surgery.

Moreau–esque thought experiments, like this: "Suppose doctors took a raccoon and shaved away some of its fur. They dyed what was left all black and bleached a single stripe all white down the center of its back. Then, with surgery, they put in its body a sack of super smelly odor, just like a skunk has. Is this animal now a skunk or a raccoon?"

Children below the age of seven tend to think the animal is now a skunk. Indeed, some are quite convinced of it:

CHILD: They made it into a skunk.
RESEARCHER: Why do you think it's a skunk?
CHILD: Because it looks like a skunk, it smells like a skunk, it acts like a skunk, and it sounds like a skunk. [The child was not told this.]
RESEARCHER: Can it be a skunk if its mommies and daddies were raccoons?
CHILD: Yes.
RESEARCHER: Can it be a skunk if its babies were raccoons?
CHILD: Yes.

Children hold this intuition not just for raccoons altered to resemble skunks, but also for zebras altered to resemble horses, lions altered to resemble tigers, goats altered to resemble sheep, mice altered to resemble squirrels, and chickens altered to resemble turkeys. With enough changes to the animal's traits, children assume that its species has changed as well.

But not all changes are viewed as equal. Surgical changes and endogenously induced changes—changes wrought by shots or pills—are viewed as species-altering, but costume changes are not. If children are questioned about the identity of a raccoon stuffed into a skunk costume, they deny that the raccoon is now a skunk, even if they are shown, in a picture, that the transformed animal looks identical to a skunk. Children are not simply appearance bound. The history behind an animal's appearance matters more than the appearance itself. External changes are viewed as relevant to species-hood only when they are believed to betray deeper, internal changes.

Children's essentialist reasoning about species-hood eventually becomes moored to an adultlike theory of inheritance, and when it does, children begin to reject the possibility of cross-species transformation, as they now appreciate the biological reasons for why it couldn't happen. Consider the following conversation between a researcher and a nine-year-old child about the possibility of transforming a goat into a sheep:

CHILD: They messed it up, and so . . . it could be part sheep and part goat.
RESEARCHER: Okay, how would that work? Tell me why you think it'd be part sheep and part goat.
CHILD: Well, when it was born it was a goat, but when he gave it the vitamin shots, it might have . . . uh . . . changed its insides.
RESEARCHER: If you had to decide whether it was really more sheep or more goat, what would you think?
CHILD: I'd mate it and see which way its babies came out.

This child has connected species-hood to inheritance and sees species-hood as a birthright. Consequently, the question of whether a goat can be transformed into a sheep is no longer just a matter of speculation. It's now an *empirical* question, to be decided by breeding.

It may seem odd that a psychologist would ask young children to contemplate a thought experiment drawn from a gothic horror novel, but the real inspiration for this thought experiment was not H. G. Wells but Jean Piaget. Recall from Chapter 2 that Piaget devised the infamous conservation task, in which children are shown a physical transformation that changes the external appearance of a material substance but not its mass (e.g., squashing a ball of clay into a pancake). Keil's species-transformation task is a conservation task in the domain of biology. To pass, the participant must recognize that an animal's species is conserved across transformations that change its external appearance but not its inner constitution (its DNA).

Although children of all ages can pass the task when the change is blatantly superficial, only nine-year-olds are able to pass when the change is more subtle. This ability comes later than the ability to pass standard conservation tasks in the domain of matter. Conservation of species is apparently more difficult to grasp than conservation of mass. Indeed, this gradient of abilities has been documented not only among children but also among people with Alzheimer's disease. When people with Alzheimer's begin to lose their conceptual knowledge because of dementia, they lose their understanding of the conservation of species before they lose their understanding of the conservation of matter. That is, they claim that shaving, dying, and surgically augmenting a raccoon will change its species before they claim that pouring water from a short, squat cylinder into a tall, thin cylinder will change its volume. The last insights attained in development are often the first to go in senescence.

✦ ✦ ✦

YOUNG CHILDREN'S MISCONCEPTIONS about the heritability of mental traits, the meaning of kinship terms, and the determinants of species-hood suggest that their earliest conceptions of inheritance are not distinctly biological. Children have ideas on the matter—they don't just shrug their shoulders when posed thought experiments about inheritance—but those ideas are grounded in essentialism, not biology. How, then, do children acquire a genuinely biological theory of inheritance? It turns out that it's as simple as learning where babies come from. They don't need to learn the lurid details of sexual reproduction; they just need to learn that babies develop from eggs inside their mother's wombs.

When my daughter Lucy was four and a half, she had some curious ideas about where babies come from. She knew that they come from their "mommy's tummy," but she hadn't quite figured out what that meant. Her primary association with tummies was eating, so she assumed that mothers must eat their babies so that the babies could get inside their tummies. As Lucy once explained to my wife, "First I was alive, then I died, and you ate me. I was in your stomach and then you burped me up."

We tried to explain to Lucy that she started as an egg inside her mother's body, not as food that her mother ate, but the explanation did not stick. A few weeks after she had provided the baby-eating explanation, Lucy and I had the following conversation:

LUCY: Can I see a picture of the egg I hatched out of?
ME: Lucy, you didn't hatch out of an egg. You came from Mommy's tummy.
LUCY: I know! I was an egg *inside* Mommy's tummy. Mommy ate a lot of eggs, and I was in one of them. And then, when I was out, I hatched.

Children typically learn the biological facts of reproduction by age nine or ten, at which point they are able to discern why some aspects of an organism's identity—its physical traits, its kinship roles, its species-hood—are fixed at birth and others are not. Studies that have charted children's beliefs about inheritance before and after they have been taught the "facts of life" suggest that learning these facts has far-ranging consequences. In one study, psychologist Ken Springer taught children between the ages of four and seven three key facts: (1) that babies are conceived internally, (2) that babies begin life as an embryo, and (3) that babies grow from an embryo into a baby inside their mother's womb.

Before learning these facts, children espoused several wrongheaded beliefs about inheritance, including the belief that similar-looking strangers share nearly as many traits as dissimilar-looking kin, that acquired traits (e.g., dyed hair) are as heritable as inborn traits (e.g., curly hair), that maladaptive traits (e.g., having a weak heart) are less heritable than adaptive ones (e.g., having a strong heart), and that parents can decide which traits they want their children to inherit. After learning the three facts about babies' conception and development, children revised their beliefs about inheritance. They recognized that dissimilar-looking kin share more traits with each other than they do with similar-looking strangers, that acquired traits are not heritable, and that maladaptive traits are just as heritable as adaptive ones. Moreover, they understood that parents transfer traits to their children by physical means—namely, by "tiny pieces of stuff" transferred from mother to baby before the baby is born.

This collection of ideas constitutes children's first real theory of inheritance. The next development in their understanding of inheritance is learning about genes. Middle-school children typically know the terms *genes*, *genetic*, and *DNA*, and associate these terms with inheritance. But they have no conception of a gene's actual role in inheritance, let alone its physical instantiation in the body.

Some middle-schoolers think that genes circulate in the blood, like hormones. Some think that genes are consumed in food, like nutrients. And some think that different types of genes are found in different parts of the body, like cells. With respect to function, most middle-schoolers believe that genes code for traits, not proteins. They see the mapping between genes and trait as one-to-one, with each gene containing the instructions for building a separate, discrete trait. Most adults believe this too. In reality, multiple genes contribute to the expression of each trait, through the interactions of the proteins they code for. Without proteins, there is no mechanism for genes to communicate with one another as growth and development unfold in real time.

Learning about inheritance is thus a two-step process. Essentialist notions of innate potential must give way to trait-based notions of information transfer, and trait-based notions of information transfer must give way to molecular notions of gene expression and gene regulation. The first step occurs during early childhood, when a child learns basic facts about conception and gestation, but the second step is more variable. This step requires detailed instruction on cellular processing, and most adults never receive such instruction.

But does the average adult need a detailed, biochemical understanding of inheritance? Or will a simple trait-based understanding suffice? It turns out that media coverage of genetics research—coverage that is increasingly plentiful in our age of modern genomics—requires a fairly sophisticated level of understanding. Between 2010 and 2011, the *New York Times* published over two hundred articles related to genes, genetics, or DNA. Education researcher Nicole Shea analyzed the articles for the types of knowledge they presuppose and discovered that readers are expected to know several biochemical facts:

1. Genes are instructions for building proteins, and those instructions are written in the same molecular language for all organisms.

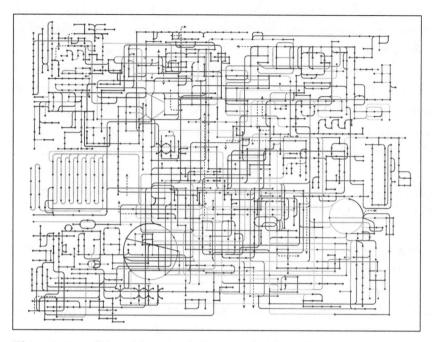

This artistic rendition of three metabolic networks (the Krebs cycle, the urea cycle, and fatty-acid beta-oxidation) illustrates the complexity inherent in biochemical systems—complexity that requires an appreciation of gene-protein interactions.

2. Proteins perform cellular functions, like transporting molecules or regulating chemical reactions, and those functions depend on their structure.
3. Many sequences of DNA vary across species (or individuals), and this variation sheds light on how differences in genetic structure yield differences in morphological structure.
4. Environmental factors can mutate genes or alter gene expression.

If most adults think that foods containing DNA require mandatory labeling, then most adults clearly do not understand genetics at this level. And understanding genetics at this level is crucial for making informed consumer decisions about genetic issues, including what foods to eat, what tests to undergo, and what medications to take. But that's not the only reason genetic literacy is important. Our understanding of genes also influences how we react to information about the relation between genes and behavior.

Genes are involved in all our behavior, at some level, but geneticists are beginning to ascertain the links between particular genes and particular behaviors. And when we learn about such links, we tend to endow them with significance—more significance than they deserve. For instance, people who endorse genetic explanations for obesity believe they have less control over their weight than do people who doubt such explanations. Merely reading a newspaper article containing genetic explanations for obesity leads people to eat more junk food than they typically would. Equally problematic, female test takers perform significantly worse on standardized math tests if they take the tests after having read a genetic explanation for why women are underrepresented in math- and science-related professions.

Our beliefs about our genes may affect our behavior more strongly than do the genes themselves. In the case of mathematics achievement, for instance, the evidence for innate gender differences is weak, but the evidence for socially primed gender differences is strong. Ironically, as scientists discern the limits of genetic influences on behavior, our knowledge of any influence at all can lead us to behave more fatalistically. Our genes do not dictate our destiny, but our beliefs about our genes may, if we let them.

11 | ILLNESS

What Makes Us Ill?
How Does Illness Spread?

I F HUMANS EVOLVED INNATE KNOWLEDGE OF ANY NATURAL PHENOME-
non, it should be disease. Avoiding disease is clearly advantageous from
an evolutionary point of view, as pathogens and parasites threaten to stop
our evolutionary lineage in its tracks. And sure enough, humans around the
globe are repulsed by the kinds of things that contain pathogens and parasites: bodily products (vomit, feces), bodily fluids (spit, sweat), violations of
the "body envelope" (mutilation, gore), visible signs of infection (swelling,
discoloration), parasites (ticks, maggots), and decomposing organic matter
(rotten meat, spoiled milk).

When we encounter such things, we make what is universally recognized as the *disgust face*—an expression characterized by a scrunched nose
and an outthrust tongue. Both characteristics have practical benefits. The
scrunched nose restricts our intake of contaminated air, and the outthrust
tongue expels any contaminated substances from our mouth.

Our repulsion toward noxious substances is mediated by an evolution-
arily ancient part of our brain, the *insular cortex*. This part of our brain,
which we share with all mammals, is a subcomponent of a larger neural
system responsible for linking visceral sensations to conscious awareness.

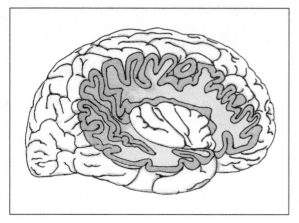

The insula (exposed white area), located in the central part of the brain, is active both when we experience disgust and when we view disgust in others.

Curiously, the insular cortex becomes active not only when we feel disgusted but also when we see that others are disgusted—that others have scrunched their noses and thrust out their tongues. Disgust is thus triggered, at a neural level, both by firsthand identification of something noxious and by secondhand identification. Our brains operate on the assumption that anything that disgusts you should disgust me, which is sensible given that both of us are probably susceptible to the same diseases. Seeing someone look disgusted even bolsters our immune response. We produce more disease-fighting proteins in anticipation of coming into contact with a disease-ridden object.

Disease-ridden objects can vary in what they look like (and what they smell like), but there are some kinds of objects that we universally regard as disgusting. In one far-ranging study, researchers asked over forty thousand adults from all major continents to rate how disgusting they found each of the following objects: a mucus-covered plate, a pus-stained towel, a feverish-looking face, a congested subway car, a swarm of parasitic worms, and a louse. People everywhere rated these objects as more disgusting than perceptually similar objects that lacked cues to disease: a jelly-covered plate, an ink-stained towel, a healthy face, an empty subway car, a swarm of caterpillars, and a wasp. On average, women found the disease-ridden objects more disgusting than men did, and younger adults found the objects more disgusting than older adults did, but everyone found them at least somewhat disgusting and thus somewhat aversive.

The evolutionary logic behind disgust is seemingly straightforward, but it does have quirks. Consider the following situations:

- Drinking a glass of spoiled milk.
- Stepping in vomit.
- Being sneezed on.
- Getting a fishing hook stuck in your finger.
- Touching the ashes of a cremated body.
- Using your mouth to inflate a new, unlubricated condom.
- Eating soup stirred with a sterilized flyswatter.
- Eating fudge shaped like dog feces.

Each of these situations typically elicits some degree of disgust, but the first four are qualitatively different from the last four. The first four entail a genuine threat of infection, whereas the last four do not. The last four are disgusting only by association—either perceptual association with a disease-ridden object (the feces-shaped fudge), functional association (the new condom, the sterilized flyswatter), or historical association (the ashes of a cremated body). The boundaries of disgust are readily extended to encompass substances that pose no real threat, because it's ultimately better to avoid something disease-neutral than to touch or ingest something disease-ridden. Avoiding a disease-neutral object is inconsequential from an evolutionary point of view, but exposure to a disease-ridden object can be a game stopper.

Our hypersensitivity toward the threat of contagion can be seen not just in our contemplation of hypothetical situations but also in our actual behavior. Adults offered a piece of fudge in the shape of dog feces typically refuse to eat it, even though they know perfectly well that the fudge is not contaminated. Adults offered juice stirred with a sterilized cockroach typically refuse to drink it, even though they know perfectly well that the juice has not been contaminated. Likewise, most adults refuse to hold a disc of plastic vomit between their teeth, eat soup out of a brand new bedpan, or eat sugar out of a bowl labeled "cyanide," even when they themselves affixed the label to the bowl.

Perhaps least rational of all, most adults refuse to eat soup from a bowl they have spit into or drink water from a glass they have spit into, even though they know that each bite of soup or each sip of water will mix with saliva the moment it hits their tongues. None of these activities are physically harmful, but they are still psychologically harmful.

Our tendency to confer disgust by association would be nothing more than a quaint feature of human cognition if it weren't for our failure to associate disgust with many things that *should* be disgusting. For centuries, infectious diseases like cholera and smallpox spread like wildfire because humans were not disgusted by cholera-infested water or smallpox-infested blankets. These disease-ridden objects betrayed no sign of their deadly nature, so they spread disease more effectively than basic human-to-human contact. Even today, highly avoidable diseases like chlamydia and HIV still plague humanity because the acts that spread them are associated with pleasure rather than repulsion.

Our evolved capacity to avoid pathogens and parasites—disgust—is thus largely ill informed. On one hand, it's triggered by sights and sounds merely associated with disease, while on the other, it's left untriggered by the pathogens and parasites imbued in everyday objects. What disgusts us is not always a threat, and what threatens us is not always disgusting.

✢ ✢ ✢

CHILDREN ARE DISGUSTED by many of the same things that adults are, as one would expect on an evolutionary account of disgust. They are not keen on smelling putrid odors or touching filthy socks; nor are they keen on holding a glass eyeball ostensibly plucked from someone's eye socket. But there are many aspects of children's disgust response that differ from adults.

For starters, children below the age of seven tend not to be disgusted by noxious things that lack the outward appearance of disease, like cockroaches, litter, or dead animals. Children also have a difficult time recognizing disgust in others. As late as age eight, they mistake expressions of disgust for expressions of anger. Their problem in identifying a scrunched nose and outthrust tongue as signs of disgust is not that they fail to understand the word *disgust* (they master that word by age five) or that they fail to make disgust expressions themselves (they make those expressions from infancy). Rather, their problem is that anger and disgust share many similarities: both are negatively charged, both are physiologically arousing, and both are associated with rejection and avoidance. Children thus assume that disgust is just a variant of anger.

Perhaps the most significant difference in children's and adults' experience of disgust is children's lack of disgust toward objects that have been contaminated by external sources of disease. Anyone who has potty-trained a toddler or taught a toddler how to use a public restroom can attest to this fact. When my son Teddy became old enough to use the urinal, he was continually distracted by the bright pink urinal cake and often tried to pick it up. After I successfully dissuaded him from doing so, I had to dissuade him from grasping the sides of the urinal with his bare hands. I also had to dissuade him from pulling down his pants so far that they would soak up whatever liquid was pooled beneath the urinal.

A fellow parent relayed to me an even more disgusting incident. Her four-year-old son was eager to use the public restroom by himself, but she was wary of letting him, for fear of lurking pedophiles. One day, while shopping, she peered into the store's single-stall bathroom and verified that no one was inside. She then let her son use the bathroom by himself. He emerged a few minutes later, with a grin of pride on his face. All seemed well until she noticed that he was chewing something: a wad of gum plucked from the bathroom wall.

Children's disgust response, or lack thereof, has been systemically documented by psychologist Paul Rozin and his colleagues. In one of Rozin's studies, children between the ages of four and twelve were asked questions about the following scenario: "A grasshopper is washing himself in the lake. After he finishes, he hops into a house. In the house, a mother goes to the refrigerator and takes out the milk. She pours the milk. How much would you like to drink the milk?" Children were shown an emoticon-based scale, ranging from a frowny face to a neutral face to a smiley face, and were asked to pick the face that best matched how they felt about drinking the milk.

After they made their selection, the thought experiment continued: "The grasshopper hops near the milk. How much would you like to drink the milk now? The grasshopper hops on the glass and falls in. He falls to the bottom. How much would you like to drink the milk now? The mother takes the grasshopper out. How much would you like to drink the milk now? The mother spills the milk. She pours new milk into the same glass. How much would you like to drink this new milk? She washes the glass with soap and water three times. She pours new milk into the same glass. How much would you like to drink this milk?"

At the start of the experiment, all children selected a smiley face to reflect their attitude towards drinking a fresh (uncontaminated) glass of milk. After told that a grasshopper fell into the milk, most then changed their selection to a frowny face. From that point onward, older children's responses differed markedly from younger children's. Older children (ages eight and above) were not happy to drink the milk again until it had been poured out and the glass had been washed before it was refilled. Younger children (ages six and below) were happy to drink the milk as soon as the grasshopper had been fished out.

The same result was found when grasshoppers were swapped for "doggie-doo." Older children said they would refuse to drink milk that doggie-doo had fallen into until the glass had been washed and the milk had been replaced, but younger children said they would drink the milk as soon as the doggie-doo had been fished out. Adults tested with the same materials typically expressed dissatisfaction with the milk even after the most extreme stage of decontamination (washing the glass and replacing the milk).

Rozin and his colleagues worried that younger children may have responded differently from older children not because their disgust response was less sensitive but because their imaginations were less vivid. To circumvent this possibility, they performed a follow-up study in which they did away with hypothetical situations and presented children with real, physical objects. They offered children foods that appeared to have been contaminated in one way or another: juice stirred with a used comb, juice laden with a dead grasshopper, and cookies sprinkled with "grasshopper powder" or "dried and ground up grasshopper parts."

None of these foods had actually been contaminated—the comb was sterilized, the dead grasshopper was sterilized, and the grasshopper powder was just green-colored streusel—but the children knew no better. And, consistent with previous studies, older children (ages seven and above) refused to consume any of the foods on offer, but younger children (ages six and below) often accepted those foods. A whopping 77 percent of the younger children drank juice stirred with a used comb, 63 percent drank juice laden with a dead grasshopper (still floating inside), and 45 percent ate cookies powdered with grasshopper parts.

Why do young children fail to be disgusted by incidental contamination? One possibility is that this form of disgust is a luxury, afforded only to those who live in modern, industrialized societies. For most of human history, anyone who refused to eat food prepared with nonsterile instruments would have starved, and anyone who refused to drink water that was not perfectly clear and odorless would have died of thirst. The same is true of anyone living in a developing country today. Indeed, the commonly held belief that food becomes inedible the moment it touches the ground is a luxury tenable only to those who have food to spare. Food picks up additional bacteria when it touches another surface—as do all objects—but the amount of bacteria depends on the type of food, the type of surface, the cleanliness of the surface, and the length of contact between the food and the surface. In most situations, eating something off the ground poses minimal risk of contagion, but many of us treat fallen food as if it were a deadly substance, to be thrown directly into the trash.

Another reason children's disgust response emerges so slowly is that this response has to be tailored to the local environment. The primary function of disgust is to defend our bodies from noxious substances, so disgust is always strongly linked to food. We willingly take food into our bodies, which is where pathogens and parasites would like to be. So disgust acts as a gatekeeper, helping us distinguish foods that are safe to ingest from foods that are not.

For some species, evolution has prespecified the foods an animal will find disgusting, because those foods were a regular feature of the animal's ancestral environmental. Ravens, for instance, have a seemingly innate disgust of bees (which sting if consumed) and monarch butterflies (which induce nausea if consumed). Ravens do not need to learn through trial and error that bees sting and monarchs are nauseating. Evolution has endowed them with an automatic defense.

Humans, on the other hand, have occupied—and continue to occupy—environments so distinct from one another that their food offerings overlap only minimally. Evolution could not have foreseen the food-based dangers present in all these varied environments. Humans must therefore discover for themselves which parts of the environment are safe to eat and which are not. The rule we seem to follow is that foods we encountered as children, provided to us by our caregivers, are safe to eat, whereas foods we did not encounter as children are not safe to eat. In this way, children growing up in

Grasshoppers are an object of disgust in Western culture but are a delicacy in several non-Western cultures.

coastal North America develop a taste for crabs (served to them by their caregivers) but are disgusted by termites (not served by their caregivers), whereas children growing up in central Africa develop a taste for termites but are disgusted by crabs.

Termites and crabs are both arthropods and are similar from a nutritional point of view, yet we have strong feelings about which animals we are willing to eat and which we are not. When a food is unavailable during our childhood, we grow to regard it not merely as distasteful but as disgusting—as outside the scope of human consumption. Across cultures, then, there are few consumable goods that are deemed universally disgusting. Ironically, Western researchers interested in the development of disgust have used grasshoppers as their stimuli. Grasshoppers are a delicacy in China, Indonesia, Thailand, Japan, Mexico, and Uganda. Young children's willingness to eat grasshopper-infused cookies and drink grasshopper-infused beverages is counterintuitive only from an Anglo-European perspective.

✦ ✦ ✦

DISGUST MAY BE our strongest defense against infectious disease—disease caused by bacteria, viruses, fungi, or parasites—but there are other reasons people fall ill and thus other facets to our conceptions of illness. Sometimes we fall ill from nutritional deficiencies (e.g., rickets, scurvy). Or we fall ill from genetic abnormalities (e.g., Huntington's disease, cystic fibrosis). And sometimes we fall ill from a combination of genetic factors and environmental factors (e.g., diabetes, heart disease, cancer). Medical science has classified the causes of most human maladies, but that taxonomy is a recent innovation. For most of human history, the dominant explanation for all maladies—microbial, nutritional, and genetic—was an imbalance in our internal fluids, or "humors."

Beginning with Hippocrates, physicians analyzed disease in terms of four primary humors: blood, the "sanguine" humor; phlegm, the "phlegmatic" humor; yellow bile, the "choleric" humor; and black bile, the "melancholic" humor. Each humor was associated with a different organ (blood with heart, phlegm with brain, yellow bile with liver, black bile with spleen), a different season (blood with spring, phlegm with winter, yellow bile with summer, black bile with autumn), and a different element of creation (blood with air, phlegm with water, yellow bile with fire, black bile with earth).

Diseases were explained in terms of a humoral imbalance. Too much blood was thought to cause headaches; too much phlegm, epilepsy; too much yellow bile, fevers; and too much black bile, depression. The prescribed cure for such diseases was to relieve the body of excess humors by inducing vomiting, defecation, or bleeding. The last of these cures—bloodletting—is particularly strange from a modern point of view. Bloodletting is a universal practice, observed in societies on all major continents, yet it invariably does more harm than good. President George Washington actually died from bloodletting, after nearly half his blood was drained from his body in an attempt to cure a respiratory illness. While modern doctors have occasionally embraced the use of leeches as a form of treatment, the animals' utility lies in the anticoagulant properties of their saliva, not in the actual bloodletting.

Bloodletting was practiced by many as an attempt to restore balance to the humors. Humors were thought to become imbalanced for a number reasons: heredity, poor diet, imprudent behavior, a change in weather, a change in dwelling, or bad air. Bad air, or "miasma," was the most popular explanation for diseases spread by infection, like plague or cholera. In the minds of early doctors, the contagious nature of these diseases was overshadowed by the bad smells associated with them. (Dying people do not smell great.) Of course, bad air was not the cause of death and dying; death and dying was the cause of the bad air. Malaria was also blamed on bad air—*malaria* literally means "bad air" in Italian—but the disease's

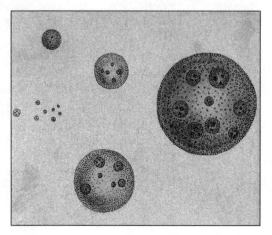

A seventeenth-century sketch of the *animalcules*, or "tiny animals," observed only under the microscope.

association with bad air is equally superfluous. Malaria was thought to be caused by inhaling swamp vapors, but it was actually caused by the mosquitos that bred in those swamps.

Despite its shortcomings, the humoral theory of disease remained popular for thousands of years, from antiquity to the mid-nineteenth century. Its successor—germ theory—was slow in coming. As early as 1546, Italian physician Girolamo Fracastoro published a treatise in which he argued that even people with well-balanced humors can become ill through the contraction of imperceptible particles, termed *seminaria*, or "seeds." Fracastoro's notion of seeds was an improvement over humors, as it emphasized the role of contagion, but Fracastoro did not conceptualize seeds as biological.

Over a century later, in 1676, the Dutch scientist Antony van Leuwenhoek observed bacteria under a microscope for the first time—bacteria scraped from his own teeth. Leuwenhoek labeled what he saw *animalcules*, or "tiny animals," but he did not link them to disease. The first person to make this link was the French scientist Louis Pasteur, nearly two hundred years later, in 1857.

Pasteur had been investigating the role of yeast in the fermentation of beer and wine and came to the realization that yeast is alive—that yeast is a microorganism that digests starch cells and leaves behind alcohol in their place. He then conjectured that the role of yeast in fermentation is similar to the role of germs in disease. The German scientist Robert Koch further developed Pasteur's ideas into a set of empirical predictions, which he and

Young children are happy to accept food that someone has sneezed on; they show no preference for the clean bowl on the right over the contaminated bowl on the left.

Pasteur later confirmed in experiments with anthrax and rabies. The result was not only a new theory of disease (germ theory) but also a new field of biology (microbiology).

Today, the concept of a germ has permeated popular consciousness and popular discourse. Even toddlers are bombarded with messages about germs: "Don't eat that; it has germs," "Wash your hands with soap to kill all the germs," "Cover your nose when you sneeze so you don't spread germs." All this talk about germs has affected the way young children think about illness. Preschoolers know that rotting food has germs and that eating rotting food can make you sick. They know that sick people have germs and that contact with a sick person can spread the sickness. They know that germs can be passed from contaminated objects (e.g., a dead bug) to uncontaminated objects (e.g., a glass of milk). And they know that germs are too small to be seen and can therefore be passed from one object to another undetected.

But for all this factual knowledge, children are still willing to touch germ-contaminated objects and eat germ-contaminated foods, as discussed above. In one shocking demonstration of children's obliviousness to germs, researchers presented children with two bowls of cereal: a bowl that was clean and a bowl that someone appeared to sneeze into. Preschoolers ate as much cereal from the second bowl as from the first, and they rated both bowls as equally yummy. Children's factual knowledge of germs clearly has limitations.

Indeed, it's presumptuous to think that preschoolers have acquired a germ theory of disease from casual exposure to germ-related talk when it took scientists hundreds of years to discover germ theory. The notion of contagion may be easy to understand, but the notion of a germ is not. To children, germs are just a label for something that makes you sick. They have no idea that germs are different from other noxious substances—pesticides, disinfectants, toxic fumes, heavy metals—let alone that germs are alive.

This point was nicely demonstrated in a study comparing children's understanding of germs to their understanding of poison. In the first part of the study, children between the ages of four and ten were asked questions like this: "A girl named Susan accidentally breathed in some germs and got a runny nose. If a friend came over to visit, do you think the friend could catch a runny nose from Susan? A boy named Sid breathed in some poison and pretty soon he got a bad cough. If a friend came over to visit, do you think the friend could catch having a cough from Sid?" In the second part of the study, children were asked whether germs eat, reproduce, and move on their own and whether poisons eat, reproduce, and move on their own.

Across both parts of the study, children below the age of ten did not distinguish between germs and poison. They claimed that poison-induced illnesses were as contagious as germ-induced ones, and they claimed that neither poison nor germs have any biological properties. Ten-year-olds, on the other hand, correctly claimed that germ-induced illnesses are more contagious than poison-induced ones and correctly attributed biological properties to germs but not to poison. Still, the overall proportion of biological properties attributed to germs was small (about half—the same amount attributed to plants, which is consistent with the developmental patterns discussed in Chapter 8).

Another study that drives home this same point looked at children's understanding of the difference between diseases caused by germs and those caused by genetics. The children in this study were asked to consider an illness-based version of the adoption scenario described in Chapters 9 and 10: "Mr. and Mrs. Robinson had a baby girl. That means that the baby came out of Mrs. Robinson's tummy. Right after she came out of Mrs. Robinson's tummy, the baby went to live with Mr. and Mrs. Jones. They named her Elizabeth. Elizabeth lived with them and they took care of her. They fed her, bought her clothes, hugged her, and kissed her when she was sad. Mr. and Mrs. Robinson have trouble seeing certain colors. They cannot see the color yellow. Mr. and Mrs. Jones don't have any trouble seeing colors. They can see the color yellow. What do you think will happen to

Elizabeth when she grows up? Will she be able to see the color yellow like Mr. and Mrs. Jones or will she be *unable* to see the color yellow like Mr. and Mrs. Robinson?"

Some of the adoption scenarios described genetic disorders, like color blindness. Others described infectious diseases, like the flu. Children below the age of ten did not robustly differentiate the two types of conditions, claiming instead that both were attributable to the *birth* parents. That is, the children claimed not only that Elizabeth is likely to be color-blind if her birth parents are color-blind but also that Elizabeth is likely to have the flu if her birth parents have the flu. If children understand that infectious diseases are transmitted through contact—that is, through the physical transfer of germs—then they should attribute such diseases to Elizabeth only when her adopted parents have them. But children rarely cited Elizabeth's adopted parents as the determinants of her current health. They seemed to think that infectious diseases, like genetic disorders, are inherited at birth. Clearly, the link between germs and disease is fuzzy in young children's minds.

✦ ✦ ✦

THE LINK BETWEEN germs and disease is fuzzy in adults' minds too. Consider the common belief that you can catch a cold from being cold. Adults in both Eastern cultures and Western cultures hold this belief, prescribing heavy coats, thick scarves, and dry socks as ways of warding off illness. But merely being cold does not increase your chances of contracting a cold. Immunologists have found no correlation between coldness and illness across a century's worth of studies. The idea that you can catch your death of cold is just an old wives' tale—or, in the parlance of psychologists, a *folk belief*.

Folk beliefs about disease are appealing because they prescribe preventative behaviors without requiring any underlying knowledge of disease transmission. Anyone can obey the advice of staying warm and keeping dry, regardless of whether they think that diseases are caused by germs or by humors. But folk beliefs are often wrong, and the behaviors they spawn are often maladaptive. Causal knowledge of disease is the only surefire means of staying healthy.

Psychologist Terry Kit-fong Au and her colleagues have demonstrated as much in studies of knowledge-focused health education programs. Drawing on the findings described above, they developed a health education program that taught the causal principles behind cold and flu prevention, dubbed Think Biology. Whereas conventional health education programs focus on behavior (the dos and don'ts of cold and flu prevention), the Think Biology program focused on knowledge (the whys and hows of cold and flu prevention). Its main objective was to get students to conceptualize germs as living, reproducing biological agents rather than as inert substances like poison. It emphasized four key principles: (1) that viruses are tiny living things too small to see with the naked eye; (2) that cold and flu viruses can survive for several hours in cool, humid air but are quickly killed by heat and disinfectants, (3) that only live strains of virus can cause colds and flu, and (4) that cold and flu viruses enter the body through the eyes, nose, and mouth.

To test the effectiveness of the Think Biology program, Au administered it to a group of third-graders in Hong Kong. She compared their progress with third-graders who received a more conventional health education program. The conventional program did not cover any of the biological underpinnings of cold and flu infection but instead covered cold and flu symptoms, treatments, complications, preventative behaviors (dos), and risk behaviors (don'ts).

Before and after each program, children's understanding of cold and flu infection was assessed by three tasks. The first was to describe behaviors that would cause people to catch a cold or flu and to explain why. The second was to watch videos of everyday situations and identify the events that posed a risk of cold and flu infection, such as rubbing one's eyes, chewing one's fingernails, or handing someone an eraser after having sneezed on it. The third task was more subtle. Each child was called into a room separate from the main classroom and asked to help put crackers into plastic bags for snack time. The crackers and bags were located on a table next to a bottle of hand sanitizer, and the measure of interest was whether children spontaneously used the hand sanitizer to clean their hands before touching the crackers.

At the conclusion of the study, children in both health education programs were better able to explain illness in terms of germ transfer. Only children in the Think Biology program, however, could explain why germ transfer was harmful (i.e., because germs, once transferred, replicate inside their new host). And only children in the Think Biology program were less likely to cite cold weather or wet weather as causes of cold and flu infection. When it came to identifying cold and flu risk behaviors, children in the conventional program could identify the risk factors they had studied (e.g., being sneezed on), but they were unable to identify risk factors they had not studied (e.g., sharing a drink with a friend). Children in the Think Biology program, on the other hand, identified both studied and unstudied risk factors. Most significantly, only children in the Think Biology program increased their use of hand sanitizer when handling food. Rates of hand sanitation more than doubled, with 15 percent of students sanitizing their hands before the program and 41 percent sanitizing their hands after the program.

Au and her colleagues achieved similar success with a program designed to teach adolescents about the biological underpinnings of sexually transmitted diseases. The power of such programs lies not just in their ability to engender more accurate reasoning but in their ability to engender more flexible reasoning. No health education program could cover all behaviors associated with the spread of a particular disease, and even if it could, no student is likely to memorize that list. An effective program provides students with the conceptual tools to evaluate risk in the moment, as new disease-relevant situations unfold.

As a case in point, Au and her colleagues observed a curious breakdown in disease-prevention behavior in the Hong Kong schools where they tested their cold and flu prevention program. The children in this school washed their hands dutifully before lunch, only to recontaminate them minutes later by touching the face masks they wore as a precaution against the 2003 outbreak of severe acute respiratory syndrome (SARS). These face masks were the most contaminated objects in the children's environment, as they were covered in microbes filtered from the children's airstream throughout the day.

"Don't touch your face masks" was not a rule covered in the school's conventional cold and flu prevention program, but it was a rule that could be inferred from the general principles conveyed by the Think Biology program. In fact, many children did infer this rule, labeling the touching of face masks as a risk factor in the risk-factor identification task administered at the conclusion of the Think Biology program.

✦ ✦ ✦

IN AU'S STUDIES, children who learned about the microbial nature of colds and flu stopped citing cold weather and wet weather as causes of infectious disease. But other folk beliefs about the causes of infectious disease are not so easily shaken—folk beliefs of a supernatural flavor. Illness raises concerns that extend beyond the realm of secular affairs into the realm of gods, angels, ancestors, and spirits.

For Christians and Jews, reprieve from illness is one of the most common forms of petitionary prayer. Christians and Jews seek God's help even in coping with infectious disease, like hepatitis or pneumonia. They do so, not because they are unaware that infectious diseases are caused by germs but because they view God and germs as complementary. God is the distal agent of human health, and germs are the proximal agent. Put differently, God is the answer to the question of *why* we fall ill, and germs are the answer to the question of *how* we fall ill.

From our Western point of view, petitioning God for help with illness seems perfectly benign, but we are less complacent about the supernatural beliefs observed in other cultures, like the Creole belief that tuberculosis is caused by sorcery, the Hmong belief that epilepsy is caused by spirit possession, or the African belief that AIDS is caused by witchcraft. Those beliefs strike many Westerners as foolish, yet psychologists have found that such beliefs take the same form and function as the Judeo-Christian belief that God has a hand in human health.

Consider the folk belief that AIDS is caused by witchcraft. Healthcare workers have spent a significant amount of effort trying to dissuade Africans from this belief on the assumption that it blocks their receptivity to scientific information about AIDS, the disease, and HIV, the virus that causes AIDS. But most African adults, and even many African children, know the basic facts about HIV. They know that HIV is passed through sexual contact or contact with blood, that HIV is *not* passed through skin-to-skin contact, that someone who is a carrier for HIV may not show any symptoms of AIDS, and that AIDS causes people to become thin and weak but that being thin and weak does not cause people to get AIDS. On top of this knowledge, they also happen to believe that AIDS is caused by witchcraft—witchcraft wrought either by jealous neighbors or displeased ancestors.

When asked to explain how AIDS could be caused both by a virus and by witchcraft, African adults provide several causally sophisticated explanations, like the following:

- "Witchcraft can fool you into sleeping with an infected person."

AIDS education in several African countries has had to combat the folk belief that AIDS is caused by witchcraft, as illustrated in this adaptation of a poster produced by Kenya AIDS NGOs Consortium, Nairobi.

- "A witch can make a condom weak and break."
- "The people that hated her paid the witches to put the virus in her path."
- "He was bewitched and sleeping with infected people."
- "Witches can use anything to kill you, evil magic or HIV."

Beliefs about witchcraft and viruses are intermingled in the minds of many Africans. Indeed, the two appear to develop hand in hand; supernatural beliefs about HIV infection emerge only after children have acquired a biological understanding of the topic. It's not biologically naive children who point to witches as the cause of AIDS; it's adults.

A similar developmental pattern has been observed in India and Vietnam as well. Many adults in these countries endorse a mixture of biological and supernatural explanations for illness, but the children raised in these countries endorse biological explanations before they endorse supernatural ones. Even in the United States, children are less likely than adults to endorse supernatural beliefs about illness, particularly the belief that illness is caused by immoral behavior.

Disease obeys no moral laws; it afflicts the righteous as often as it afflicts the wicked. Yet many adults—even college-educated ones—believe otherwise. Consider the following vignette from a study on childrens' and adults' beliefs about the moral underpinnings of illness: "Peter and Mark were talking about a person who just came down with a mysterious and deadly illness. The person led a healthy life, and there was no known reason why this person should have contracted the illness. Peter said, 'I know that bad things happen to both good and bad people but I believe there is a greater chance of bad things happening to bad people. This person was not a good person. He has cheated and lied and has robbed many decent people of their money. What goes around comes around.' Mark said, 'I disagree. People who are bad get serious illnesses just as often as people who are good. What goes around doesn't come around.'"

When twelve-year-old children heard this vignette and were asked who they agreed with—disease-is-random Mark or disease-is-deserved Peter—80 percent sided with Mark and 20 percent sided with Peter. When adults heard this same vignette, 60 percent sided with Mark and 40 percent sided with Peter. In other words, adults were twice as likely as children to blame the ill character for his own illness. These findings echo the popular belief among adults that cancer victims have caused their own cancer. Cancer looms as large in the minds of Americans as HIV in the minds of Africans, and no health-care topic aside from vaccination seems to have attracted the same level of anti-intellectualism. Quackery about cancer abounds on the internet, in self-help books, and on talk shows, perpetuating myths both about the causes of cancer (sugar, citrus, fungi, modern living, negative thinking) and its cures (cannabis, baking soda, ginger, meditation, coffee enemas).

Adults may know more about disease and disease transmission than children do, but knowing how we got sick does not answer the question of why we got sick, and adults are universally bothered by this second question. It haunts us when we confront illness in ourselves or in our loved ones, and it causes us to turn from the realm of science to the realm of the supernatural. People across cultures are compelled to seek explanations that transcend mere happenstance, regardless of their biological knowledge. Blaming one's illness on a jealous witch or a vengeful god is sometimes better than having no one to blame at all.

12 | ADAPTATION

Why Are There So Many Life-Forms?
How Do They Change Over Time?

W HEN I LEARNED AS A CHILD THAT ISAAC NEWTON "DISCOVERED
gravity," I thought to myself, "Boy, science must have been easy back
then." It didn't seem to take a genius to realize that unsupported objects
fall. Of course, Newton didn't merely discover the fact of gravity; he discovered an explanation for gravity—that gravity is a by-product of mass,
pulling any two objects together with a force directly proportional to the
product of their masses and inversely proportional to the square of the distance between them.

The same is true of Charles Darwin and his "discovery of evolution."
Darwin did not discover the mere fact of evolution. Evolution had been
contemplated as a theoretical possibility since antiquity and had been investigated as a biological reality for decades before Darwin was even born.
Darwin's fame comes from his discovery of an explanation for evolution—
that evolution results from the selective survival and reproduction of some
members of a species relative to others over successive generations.

What Darwin discovered was a mechanism for evolution—natural selection—and this discovery entailed a series of interrelated insights. The
first was that populations of organisms possess the reproductive potential

to grow exponentially. This is as much a mathematical truth as it is a biological one. If every organism in a population produced just two offspring, the size of that population would double with each passing generation, leaping from 2 in the first generation to 32 in the fifth to 1,024 in the tenth.

Darwin himself illustrated the point, in his magnum opus, *On the Origin of Species*, by showing that a single pair of elephants would leave over fifteen million descendants in just 500 years. Clearly, populations do not grow this large—the earth is not overrun by elephants or any other kind of organism—which means that most organisms do not leave behind offspring. This was Darwin's second insight: population growth is curbed by limited resources. The environment contains only so much food, so much shelter, and so many mates, which means that organisms must fight for those resources—even organisms within the same species. All life-forms are embroiled in a struggle for existence, and only a fraction survive the struggle to reach reproductive maturity.

Who survives the struggle? Those born with traits that help them secure resources and avoid predators. This was Darwin's third insight: that the struggle for existence is not waged on a level playing field. Some organisms, by happenstance, are born with traits that make them more likely to survive the struggle and contribute offspring to the next generation. The offspring, in turn, are likely to inherit the traits that helped their parents survive and reproduce. The fact that traits are heritable was Darwin's fourth insight. Genetic winners pass on their winnings to their offspring.

Darwin's final insight was that this process is iterative. As organisms with useful traits outlive and out-reproduce those with less useful traits, the proportion of the population that possesses the useful traits will increase. Eventually, those traits will become characteristic of the population as a whole. A trait that started as a random variation in a single individual—a longer trunk, a harder shell, a sharper claw—will become a staple of the entire population, as long as that trait continues to prove useful in the never-ending struggle for existence.

In short, Darwin's key insights were (1) organisms produce more offspring than the environment can support; (2) organisms are thus locked in a struggle for existence; (3) some organisms fare better in that struggle than others because of inherent differences in their traits; (4) those differences are heritable; and (5) the differences will become more pronounced over time, as organisms born with less useful traits (genetic losers) die off and organisms born with more useful traits (genetic winners) come to dominate the population.

Darwin's insights led to a qualitatively different view of evolution—a view that emphasized the winnowing of nonadaptive forms rather than the emergence of adaptive ones. His view also emphasized changes to populations rather than changes to individuals. Darwin was not the first biologist to put his mind to the question of why species are adapted to their environment. His predecessors and contemporaries had posited several theories of their own. But those theories carved up the biological world in the wrong ways. They treated species as holistic entities, not populations of varied individuals, and they treated evolution as uniform adaptation, not differential survival.

The most famous alternative theory to Darwin's was a theory proposed by the French biologist Jean-Baptiste Lamarck. Lamarck argued that organisms acquire adaptive traits throughout their lives, through the use and disuse of preexisting traits, and then pass those traits onto their offspring. A giraffe, for instance, might acquire a longer neck through years of stretching for distant leaves, or an eagle might acquire better eyesight through years of focusing on distant targets. These changes would then be transmitted to the organisms' offspring at birth, such that the next generation of giraffes would be born with slightly longer necks and the next generation of eagles would be born with slightly better eyesight.

Lamarck was wrong about the inheritance of acquired traits. Offspring do not inherit traits acquired during their parents' lifetime. But that's not what makes Lamarck's theory qualitatively different from Darwin's. Lamarck's theory assumed that all members of a species evolve collectively, as a cohesive unit. All giraffes strive for longer necks and all eagles strive for better eyesight, the result being that the next generation of each species is born slightly more adapted to the environment than its predecessors were.

In reality, however, there is no biological mechanism to ensure that all members of the next generation be born adapted to the environment. Some organisms are born adapted, and others are not. The latter are simply removed from the gene pool, as they die without offspring. What Darwin realized—and what Lamarck had not—is that biological adaptation is not one process but two: mutation and selection. Mutation is blind; offspring vary from their parents (and from each other) in unpredictable ways. But selection is discerning. It weeds out nonadaptive mutations from the adaptive ones, altering the overall landscape of available mutations. The result is not a population of more-adapted individuals but a population in which more of the individuals are adapted.

It took the scientific community several decades to recognize the genius of Darwin's theory. Fifty years after he proposed it, many biologists still favored alternative theories, including Theodor Eimer's theory of orthogenesis (which explained evolution as a by-product of the laws of organic matter), Edward Cope's theory of accelerated growth (which explained evolution as a form of accelerated embryonic development), and even Lamarck's theory of the inheritance of acquired traits. What ultimately convinced biologists of the correctness of Darwin's theory was its synthesis with a genetic understanding of inheritance—an understanding developed several decades after Darwin's death. Genes provided an explanation for the origin of trait variation, which Darwin assumed but did not explain. Today, biologists not only have embraced natural selection as an explanation for evolution but have also come to see evolution by natural selection as a unifying framework for the biological sciences. As one modern biologist put it, "Nothing in biology makes sense except in the light of evolution."

✦ ✦ ✦

HISTORY REPEATS ITSELF. The early twentieth-century biologists who failed to appreciate the importance of natural selection may be dead, but students in today's biology classrooms still fail to appreciate its importance. Many don't believe that evolution occurs at all, subscribing instead to creationist explanations for biological adaptation—something we will return to in Chapter 13. Among those who do accept evolution, many tend not to understand how it works.

Consider the following scenario. Let's say that biologists have recently discovered a new species of woodpecker that lives in isolation on a secluded island. These woodpeckers have, on average, a one-inch beak, and their only food source is a tree-dwelling insect that lives, on average, 1½ inches under the tree bark. If two woodpeckers mate, what type of beak is their offspring likely to develop? (1) A longer beak than either parent had, (2) a shorter beak than either parent had, or (3) either a longer beak or a shorter beak, neither being more likely.

The correct answer is option 3, because offspring vary randomly from their parents. Selection may favor long beaks over short beaks, but the sources of variation between parents and their offspring—mutation and genetic recombination—are blind to the offspring's needs. Most people do not pick option 3 as their answer, however. They pick option 1, reasoning that evolution guarantees that offspring are born more adapted to the environment than their parents were at birth. Typical justifications for selecting this option include "They need a longer beak to get their food," "It's required for survival," "They'll adapt to their environment," or simply "That's evolution."

This question is one of several that my colleagues and I have developed as a litmus test for whether students appreciate the role of natural selection in evolution. Of all the intuitive theories covered in this book, intuitive theories of evolution are the ones I know best. I've spent over a decade studying their content, structure, and origin, and I am continually surprised by how similar these theories are to pre-Darwinian theories of evolution. When most of us put our minds to the topic of evolution, we follow Lamarck's lead, not Darwin's. It's as if Darwin never existed and the concept of natural selection had never been formulated. Organisms are thought to inherit the traits they need to inherit so that they can thrive in their current environment, and this process is thought to occur uniformly across the entire species. Mutation and selection play no role in most people's understanding of evolution.

Here's another question about evolution that most people get wrong: "During the nineteenth century, England's native moth species, *Biston betularia*, or the peppered moth, evolved darker coloration in response to the pollution produced by the Industrial Revolution. Imagine that biologists gathered a random sample of *Biston betularia* once every twenty-five years from 1800 to 1900. What range of coloration would you expect to find at each point in time?" To answer this question, you would be given a five-by-five matrix of moth outlines, five rows of five moths each. The rows would be labeled with the years 1800, 1825, 1850, 1875, and 1900, and your task would be to shade the moths within each row to depict random samples gathered during those time periods.

The correct response, produced by only a handful of people, is to shade an increasing number of moths per row, to depict a random mutation—darker coloration—spreading through the population over time. The first

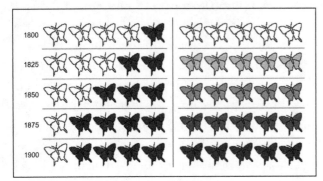

Evolution is often erroneously construed as the holistic transformation of an entire species (right panel) rather than the selective survival and reproduction of a subset of the species (left panel).

row of the matrix might contain four white moths and one gray moth; the second, three white moths and two gray moths; the third, two white moths and three gray moths, and so forth. The other, more popular response is to shade the moths uniformly darker from one row to the next—say, leaving all the moths in the first row white but shading all the moths in the second row light gray, all the moths in the third row a darker shade of gray, and so forth.

The key difference between these two patterns is whether they include any variation (in coloration) within the same generation. Whereas the first pattern depicts variation both within and across generations, the second pattern depicts variation only across generations. Each moth is portrayed as evolving darker coloration in lockstep with every other moth.

When I first developed this task, I knew, from the behavior of one of my earliest subjects, that the task would successfully discriminate people who understand evolution (as a selection-driven process) from those who do not. She shaded a single column of moths from light to dark and then stopped. "Do I need to shade them all?" she asked. "Yes," I said, confused by why she thought she didn't. She went on to shade the moths in the four remaining columns identically to those in the first column: white to light-gray to medium-gray to dark-gray to black. She had made this pattern apparent in just one column. Why shade anymore?

The moth-shading task assesses participants' understanding that within-species variation is a precondition for adaptation. It's one of dozens of tasks that my colleagues and I have developed to distinguish those who understand evolution from those who do not. The other tasks assess different

facets of evolution: inheritance, population change, domestication, speciation, and extinction. It turns out that participants who hold non-Darwinian
misconceptions about one topic tend to hold non-Darwinian misconceptions about all the other topics as well. For instance, participants who select
option 1 on the woodpecker question described above, indicating a belief
in directed mutation, also tend to produce a moth-shading pattern devoid
of any within-generation variation.

Extinction and speciation are particularly interesting cases. From a
post-Darwinian point of view, extinction is selection writ large; species go
extinct when their death rate exceeds their birth rate. And speciation, from
this point of view, is selection operating over geographically isolated populations; new species emerge when subpopulations of the same organism are
driven apart by different selection pressures in different environments. But
most people do not see extinction or speciation in these terms. Instead, they
see extinction as the rare event in which a species is wiped off the planet
by a natural disaster (say, a comet or a flood), and they see speciation as the
rare event in which evolution transforms one population into another (say,
monkeys into apes).

Pre-Darwinian biologists also held these views. To them, extinction and
speciation were rarities, arising from extraordinary circumstances rather
than the ordinary operation of natural selection. The tendency of today's
students of evolution to hold the same misconceptions as pre-Darwinian
biologists suggests that these misconceptions are not isolated errors, im-
planted by a few bad teachers or a few misleading texts. Rather, they are
a deep-seated confusion arising from a theory of evolution that lacks the
post-Darwinian concepts of mutation and selection.

Consistent with this idea, evolutionary misconceptions have proven
robust and widespread. They have been documented in students who
have had no instruction in evolution, as well as those who have had several
years of instruction. They have been documented in elementary-schoolers, middle-schoolers, high-schoolers, and college-educated adults. And
they have been documented in populations who really should know better: undergraduate biology majors, medical school students, masters-de-
gree students training to teach biology, and even high school biology
teachers. Evolutionary misconceptions are apparently hard to shake. The
problem is not that your average biology student believes that acquired

Dog shows epitomize essentialist thinking. Each dog is compared with an ideal proto-type, and deviations from that prototype are seen as anomalous and problematic rather than as natural and expected.

traits are inherited (Lamarck's theory) or that evolution is driven by ac-celerated embryonic development (Cope's theory). The problem is that they believe that adaptation occurs uniformly across all members of a species in accordance with the species' needs. Their views of evolution are pre-Darwinian in spirit, not detail.

✦ ✦ ✦

Physicists tell us that nature abhors a vacuum, but biologists tell us that nature abhors a category. Life on earth is profoundly varied—too var-ied to fit into neat categories. Darwin appreciated this fact more than any biologist before him. His voyage to the Galapagos in his early twenties, and his observation of the several types of finches that inhabited those islands, impressed on him how varied a species (or a genus) could be.

But Darwin's appreciation of variation was unusual—unusual both for the biologists of his time and for people in general. Most of us see variation as nothing more than error, as deviations from something's "true" form. Dog shows are the epitome of this kind of thinking. Judges and contestants pore over the decision of which dog best exemplifies its breed. Variations like shorter-than-usual snouts or longer-than-usual legs are seen as problems, when, in reality, they are assets. They are what made it possible for breeders to differentiate dachshunds from dalmatians and retrievers from rottweilers in the first place, let alone dogs from wolves.

Biologist Stephen Jay Gould has written at length about how we misinterpret the variation inherent in a biological system. We attend to the system's average values—for example, the average length of a setter's snout or the average length of a dachshund's legs—and ignore or dismiss its more extreme values. Gould traces our misinterpretation of variation back to Plato, who argued that our sensations of worldly objects are illusions masking a deeper, truer reality akin to how the shadows on the wall of a cave are illusions of the objects that cast them. According to Gould, "[Our] Platonic heritage prompts us to view means and medians as the hard 'realities,' and the variation that permits their calculation as a set of transient and imperfect measurements of this hidden essence. . . . But all evolutionary biologists know that variation itself is nature's only irreducible essence. Variation is the hard reality, not a set of imperfect measures for a central tendency. Means and medians are the abstractions."

Gould points to Plato as the reason we posit "hidden essences," but essentialism is a core feature of human cognition, as we've seen in Chapters 9 and 10. We'd all still be essentialists even if Plato had never existed. Consider Hans Christian Andersen's tale of the Ugly Duckling. In this tale, a swan hatches from an egg that somehow found its way into a duck's nest. The fledgling swan is mocked for failing to conform to the appearance and behavior of a duck until it grows up and takes on the appearance and behavior of its true form: a swan. This tale makes sense to readers of all ages—even toddlers—because we instinctively know, in Andersen's words, that "to be born in a duck's nest in a farmyard is of no consequence to a bird if it is hatched from a swan's egg."

We know that the Ugly Duckling grew into a beautiful swan for reasons that have nothing to do with what it ate, where it lived, or what it desired; it was simply born a swan. And we know that it was born a swan for reasons that have nothing to do with what its parents ate, where its parents lived, or what its parents desired; the parents had been born swans. Like begets like. This assumption serves us well when we are reasoning about the traits of individual organisms, because an organism's species is a reliable predictor of its traits. Knowing that an organism is a swan allows us to make accurate predictions about what that organism should look like (brown as an infant, white as an adult), where it should live (by water), what it should eat (vegetation), and how it should reproduce (by laying eggs).

Yet, despite the benefits of essentialism for reasoning about individuals, it has proven detrimental for reasoning about populations. Offspring resemble their parents, but that resemblance is not exact. Every organism is unique, and every population is full of variation. But essentialism leads us to overlook those differences or to treat them as inconsequential. A swan is a swan is a swan.

Our tendency to essentialize biological kinds is codified not just in cultural practices like dog shows or flower shows but also in our language. We refer to biological kinds by a single label—*duck* or *swan*—and these labels invite us to extend what we know about one member of the kind to the kind as a whole. If someone told you that swans can swim the moment they are born (which is true), you wouldn't assume the person meant that *most* swans can swim the moment they are born. You'd assume the person meant that *all* swans can—that being a swan confers an organism with the essence-laden ability to swim at birth.

In my own lab, we've investigated this phenomenon by asking people to gauge the variability of different traits in different organisms. In one study, we presented children (ages four to nine) and adults with six kinds of animals—giraffes, kangaroos, pandas, grasshoppers, ants, and bees—and asked them to decide whether each kind of animal varies in its traits. We asked about behavioral traits and two kinds of anatomical traits: external traits and internal traits.

For instance, we asked whether giraffes vary in the behavioral trait of sleeping on their feet, the external trait of having spots on their coats, or the internal trait of having an extra neck joint (all true properties of giraffes). Likewise, we asked whether ants vary in the behavioral trait of living in mounds of dirt, the external trait of having feelers on their head, or the internal trait of having a tube-shaped heart (all true properties of ants).

We posed our questions in two parts, first by asking whether all animals of that kind have the trait or just most animals ("Do all giraffes have spots on their coat or just most giraffes?") and then by asking whether an animal could be born with a different version of the trait ("Could a giraffe be born with a different kind of coat?"). The first question was intended to assess participants' beliefs about the *actual* variability of the trait in the current population, and the second question was intended to assess their beliefs about the *potential* variability of the trait in some future population.

Regardless of the animal or the trait, most children denied that animals actually vary in their traits and were equivocal as to whether the traits could vary in the future. The one type of trait for which children were most accepting of variation was the behavioral trait, perhaps because they believed that animals can control (and thus change) their behavior. Adults, on the other hand, responded in one of two ways depending on whether they understood evolution—something we measured in a separate set of tasks. Adults who understood evolution claimed that all types of traits are variable, both actually variable and potentially variable. And if they ever denied that a trait was variable, it was almost always for internal traits, as the variability of such traits could compromise the animal's viability. Adults who did *not* understand evolution, on the other hand, responded just like children. They denied that animals vary in their traits, though they were more accepting of variation for behaviorial traits.

All traits have to have emerged from somewhere; thus, all traits must have existed in other forms at some point in an animal's evolution. Yet only adults who understood evolution (as a selection-driven process) demonstrated an appreciation of this fact. Adults who did not understand evolution—and children who had yet to learn about evolution—seemed to think that variation is an atypical feature of biological kinds.

In a follow-up study, children continued to deny the variability of traits even when that variability was illustrated for them. The researchers who conducted this study were concerned that the children in our original study may have denied the possibility of variation because they couldn't imagine it for themselves. What, for instance, would a giraffe look like if it didn't have spots? And where, for instance, would an ant live if not in a mound of dirt?

To address this concern, the researchers introduced children (ages five and six) to a novel, fictitious animal with fictitious traits and asked about the variability of those traits with pictures. For instance, they showed children a rodent called a "hergob," which had fuzzy ears, and they asked the children whether all hergobs have fuzzy ears or just some hergobs do. The first option was illustrated with a picture of four fuzzy-eared hergobs, and the second option was illustrated with a picture of two fuzzy-eared hergobs and two bare-eared hergobs. Even under these conditions, children claimed that animals are unlikely to vary in their traits. The first hergob they saw determined what they believed all hergobs should look like. Once you've seen one hergob, you've seen them all.

✦ ✦ ✦

KNOWING ABOUT VARIATION is not the same as appreciating its role in evolution. The biologists of Darwin's day certainly knew about variation—it was implicit in their vast collections of flora and fauna—but they did not see variation as related to evolution. Historians of science who have analyzed the transition from pre-Darwinian theories of evolution to post-Darwinian ones have often pointed to Darwin's appreciation of variation as the crucial difference between his views and those of his peers. But Darwin's appreciation of selection is just as important. And just as counterintuitive.

This point is well captured by the *Onion* in its satirical news story "Natural Selection Kills 38 Quadrillion Organisms in Bloodiest Day Yet." It reports that "natural selection left a trail of dead in such conflict-plagued regions as sub-Saharan Africa, the Pacific Ocean, and the troposphere, with the fatalities including slain emperor penguins, coral snakes, and blue-green algae, as well as several swarms of blue-winged wasps, an assortment of hyacinth clusters, 131 orangutans, and various microorganisms. All were reportedly unequipped to escape the terror sweeping their ecosystems. In what many are calling its most grotesque tactic, the killer appeared to single out the most vulnerable organisms—particularly the young and the physically weak—for its murderous rampage, slaughtering them without mercy as other members of their species fled in panic."

The struggle for existence is not pretty. Darwin gleaned as much from the economist Thomas Malthus, who wrote at length about the consequences of limited resources on growing populations. Through a combination of math and logic, Malthus demonstrated that populations cannot grow unchecked and that, if they do, the result will be misery and strife.

But misery and strife are not common experiences for humans in today's industrialized societies, despite the numerousness of our species. Technological advances in agriculture, engineering, and medicine have enabled humans to defy the struggle for existence that characterizes the lives of all other species. We are in fact oblivious to it. Most humans living in industrialized societies have enough to eat and no predators to fear, and we assume that the same is true for other organisms as well. As a case in point, a study of introductory ecology students found that they believe that stable ecosystems are characterized by (1) ample food, water, and shelter; (2) a harmonious balance between overpopulation and extinction; (3) a mutually beneficial relationship between the earth and its organisms; and (4) the capacity for all species to survive and reproduce.

In my own research, I discovered how counterintuitive a Malthusian view of the world is. I was analyzing the results of a survey in which college-educated adults made true-or-false judgments for two hundred scientific statements, and one statement emerged as an outlier: "Most organisms die without leaving offspring." It was recognized as true by only 33 percent of participants, far fewer than those who recognized that "germs have DNA" (71 percent), that "ice has heat" (66 percent), and that "atoms are mostly empty space" (50 percent).

Inspired by this finding, I decided to compare college students' understanding of evolution with their perceptions of nature—whether they perceive nature as a peaceful and cooperative place or as a violent and competitive place. To measure the latter, I asked participants to estimate how frequently animals engage is several specific behaviors, some "naughty" and some "nice." The nice behaviors were cooperation within a species (e.g., nursing the offspring of an unrelated member of the same species, or *allonursing*) and cooperation between species (e.g., sharing a nest or burrow with an animal from a different species). The naughty behaviors were competition within a species (e.g., eating other members of the same species) and competition between species (e.g., tricking an animal from a different species into raising one's young).

Each behavior was paired with six animals, and participants were asked to decide whether each animal did or did not exhibit the behavior. I selected unfamiliar animals (e.g., plover birds, bluestreak wrasse) so that participants would be unlikely to know the correct answers and would have to guess. In reality, half the animals exhibited the target behavior and half did not.

On the whole, participants overestimated the frequency of cooperative behaviors relative to competitive ones, particularly for behaviors directed at members of the same species. They thought that behaviors like allonursing were more widespread among our animal exemplars than behaviors like

Edward Hicks's *Peaceable Kingdom* (1826) exemplifies a view of nature at odds with natural selection, that is, at odds with the idea that organisms must compete to survive and that most die without leaving any offspring.

cannibalism. Critically, the more a participant overestimated cooperative behaviors, the less he or she understood evolution, as measured by a separate set of tasks. In other words, participants who held sugar-coated views of nature, in which animals are more likely to share resources than compete for them, construed evolution as the uniform adaptation of all members of a species. Participants who held a more realistic (competitive) view of nature, on the other hand, construed evolution as the selective survival and reproduction of some members of the species over others.

From an empirical point of view, it's debatable whether nature is better characterized as a peaceable kingdom or as red in tooth and claw—biologists have certainly argued for both characterizations—but the latter characterization appears to foster a more correct understanding of evolution. Indeed, what mattered most in the correlation between participants' perceptions of nature and their understanding of evolution was not their recognition of competition in general but their recognition of competition *within a species*. The more participants recognized that members of the same species fight for resources, the better they understood evolution.

The image of fluffy white bunnies fighting over territory or fluffy brown foxes fighting over a carcass can be unsettling. As a case in point, consider the public's reaction to live video feeds of osprey nests or eagle nests. These nests are the site of much "nasty" behavior: hatchlings attacking one another, hatchlings stealing food from one another, mothers feeding house pets to their young, mothers neglecting their young, mothers eating their young. Members of the public who have observed such activities have launched campaigns to save the abused and neglected hatchlings. They have also posted several vitriolic comments on social media: "I realize this is nature but . . . you have a responsibility to help save when in need," "I for one will not stop fighting to get [the hatchling] removed from this nest . . . shame on all involved," "It is absolutely disgusting that you will not take those chicks away from that demented witch of a parent!!!!!"

Another telling illustration of our distaste for the struggle for survival comes from a student's answer to a biology quiz, circulated on the internet. The student was asked to interpret a three-panel diagram. In the first panel, two giraffes munched leaves from a tall tree while a third giraffe strained for the leaves but was not tall enough to reach them. In the second panel, the short giraffe lay at the feet of the two taller giraffes, who were still contentedly munching leaves. And in the third panel, the short giraffe had died, leaving behind a pile of bones.

Next to the diagram was the instruction to select the principle it best illustrated: (a) Lamarck's theory of evolution, (b) Darwin's theory of evolution, (c) Malthus's principles, or (d) Lyell's theory about past changes. Scrawled in pencil beneath those options was an added suggestion: "(e) Giraffes are heartless creatures." We want to believe that all animals take care of their own, but if they did, there would be no competition within a species and hence no evolution. The giraffe's majestic long neck did not materialize out of thin air; it came at the cost of several short-necked giraffes who never got enough to eat.

✦ ✦ ✦

As we've seen, evolution defies two deep-seated misconceptions about the biological world. One misconception is that all members of a species are essentially the same. The other is that all members of a species have plenty of resources at their disposal. If biology educators hope to head off

The idea that some organisms are inherently predisposed to starvation, predation, or disease is hard for most people to swallow.

these misconceptions and keep them from growing larger or deeper, they should introduce evolution as early as possible in the biology curriculum. But in the United States, we do the opposite: we exclude evolution from the biology curriculum until high school. The US National Science Teachers Association, for instance, recommends that elementary-schoolers learn about anatomy, physiology, taxonomy, and ecology but not evolution. As a consequence, elementary-schoolers learn about biological adaptations without reference to the historical pressures that shaped the adaptations and, accordingly, without explanation for their form or function. In some school systems, students will never be provided with such explanations, as evolution remains absent from the high school curriculum as well.

If, and when, students are finally introduced to evolution, the result is typically a schizophrenic view of biological adaptation. Sometimes adaptation is analyzed in terms of selection, but more commonly it is analyzed in terms of essentialism (what is the organism's core nature?), intentionality (what does the organism *want*?), or teleology (what does the organism *need*?). Teleology, or need-based reasoning, is particularly pernicious. The needs of individual organisms are irrelevant to the evolution of the species as a whole. Evolution does not provide individual organisms with the traits they need; some organisms just happen to be born with those traits, and they outlive and out-reproduce everyone else.

Still, students who have been taught evolutionary explanations for adaptation have great difficulty divorcing considerations of need from considerations of selection. They explain adaptation in terms of both considerations, as in these responses to the woodpecker question described above: "Woodpeckers will be born with longer beaks because they need longer beaks to survive," "Longer beaks will ensure the survival of the species," "Birds will be born with longer beaks so they can eat more and live longer." The logic here is backward: adaptation is the consequence of prolonged survival (and increased reproduction), not its cause.

Why do we have such difficulty letting go of need-based reasoning and embracing only selection-based reasoning? One possibility is that evolution is portrayed as a need-based process in popular media. In the video game *Spore*, for instance, players "evolve" their avatars by selecting whatever traits the avatar might need to meet the challenges of its current environment. Likewise, in the 2001 movie *Evolution*, an alien organism arrives on earth and spawns ever-more-adapted offspring, with each offspring inheriting whatever traits it might need to overcome the obstacles in its path.

Misrepresentations of evolution are probably not the only reason we cling to need-based explanations, there's also something inherently dissatisfying about selection-based ones. Selection-based explanations don't answer the question of why individuals are adapted to their environment. They answer the question of why species are adapted to their environment, with the unsettling implication that evolution cares nothing for individuals. Individual organisms come and go, their reproductive success largely predetermined by their luck in a random genetic lottery. Only species endure and thus only species evolve.

Evolution is an emergent phenomenon, like heat or pressure, in that biological adaptations emerge from the collective interaction of innumerable organisms over innumerable generations. But we don't like emergent phenomena, as noted in Chapter 3. Emergent phenomena defy simple analysis (e.g., all members of a species are basically the same) and simple explanation (e.g., organisms inherit the traits they need to inherit). There may be grandeur in this view of life, as Darwin suggested in the *Origin of Species*, but there's also doubt and uncertainty. It takes an evolved mind to embrace evolution—and only evolution—as the reason for why living things are so exquisitely adapted to their environment.

13 | ANCESTRY

Where Did Species Come From?
How Are They Related?

On a trip to the zoo, when my son Teddy was seven and my daughter Lucy was two, we found ourselves in front of the howler monkeys. The monkeys were engaged in humanlike behavior—grooming, playing, bickering—and I took the opportunity to explain that the reason humans and monkeys seem so similar is that humans and monkeys came from the same ancestor. Teddy nodded his head and then turned to Lucy and repeated the explanation in his own words: "See that monkey, Lucy? That monkey is your ancestor."

Teddy assumed, like most people, that humans are related to monkeys through *direct* ancestry rather than *shared* ancestry. He assumed that monkeys are our ancestors, not our cousins, despite my explanation to the contrary. This view of the relationship between humans and monkeys is crystalized in evolution's most canonical illustration: a parade of primates arrayed from monkey to ape to caveman to human, intended to imply that monkeys gave rise to apes, which gave rise to cavemen which gave rise to humans.

The implication is wrong, though. Modern-day monkeys (marmosets, macaques, capuchins) did not give rise to modern-day apes (chimpanzees, gorillas, orangutans); they share an ancestor that was neither monkey nor

Evolution is frequently depicted as a kind of metamorphosis, in which one member of a taxonomic family (e.g., chimpanzees) metamorphoses into another (e.g., humans).

ape but a precursor to both. Likewise, modern-day apes did not give rise to modern-day humans (or cavemen); they share an ancestor that was neither ape nor human but a precursor to both. Apes may seem more primitive than humans, but apes have been evolving independently of humans for as long as humans have been evolving independently of apes. Apes are our closest living relatives, not our closest living ancestors. Mistaking an ape for an ancestor is akin to mistaking a cousin for a grandmother.

What makes common ancestry so counterintuitive is that it turns a simple line (monkeys begat apes begat humans) into a nested hierarchy (humans share a common ancestor with apes, which in turn share a common ancestor with monkeys). The implication is that apes are more closely related to humans than to monkeys, despite the common perception (or misperception) that apes look and act more like monkeys than like humans. We might mistake an ape for a monkey, but we'd never mistake an ape for a human.

A case in point is Curious George. This cartoon primate is anatomically an ape—his arms are longer than his legs (like apes) and he has no tail (unlike monkeys)—but he is described in his books and his TV shows as a "curious little monkey." And no one seems to care, not even the educationally minded PBS staff who air the Curious George cartoon. We lump apes with monkeys because both seem so different from humans and because we

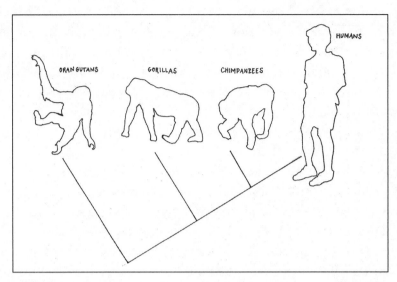

All living organisms are related through common ancestry, meaning that chimpanzees, gorillas, and orangutans are our cousins, not our ancestors.

don't really know where monkeys and apes came from in the first place. We don't understand speciation.

From a scientific point of view, the emergence of new species is a by-product of natural selection operating on populations that have been split apart by distance or physical barriers. Humans and apes descended not from a single primate but from a whole population of primates—a population that fractured into different subpopulations. Each subpopulation continued to evolve independently from the others; their gene pools diverged as the surviving members of those subpopulations left behind slightly different genetic contributions. Over time, small genetic differences between the subpopulations became large genetic differences—so large that the two subpopulations were no longer able to interbreed.

Such is the nature of speciation from a selection-based view of evolution. But, as noted in Chapter 12, most people do not hold a selection-based view. Instead, they hold an essentialist view, according to which all members of a species evolve together, their fates intertwined by a common essence. In such a view, it makes no difference whether a population has been split in two, because all members of the population are united by a common essence. The only way a new species could emerge from an old one is if the old species metamorphosed into a new one—hence, the presumption that monkeys metamorphosed into apes, and apes metamorphosed into humans. Evolution is depicted as metamorphosis not just in the canonical "parade of primates" but in most popular representations of evolution, including evolution-based video games like *Spore* and *Pokémon Go*. To "evolve" a creature in *Pokémon Go*—say, Pikachu—you don't track a population of Pikachus as they selectively survive and reproduce. You feed a single Pikachu until it is nourished enough to metamorphose into a more advanced form (Raichu).

This type of evolution has been termed *anagenesis*, or linear evolution, and it contrasts with *cladogenesis*, or branching evolution. Anagenesis is consistent with an essentialist view of life, but is inconsistent with a selection-based view—in other words, it is inconsistent with reality. And anagenesis is not a particularly satisfying view, either, as it makes a mystery of why ancient life-forms would continue to exist after they had metamorphosed into new ones. Why would monkeys continue to exist if monkeys had metamorphosed into apes? And why would apes continue to exist if apes had metamorphosed into humans? Creationists sometimes put these questions to evolutionists, as a way of undermining their belief in evolution. But the only belief undermined by such questions is the creationists' belief that they understand how evolution actually works. Speciation is a process of divergence, not metamorphosis, and common ancestry is a branching relationship, not a linear relationship. Monkeys are as much our ancestor as Curious George is an example of a monkey.

✦ ✦ ✦

ONE OF THE most profound insights of evolutionary theory is that all life is interconnected. Every organism on the planet is connected to every other organism through common ancestry. Humans share a common ancestor not only with apes and monkeys but also with sparrows, frogs, jellyfish, and algae. The common ancestor of humans and algae lived a long time ago—billions of years ago—and it most certainly resembled algae more than it resembled a human. No one has found a specimen of this ancestor, but we are sure that it existed because there is no other way to explain why humans and algae are so similar at a cellular level. We share chromosomes, ribosomes, mitochondria, and endoplasmic reticula, not to mention the same mechanisms for transmitting genetic information (DNA and RNA).

Common ancestry has profound implications for our understanding of the biological world and humans' place within it. Biologists have been grappling with these implications for decades, but most nonbiologists are oblivious to them, thinking that species are only minimally interconnected. It's conceivable, from an essentialist point of view, that humans share an underlying essence with other primates, but it's inconceivable that we share an underlying essence with jellyfish or algae.

Biology educators have become increasingly aware of this problem and have responded by including more visual representations of common ancestry in their instruction, particularly *cladograms*. These visual representations of common ancestry were developed by biologists in the 1960s to depict when and how a group of organisms diverged from one another. In recent years, cladograms have spread beyond the scientific domain into the public domain, becoming a stock representation of evolution in science textbooks and science museums. Here's a sample cladogram, one that depicts the evolutionary relationships between the four great apes:

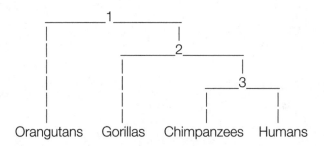

It's the same cladogram as the one on page 223 (with the silhouettes of the orangutan, gorilla, chimpanzee, and human), but just formatted differently. Cladograms depict common ancestry by means of their branches. Given a predefined group of species, the pair that shares a common ancestor more recently than any other pair is connected with lines that converge at a node. The node represents the pair's common ancestor. This pair is then connected to every other species using the same logic: species that share more recent ancestors are connected before those that share less recent ancestors, until all species in the group are interconnected. Each new connection yields a new node, with deeper nodes signifying ancestors that are both more distant (time-wise) and more common (descent-wise).

For example, the cladogram above indicates that humans and chimpanzees share a more recent ancestor (node 3) than do any other pair of apes. Humans and chimpanzees, in turn, share a more recent ancestor with gorillas (node 2) than with orangutans. Orangutans are the most distantly related member of the group; they share a common ancestor with the other members (node 1) the furthest in the past. Orangutans, gorillas, and chimpanzees are not technically species—they are *genera*, a higher-level taxonomic category—but the same logic holds for any taxonomic category: species, genus, family, order, class, phylum, or kingdom.

Cladograms have become a mainstay of modern evolutionary research because it is now possible, through gene sequencing, to discern common ancestry at a molecular level. Still, a person needn't know anything about the genetic basis of a cladogram to glean profound insights from these models. Cladograms can greatly alter our commonsense notions of how different life-forms are related. Consider the evolutionary relationships between mongooses, weasels, hyenas, and jackals. By their appearance, we might group mongooses with weasels, and hyenas with jackals. But genetically derived cladograms tell us that mongooses are more closely related to hyenas than to weasels and that weasels are more closely related to jackals

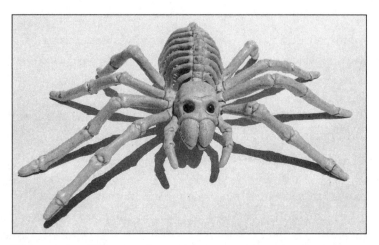

This popular Halloween decoration is a testament to our poor understanding of the relationships between living creatures. Only vertebrates have bones. Invertebrates, which include spiders, split off from vertebrates over five hundred million years ago. A spider with bones is as biologically implausible as a spider with wings.

than to mongooses. Or consider the evolutionary relationships between manatees, dolphins, elephants, and cows. By their habitat, we might group manatees with dolphins, and elephants with cows. But genetically derived cladograms tell us that manatees are more closely related to elephants than to dolphins and that dolphins are more closely related to cows than to manatees.

Cladograms, and the genetic analyses that underlie their construction, cut through superficial similarities in appearance and behavior and reveal deeper, more meaningful relationships. They expose a hidden history of evolutionary pressures otherwise masked by the observable properties of current life-forms.

For all their benefits, cladograms turn out to be highly confusing to non-biologists. These models represent patterns of cladogenesis, or branching speciation, but most nonbiologists construe speciation as a linear process (anagenesis). Accordingly, they misinterpret what cladograms are intended to illustrate. For starters, most nonbiologists misinterpret the ordering of the species along a cladogram's tips, reading information into the ordering that is not supported by the cladogram's branches. The ordering of species along a cladogram's tips is, to a large extent, arbitrary. Species that share a most recent common ancestor must be adjacent, but their ordering relative to one another can be changed. For instance, in a cladogram that contains humans, chimpanzees, gorillas, and orangutans, humans must be adjacent to chimpanzees, but they can appear either to the left of chimpanzees or the right. Likewise, gorillas must be adjacent to the human/chimpanzee branch, but they can appear either to the left of this branch or to the right. Indeed, there are eight biologically legitimate ways to order the four great apes. Here is one such way:

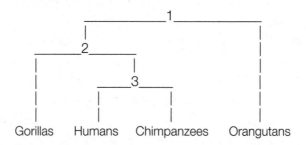

These alternative orders are possible because a branch between two species indicates only that those species share a more immediate ancestor with each other than with any other species, in the same way that two siblings share a more immediate ancestor with each other than with any of their cousins. Nevertheless, most nonbiologists wrongly assume that species are ordered along a cladogram's tips according to their ancientness (from most to least ancient) or their primitiveness (from most to least primitive).

An associated misconception is that the further apart two species appear at the cladogram's tips, the more distantly they are related. Orangutans, for instance, appear closer to chimpanzees than to humans in the above cladogram, but that's just a coincidence of how humans and chimpanzees were ordered. Orangutans have evolved independently of chimpanzees for as long as they have evolved independently of humans and are thus no more closely related to one than the other. All three apes share the same common ancestor (node 1), even though humans and chimpanzees share a more immediate ancestor.

Two other common misconceptions about cladograms are that lines connecting species to nodes convey information about the species' age (the longer the line, the older the species) and that the number of nodes between species conveys information about their relatedness (the more nodes, the more distantly they are related). In reality, the lengths of the lines in a cladogram are essentially arbitrary, as are its number of nodes. Both the length of the lines and the number of nodes depend on which species happen to be included. For example, the longest line in the cladogram above—the line connecting orangutans to its nearest node (node 1)—is long only because orangutans are not differentiated into subgroups (e.g., Bornean orangutans versus Sumatran orangutans). And the number of nodes between orangutans and humans is greater than the number of nodes between orangutans and gorillas, only because chimpanzees are included in the cladogram. Remove chimpanzees, and the number of nodes between orangutans and humans would now be equivalent to the number of nodes between orangutans and gorillas (as node 3 would disappear).

Still, most nonbiologists read meaning into the lengths of a cladogram's lines and the frequency of its nodes because line length and node frequency are often meaningful properties of other types of diagrams: line graphs, flow charts, roadmaps, or blueprints. Further complicating matters, textbook authors and museum curators often jazz up cladograms by including design features that have no biological significance: lines that vary arbitrarily in thickness or orientation, tips that vary arbitrarily in color or placement, and nodes that vary arbitrarily in shape or labeling. Even a biologist couldn't make sense of these features, as they have been included simply for show. These extra features are, in the parlance of graphic designers, "chart junk."

+ + +

FOR ALL THE information that cladograms represent, there is still more information that they fail to represent—information that might actually be helpful to nonbiologists. For example, cladograms typically lack information about the relationship between living species and extinct species. This information has been left out mainly for methodological reasons. Cladograms have come to dominate the biological sciences because they can be constructed from highly objective genetic information. It's possible to construct cladograms from anatomical information, but such information is inherently less reliable, as it's rarely clear whether a trait observed in two species was inherited from a common ancestor (like monkey tails and lemur tails) or emerged independently in two separate lineages (like bat wings and bird wings).

The inclusion of extinct species in cladograms can be problematic because our knowledge of such organisms is almost always limited to anatomy. Extinct species leave behind fossils, but fossils are rocks and rocks contain no DNA. As a consequence, extinct species are either left off cladograms or placed amid their branches, as if to imply that these species are the common ancestors of the living species at the cladogram's tips when, in truth, we have no way of knowing that. The likelihood that an extinct species left behind no descendants is several times greater than the likelihood that it left behind descendants who are still roaming the earth. As many as 99.9 percent of the species that once existed are now extinct, and cladograms, by representing a small subset of the 0.1 percent of species that still happen to be alive, present a skewed picture of the typical outcome of evolutionary change. For every tip, there are 999 tips not represented.

Cladograms also present a skewed picture of evolutionary change itself in that the blind and messy process of mutation-plus-selection is represented as a series of straight and orderly lines. The historical record is wiped clean of false starts and blind paths, leaving only the "successful" lineages present today. In a study I conducted with my students at the Los Angeles Natural History Museum, I saw firsthand how the absence of extinct species from cladograms can be confusing to nonbiologists. The study took place in the museum's Age of Mammals exhibit, which showcases an interactive cladogram of the nineteen orders of mammals. Museum visitors can select icons representing each order and learn more about the order's evolution. They can also drag a slider at the bottom of the screen to watch the orders diverge over time, from the earliest divergence (between placental mammals and marsupial mammals) to the latest (between manatees and elephants).

Next to the cladogram is a case containing the skeletons of several extinct species, including an "entelodont," an ancient cousin of modern-day pigs that went extinct sixteen million years ago. The entelodont was not depicted in the adjacent cladogram, and we asked museum visitors whether it *could* be depicted there, and, if so, where. Although virtually everyone agreed that the entelodont could be depicted somewhere in the cladogram, only a few were able to tell that it should be on the ungulate branch (encompassing deers, horses, cows, and pigs). Most people thought the entelodont should be located either at the cladogram's root node—the node representing the earliest common ancestor—or on a separate branch altogether. In other words, most people were inclined to treat the entelodont either as a common ancestor to *all* mammals or as an isolated lineage not closely related to *any* mammal.

Just as extinct species tend to be omitted from cladograms, so are many living species within the same taxonomic group. Consider the great ape cladograms shown above. Only one tip of these cladograms represents a single species: the tip labeled "humans." The other three tips represent two species each: Bornean orangutans (*Pongo pygmaeus*) and Sumatran orangutans (*Pongo abelii*); eastern gorillas (*Gorilla beringei*) and western gorillas (*Gorilla gorilla*); and common chimpanzees (*Pan troglodytes*) and pygmy chimpanzees (*Pan paniscus*). The great ape family is nearly twice as diverse as most cladograms suggest it is.

Cladograms in general represent diverse taxonomic groups with a single tip, labeled with a single exemplar. This practice probably affects how we think about those groups. The genus *Pan*, for instance, is almost always represented by *Pan troglodytes*, the common chimpanzee (seen in most

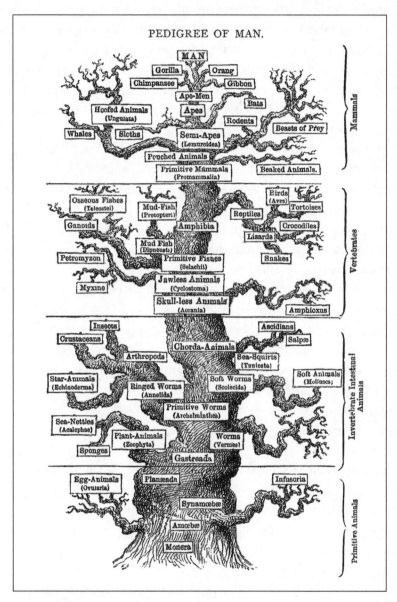

Nineteenth-century biologist Ernst Haeckel introduced the notion of a "tree of life," but his tree vastly underrepresented the diversity of some classes (e.g., insects) compared with others (e.g., mammals).

zoos), but it also includes *Pan paniscus*, the pygmy chimpanzee or bonobo. These two species differ widely in behavior. Common chimpanzees are hostile, patriarchal, and meat eating, whereas pygmy chimpanzees are docile, matriarchal, and vegetarian. We humans are as closely related to pygmy chimpanzees as we are to common chimpanzees—humans diverged from chimpanzees 3.5 million years before common chimpanzees diverged from pygmy chimpanzees—yet we emphasize our relation to common chimpanzees over our relation to pygmy chimpanzees, given how frequently the former is depicted in cladograms but the latter is not.

I first learned that humans are as closely related to bonobos as we are to common chimpanzees while preparing a lecture on primate sexual behavior (for which the hypersexual bonobo is a standout example). When I learned this fact, I was incredulous. How could I, someone who studies popular misconceptions about evolution, not know that bonobos are a kind of chimpanzee and, accordingly, share over 98 percent of their genes with humans just as *Pan troglodytes* do?

I blame the omission of bonobos from primate cladograms for my ignorance. This kind of omission has a long history in the visual representation of evolutionary ancestry, dating back to the very first such representation: Ernst Haeckel's "tree of life." This tree, which appears in Haeckel's *General Morphology of Organisms* (published in 1866), depicts the ancestral relations among all manners of organisms, from insects to mammals, but the proportion of the tree devoted to each type of organism does not accord with its actual frequency. Haeckel devoted an entire layer of branches to the mammals—branches that appear at the top of the tree, with humans in the center—but devoted only one branch to the insects, even though insects outnumber mammals, at the species level, 175 to 1. If any group of organisms were to be relegated to a single branch, it should have been the mammals.

Admittedly, cladograms are designed to depict the ancestral relations among a specific set of groups (e.g., mammals) at a specific level of abstraction (e.g., orders), and depictions of variation within those groups would detract from that goal. Still, the routine omission of several dozen—or several hundred—species within the same group is likely to exacerbate our naive, essentialist views of evolution. The few token species represented in a cladogram are pulled from a continuum of variation that has no representation at all. How might our impression of humans' place in the biological world change if every primate cladogram included all 7 species of great apes or all 22 species of apes in general (the 7 species of great apes and the 15 species of lesser apes or gibbons)? Or what if every primate clado-gram included all 400 species of primates (the 7 species of great apes, the 15 species of lesser apes, the 18 species of tarsiers, the 100-plus species of lemurs, and the 260-plus species of monkeys)? Add in the dozens of extinct primates known from their fossils, and humans would become difficult to locate among all those varied forms.

And that's just the primates. Primates are a small subset of the approx-imately 5,400 species of living mammals; 66,000 species of living verte-brates; 7.8 million species of living animals; and 8.7 million species of living organisms. The depth and breadth of our ancestral relations with other organisms is staggering, as is the history of those relations.

One biologist, David Hillis, has created a cladogram that contains 3,000 species, one of the largest cladograms to date. Even though this cladogram contains less than 0.1 percent of all living species, the labels at its tip are legible only if the cladogram is enlarged to 1.5 meters in length. Such a large diagram may not be useful for extracting specific pieces of evolution-ary information—for example, whether narwhals are more closely related to porpoises or to orcas—but it sure puts our understanding of human evo-lution in a new perspective.

✦ ✦ ✦

WE'VE SEEN THAT cladograms are confusing to nonbiologists, as is the process they represent (cladogenesis). But to be confused by a cladogram, you must first accept that cladograms represent a genuine fact of biology: that all current life-forms evolved from earlier life-forms. Many people do not accept this fact. They look at cladograms as works of fiction—or, worse, as insidious lies. They prefer a creationist explanation for the origin of spe-cies: that the species in existence today were created in their current form by a divine being (God) less than ten thousand years ago.

This explanation has been popular throughout human history, and for good reason: it's much simpler than evolution. Creation is instantaneous, whereas evolution is slow and complex. Creation involves the well-under-stood process of intentional design, whereas evolution involves the not-so-well-understood processes of mutation and selection. Creation yields

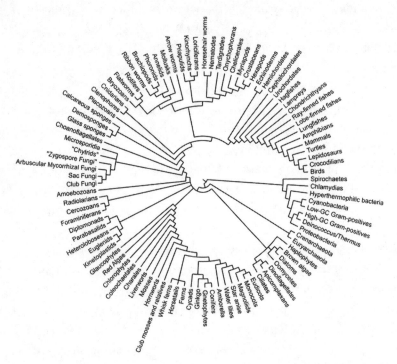

Trees of life based on modern phylogenics, like this one created by biologist David Hillis (and containing ninety-seven types of life), place mammals in a more humbling context than those based on earlier methods of analysis.

perfect forms, whereas evolution yields adequate forms (adequate for survival). And creation implies that species are eternal, whereas evolution implies that species have changed—and continue to change—in ways that are largely unpredictable.

Because creation is simpler than evolution, it tends to be children's preferred explanation for the origin of species. If you ask a preschooler or young elementary-schooler where the first lizard came from or where the first bear came from, they typically cite creation, either divine creation ("God made the animals") or a less specific form of creation ("Something made it," "Someone made it," "It just appeared one day"). They cite creation regardless of the species they are asked to consider and regardless of whether evolution is explicitly proposed as an option ("Did God make it? Or did it change from a different kind of animal?"). Most surprising, they cite creation regardless of whether their parents are creationists or evolutionists. In other words, young children cite creation even if their parents cite evolution when asked the same questions.

Children's inclination toward creationism serves as the foundation for more theologically elaborate systems of belief (e.g., the seven days of creation described in Genesis). These beliefs, in turn, block acceptance of evolution later in life. Several studies have shown that religious beliefs are the strongest predictor of skepticism toward evolution—stronger than age, gender, level of education, political beliefs, genetic literacy, aptitude for analytic reasoning, and attitudes toward science in general.

Religiosity predicts evolution acceptance by country as well. Countries with high levels of religiosity, like Turkey and Egypt, report low levels of evolution acceptance, whereas countries with low levels of religiosity, like Denmark and France, report high levels of evolution acceptance. Within the United States—where about 60 percent of the population accepts evolution and 40 percent does not—religiosity and evolution acceptance are negatively correlated across states. States with high levels of religiosity, like Alabama and Mississippi, report low levels of evolution acceptance, whereas states with low religiosity, like Vermont and New Hampshire, report high levels of evolution acceptance. These findings hold even when controlling for high school graduation rates, college attendance, teacher salaries, general science literacy, and gross domestic product per capita.

These kinds of demographic data, though compelling, fail to capture the true fervor with which many creationists reject evolution. That fervor is better captured by the hate mail sent to Richard Dawkins, the famed evolutionist and atheist. Here's a sample:

- "I'm sick of hearing about you and your theory of evolution. You may have evolved from monkeys but leave me out of it. Have you ever tried to make love to a monkey? I wouldn't be surprised if you have."
- "You suck, stupid atheist scum. . . . You only believe what you want to believe and have an unshakeable faith that your great, great grandparents were actually bacteria and that's how you evolved. For some odd reason, you wish you could be a bacteria instead of a human."
- "You, sir, are an absolute ass. Your famed intelligence is nothing more than the fart of God."
- "How can you justify the theory of evolution when you are possibly the most revolting, ugly, pile of crap on earth."

- "Richard Dawkins: he is a dick and needs to be killed in a plane crash or a flame thrower accident."
- "Richard Dawkins, I hope you die of rabies."

This hostile reaction toward evolution (and evolution advocates) has had a chilling effect on science teachers' willingness to teach evolution, particularly in the United States. A recent survey of US high school biology teachers found that only 28 percent teach evolution as an uncontroversial fact of science. That is, only 28 percent explain what evolution is and what evidence supports evolution. Most teachers (60 percent) try to avoid the topic. They do so either by teaching evolution only as it applies to the microevolution (adaptation) of nonhuman species, by justifying the inclusion of evolution in terms of state standards ("you need to learn about evolution because the biology curriculum is organized *as if* evolution were true"), or by presenting both evolution and creationism as equally plausible alternatives.

The remaining 12 percent of biology teachers advocate creationism. When asked why, one biology teacher said, "I don't teach the theory of evolution in my life science classes, nor do I teach the Big Bang Theory in my earth science classes. . . . We do not have time to do something that is at best poor science." Another said, "I am always amazed at how evolution and creationism are treated as if they are right or wrong. They are both belief systems that can never be truly or fully proved or discredited." Both teachers were employed by public schools, where advocating creationism is illegal.

✢ ✢ ✢

RELIGION AND EVOLUTION have been at odds with one another since evolution was first studied, when the concept of natural selection was just a twinkle in Darwin's eye. Darwin started life as a devout Christian, intending to join the Anglican clergy, but during his college years at Cambridge, he decided to study biology instead. This decision led to a lifelong conflict between the religious beliefs he had formed as a child and the scientific beliefs he formed as an adult. Early in his studies, Darwin recognized that an evolutionary view of life was inconsistent with a creationist one. In a letter to his friend Sir Joseph Dalton Hooker, fifteen years before the publication of *On the Origin of Species*, he wrote, "I am almost convinced (quite contrary to [the] opinion I started with) that species are not (it is like confessing a murder) immutable." For the young Darwin, acknowledging that species are mutable was "like confessing a murder."

Today, many people continue to see religion and evolution as fundamentally incompatible, but others see them as complementary. We know this from three decades of polling data from the Gallup organization. Gallup has polled Americans' attitudes toward evolution with this question: "Which of the following statements comes closest to your views on the origin and development of human beings? (1) Human beings have developed over millions of years from less advanced forms of life, but God guided this process; (2) Human beings have developed over millions of years from less advanced forms of life, but God had no part in this process; or (3) God created human beings pretty much in their present form at one time within the last 10,000 years or so."

After one of these polls, the news headline is usually, "Four in 10 Americans believe in strict creationism," but the same polls reveal that four in ten Americans believe that "human beings developed over millions of years from less advanced forms of life, but God guided this process." That is, 40 to 45 percent of Americans endorse statement 3, the strict-creationist option; 10 to 15 percent endorse statement 2, the secular-evolution option; and 35 to 40 percent endorse statement 1, the theistic-evolution option. Creationists are a sizable minority but a minority nonetheless.

Should science educators and science advocates rejoice over the fact that 40 percent of Americans endorse theistic evolution? From a sociological point of view, I would say yes. Less than a century ago, the topic of evolution was so taboo as to be prohibited from US public schools. Now it's a mandated part of the US biology curriculum. Attitudes toward evolution have changed dramatically in just three generations' time, and widespread endorsement of theistic evolution is a sign of that change. That said, there are still many communities in the United States where attitudes toward evolution have not changed—saying that you believe in evolution (theistic or otherwise) is tantamount to saying that you are immoral, disloyal, lawless, and godless. Belief in evolution is not just a stance on empirical reality; it's a marker of social identity, as potent a label as *liberal*, *pro-choice*, or *feminist*.

But it doesn't have to be. Many who reject evolution on religious grounds accept other scientific facts that are equally inconsistent with religious doctrine: the fact that dinosaurs once roamed the earth, that earth-quakes and floods are caused by natural forces, that the earth moves, that the earth orbits the sun, and that the earth is not the center of the universe. People were once burned at the stake for endorsing such facts, which are now endorsed by the religious and the secular alike. Evolution is just one scientific fact among many that have become sociopolitically charged, but it could lose that charge if enough people endorsed it as true—even if they endorsed it while maintaining that God played some role in the process.

Widespread endorsement of theistic evolution is thus good from a so-ciological perspective, but it may not be good from a cognitive perspective, as theistic evolution is logically problematic. The evolutionary machinery of mutation plus natural selection (see Chapter 12) leaves no role for divine intervention—at least no role beyond what scientists can learn about evo-lution without making such an assumption. Theistic evolution also flies in the face of what most people believe to be true of God, namely, that God is omnipotent (all-powerful), omniscient (all-knowing), and omnibenevolent (all-good). Why would an omnipotent being chose random mutation as a starting point for evolutionary change rather than directed mutation or, for that matter, plain old creation? Why would an omniscient being produce superfluous or imperfectly designed forms, like the human tailbone, the whale hipbone, the snake leg bone, the ostrich wing, or the rabbit stomach (which is so inefficient at extracting nutrients that rabbits must eat their feces so as to digest their food twice)?

And, most troubling, why would an omnibenevolent being use natural selection as a tool for creation? Natural selection is a cruel process, as noted in Chapter 12. Most organisms die of starvation, predation, or disease be-fore reaching reproductive maturity. Does God delight in watching orcas drown baby seals by the dozens? Watching wasp larvae devour caterpillars from the inside out? Watching viruses annihilate entire populations of hu-mans, including infants and children? Billions of "God's creatures" have died violent, painful deaths, and 99.9 percent of earth's species have gone extinct. Why would an omnipotent, omniscient, and omnibenevolent being have created all those life-forms just to destroy them?

On top of these intellectual concerns about the nature of God are moral concerns about humans' place in nature. Religion dictates that humans are the apex of all life-forms, whereas evolution dictates that humans are just one twig on a vast tree of life. Religion dictates that humans are blessed with an immaterial soul, whereas evolution dictates that humans are material creatures through and through. And religion dictates that good people are fated for eternal salvation, whereas evolution dictates that life is short, brutal, and unfair.

Evolutionary implications for humans' place in nature may be unpalatable from a religious point of view, but from a secular point of view, they can be inspiring and motivating. The idea that humans are just one twig of millions on a vast tree of life can inspire a sense of unity with nature and can motivate actions toward conservation. The idea that humans are thoroughly material creatures can inspire a deeper appreciation for the here and now and can motivate self-understanding and self-fulfillment. And the idea that life is inherently unfair can inspire a broader awareness of discrimination and can motivate actions toward social justice.

Evolutionists have been castigated as the evilest of evil—"revolting, ugly, piles of crap"—but nothing about accepting evolution predisposes a person toward cruelty, selfishness, or indifference. If anything, it predisposes us toward the opposite—toward embracing human existence as a precious and improbable gift and toward making the most of that gift, for ourselves and for others.

✢ ✢ ✢

IN CHAPTERS 8 through 13, we covered several intuitive theories of the biological world:

1. An intuitive theory of life, where animals are viewed as psychological agents rather than organic machines composed of life-sustaining organs.
2. An intuitive theory of growth, where eating is viewed as a means of satiation rather than nourishment and aging is viewed as a series of discrete changes rather than one continuous change.
3. An intuitive theory of inheritance, where parent-offspring resemblance is viewed as the consequence of nurture rather than the reproductive transmission of genetic information.
4. An intuitive theory of illness, where disease is viewed as the consequence of imprudent or immoral behavior rather than the spread of microscopic organisms.

5. An intuitive theory of adaptation, where evolution is viewed as the uniform transformation of an entire population rather than the selective survival and reproduction of a subset of the population.

6. An intuitive theory of ancestry, where speciation is viewed as the linear process of direct ancestry rather than the branching process of common ancestry.

These theories provide us with systematic explanations of natural phenomena, as do the theories covered in Chapters 2 through 7, but their source is different. They arise not because our observation of the relevant phenomena is inherently biased, but because our observation is inherently limited. We cannot observe with our eyes the functional relations among internal organs, the biochemical pathways of growth and aging, the genetic underpinnings of inheritance, the microbial causes of illness, the selective survival of individuals within a population, or the ancestral relations among diverse life-forms. We have no perceptual access to the inner working of biological systems, so we default to more general forms of reasoning: animism, vitalism, essentialism, teleology, or intentional design. These forms of reasoning give us some understanding of the biological world but not enough to make consistently accurate predictions or consistently optimal decisions. For that, we need the detailed, mechanistic understanding of biological phenomena afforded to us only by scientific theories.

14 | HOW TO GET THE WORLD RIGHT

IN 1802, A FARM BOY IN SOUTH HADLEY, MASSACHUSETTS, MADE AN unusual discovery while plowing his father's fields. The boy, Pliny Mood, unearthed a stone imprinted with several large, birdlike footprints. The footprints were dinosaur tracks—some of the first dinosaur tracks ever discovered—but the Mood family knew nothing of dinosaurs. They excavated the stone and placed it at their doorstep, raising speculation from the neighbors that they had been breeding some very heavy poultry.

Several years later, the stone was purchased by a physician named Elihu Dwight, who spread word that he had discerned the origin of the unusual tracks: Noah's raven. Noah, according to the Bible, sent a raven from his ark to find dry land as the waters of the Great Flood receded. The raven never returned to the arc, apparently because it found a new home in South Hadley. Paleontologists have now identified the tracks as belonging to *Anomoepus scambus*, a birdlike dinosaur that roamed the Connecticut River Valley around two hundred million years ago.

The correct interpretation of the tracks required theoretical advances in biology and geology that had yet to occur when the tracks were discovered, so Dwight relied on intuition. The tracks looked like bird tracks, so he assumed they had been made by a known species of bird. And they

These dinosaur tracks were discovered on a farm in Massachusetts before dinosaurs were known to exist (1802) and were interpreted as the footprints of Noah's raven.

looked very old, so he assumed they had been made at one of the earliest known points in time (the Great Flood described in Genesis).

This interpretation highlights several characteristics of intuitive theories discussed in the previous chapters. First, it shows how intuitive theories influence not just our beliefs about the world but our very perception of the world. The fossilized footprints were each twelve inches long—much larger than the feet of a raven—but the discrepancy did not stop Dwight from seeing the footprints as left by a raven. A more reasonable guess would have been a turkey, but Dwight also had to explain why the footprints had been fossilized. The Great Flood provided such an explanation. Not only was the flood assumed to be an ancient event—ancient enough for the footprints to have become fossilized—but it would also have left the earth muddy and thus receptive to the footprints of a mere three-pound bird.

Dwight's interpretation of the tracks also highlights how intuitive theories are anthropocentric, grounded in a human timescale, a human perspective, and a human sense of value and purpose. His interpretation entailed a time known to humans (a few thousand years ago), a creature known to humans (a raven), and circumstances significant to humans (a flood sent by

God to punish humans). A correct interpretation of the tracks, on the other hand, entails events that occurred long before humans ever existed (two hundred million years in the past), creatures never observed by humans (dinosaurs), and circumstances having nothing to do with humans (a day in the life of an ancient reptile).

A final characteristic of intuitive theories highlighted by Dwight's interpretation is that intuitive theories, while grounded in experience, are elaborated by culture. Dwight would never have identified a raven as the creator of those tracks if it were not for the biblical account of Noah's raven. If the biblical account were different—if Noah had sent an owl in search of land rather than a raven or if Noah had saved the earth's creatures from a fire rather than a flood—then the interpretation of those tracks would surely have been different (e.g., owl tracks imprinted in petrified ash).

Scientific theories, like intuitive theories, are products of culture, and Dwight cannot be faulted for failing to identify the tracks as dinosaur tracks, because his culture had not yet formulated the notion of a dinosaur, let alone the notions of evolution, extinction, and deep time. Our ability to transcend the limitations of our intuitive theories is as much a cultural achievement as it is an individual achievement. Dwight may not have identified those tracks, but anyone—even a child—living in South Hadley today could. Science has refined and expanded human thought, allowing us to entertain ideas that previous humans had never been able to entertain before, as long as we are receptive to those thoughts and not completely blinded by our intuitive theories.

✦ ✦ ✦

THE MAIN GOAL of this book was to introduce you, the reader, to your own intuitive theories—theories you held explicitly in the past but only implicitly today, as well as theories you may still hold explicitly. The twelve intuitive theories covered in this book are not the only such theories we humans hold. We also hold intuitive theories about psychology (e.g., intuitive theories of knowledge and memory) and mathematics (e.g., intuitive models of arithmetic and rational number). But the twelve discussed here are rich enough and varied enough to show that intuitive theories do not fit a single mold. Each theory arises for different reasons, though some of those reasons cohere to common themes.

One common theme is that intuitive theories are grounded in perception. They rest on properties that we can perceive, to the detriment of those that we cannot. In many cases, the properties we can perceive remain undifferentiated from those we cannot. Intuitive theories of matter, for instance, do not distinguish between the imperceptible property of density and the perceptible properties of heft and bulk, and intuitive theories of thermal phenomena do not distinguish between the imperceptible property of heat and the perceptible property of warmth. Other imperceptible notions absent from intuitive theories include atoms, elements, molecules, electrons, photons, forces, inertia, gravity, orbits, tectonic plates, organs, genes, cells, nutrients, embryos, germs, common ancestors, and natural selection.

Intuitive theories also tend to be thing-based. They carve up the world into discrete, tangible things, whereas scientific theories carve up the same aspects of the world into processes. Heat, sound, electricity, lightning, fire, magnetism, pressure, climate, weather, earthquakes, tides, rainbows, clouds, life, vitality: these are processes, not things. They are processes that emerge from the collective interaction of an entire system of things, operating at a lower level of organization than the processes themselves (e.g., electricity arises from the collective interaction of electrons, life arises from the collective interaction of organs). Historically, the reclassification of emergent phenomena from *things* to *processes* was a critical first step in establishing several domains of science. But such reclassifications rarely permeate popular consciousness, because the cognitive demands of systems-based thinking are too high (as discussed in Chapter 3).

Finally, intuitive theories tend to focus on objects rather than contexts. Properties that vary by context are assumed to be intrinsic to the objects that manifest them. Buoyancy, for instance, is not an all-or-nothing property; objects that are buoyant in some liquids may sink in others (e.g., raspberries float in water but sink in oil). Likewise, weight varies by altitude, volume by temperature, and color by viewing conditions. Taking context into account requires a broader perspective than that afforded by intuitive theories because intuitive theories are concerned with what is *typically* true (e.g., bananas are yellow) not what is *universally* true (e.g., bananas absorb all wavelengths of light except those that appear yellow to the human eye).

In short, intuitive theories focus more on the perceptible than the imperceptible, more on things than processes, and more on objects than contexts. Each of these themes extends to several intuitive theories but not all.

Intuitive theories differ in form and function, and it would be a mistake to try to shoehorn all such theories into a single category. Failing to appreciate the role of molecular motion in heat transfer is substantively different from failing to appreciate the role of tectonic plates in volcanism. Failing to abstract a notion of density from the perceptual experience of heft is substantively different from failing to abstract a notion of germs from the perceptual experience of contagion. Any educator who wants to help students confront and correct their intuitive theories needs to tailor his or her instruction to those theories.

There is, however, at least one common thread running through all intuitive theories: they are narrower and shallower than their scientific counterparts. They are narrower in what they explain, and they are shallower in how they explain it. Intuitive theories are about coping with present circumstances, the here and the now. Scientific theories are about the full causal story—from past to future, from the observable to the unobservable, from the minuscule to the immense.

Our intuitive theories of the cosmos, for example, treat the earth as the center of the universe, but scientific theories treat the earth as one planet among many, in one solar system among many, in one galaxy among many. Our intuitive theories of life construe bodies as structurally and functionally unified entities, but scientific theories construe bodies as collections of organs, composed of collections of cells, composed of collections of organelles, composed of collections of molecules. And our intuitive theories of ancestry place us at the apex of creation, whereas scientific theories place us on one of many branches of primates, within mammals, within vertebrates, within animals, within a vast tree of life. Intuitive theories may help us answer the small questions in life (e.g., what should I eat, where should I step, how can I get well?), but only scientific theories help us answer the big ones (e.g., who are we, where did we come from, where we are going?).

✦ ✦ ✦

IN CHAPTER 1, I likened the acquisition of new knowledge to the building of new Lego creations. In the same way that many Lego creations can be built from a basic set of Lego blocks, many forms of knowledge can be built from our innate repertoire of concepts. But some forms of knowledge require new types of concepts (e.g., inertia, planet, germ) just as some

Lego creations require new types of Lego pieces (e.g., wheels, axles, gears). This analogy aptly characterizes the gap between intuitive knowledge and scientific knowledge, but doesn't easily characterize how we traverse that gap—how we acquire scientific concepts. We can't just go to the concept store (down the street from the Lego store) and buy a shiny new concept. We have to acquire the new concept in increments, starting with the concepts we have and forging our way to the concepts we do not.

A better analogy for this process is Otto Neurath's analogy of building a ship in the middle of the ocean (Chapter 4). Just as sailors are stuck with a particular ship once they've set sail, cognitive creatures are stuck with a particular set of beliefs once they've begun observing and interacting with the world. If the sailors realize midvoyage that their ship is inadequate for confronting the challenges ahead, they cannot rebuild the ship from scratch. But they can restructure the ship by repurposing its constituent materials. Likewise, if we humans realize mid-development that our knowledge is inadequate for confronting the challenges ahead, we cannot rebuild the knowledge from scratch, but we can restructure our knowledge by repurposing its constituent concepts.

So how do we do that? How do we restructure our own knowledge, which is constrained by our prior beliefs and our evolved cognitive capacities? When framed at such an abstract level, the problem sounds harder than it actually is. It cannot be addressed at an abstract level, either. To restructure our knowledge, we have to get our hands dirty in the details of the knowledge itself: the concepts that need to be differentiated, collapsed, reanalyzed, or discarded.

One nice example of this dirty-hands approach is a tutorial designed to help poultry farmers determine the sex of day-old chickens. Chicken sexing is surprisingly difficult. At birth, male and female chicks are indistinguishable in size, shape, and plumage. Sex-distinctive characteristics, like the comb on a rooster's head, do not emerge until several weeks after birth, at which point the hatcheries will have wasted resources on chicks that will never lay eggs (the males). Male chicks are also disruptive to the operation of a hatchery, blocking female chicks' access to food and water. It is thus an economic priority for hatcheries to sort males from females as early as possible.

Doing so, however, requires examining a pin-sized structure—the chick's *genital eminence*, or "bead"—that looks virtually identical between males and females, at least to the untrained eye. Trained observers can identify the sex of day-old chicks with 99 percent accuracy at a rate of two chicks per second, but this level of proficiency requires several years of trial-and-error learning at the side of an expert chick sexer.

When vision scientists learned of this intriguing perceptual problem, they applied the tools of their trade—an analytic framework for distinguishing recurrent visual features from random ones—to hundreds of pictures of chick beads. They discovered that male beads do not consistently differ from female beads in size, location, texture, or segmentation but do consistently differ in one feature: convexity. Male beads are generally rounder than female beads. The researchers then created a tutorial for teaching novice chicken sexers how to differentiate males from females by focusing on bead convexity.

Their tutorial proved highly effective. Chicken-sexing novices—adults who had never laid eyes on a chick's bead, let alone wanted to—were given eighteen photographs of chick beads and asked to sort the photos by sex. Before the tutorial, they sorted the photos at random. After the tutorial, they sorted the photos with 90 percent accuracy—a rate comparable to that of experts asked to sort the same photos. The experts had an average of three years of chicken-sexing experience. The novices, in contrast, had undergone only five minutes of training.

Targeted training—that is, training grounded in an in-depth analysis of the relevant domain of knowledge—is thus several times more effective than unguided (or minimally guided) exploration of the domain, as discussed in Chapter 5. Another nice demonstration of this finding comes from research on how to teach second-graders the concept of mathematical equivalence. All branches of mathematics, from arithmetic to calculus, rely on the idea that quantities can be expressed in different ways across an equation. Quantities on the left side of an equation (e.g., $1 + 5$) must equal those on the right side (e.g., $8 - 2$). The notation separating the two sides—the equal sign—means "is the same as."

Young children don't quite see the equal sign in those terms. They interpret it as a prompt to perform a computation. The equal sign in $4 + 3 = \_\_$, for example, is interpreted as a prompt to add 4 and 3 and to write their sum in the space provided. Equations in which mathematical operations are placed on the right side of the equal sign ($\_\_ = 4 + 3$) or on both sides of the equal sign ($4 + 3 = \_\_ + 1$) throw young children for a loop, as these arrangements defy a strictly procedural interpretation. Math educators have long known that young children fail to grasp the conceptual meaning of the equal sign, but adults' approach to conveying this meaning is typically to give them more of the same—namely, more problems formatted as "operations = answer." The teachers assume that children must learn to solve standard problems before they can move on to nonstandard problems, where a procedural definition of the equal sign does not apply.

As it turns out, teaching mathematical equivalence with both standard and nonstandard problems is more effective than starting out with only standard problems. In one study, researchers created two workbooks. One workbook contained only standard problems ($4 + 3 =$ __), and one had problems with the same addends arranged in nonstandard formats (__ $= 4 + 3$). They then tested second-graders' ability to answer each type of problem, standard and nonstandard, after completing each type of workbook. Not surprisingly, children who practiced nonstandard problems in their workbooks answered more nonstandard problems correctly than did children who practiced only standard problems. But children who practiced non-standard problems also answered more *standard* problems correctly—twice as many, in fact. And this difference was observed even six months later. Both groups of children solved the same problems content-wise, but subtle differences in the formatting of these problems led to large and reliable differences in how much children learned from them.

The point of this study, as well as the chicken-sexing study, is not just that some study materials are better than others. It's that effective instruction requires an in-depth analysis of what concepts need to be learned and how those concepts are best conveyed. We've encountered several other examples of conceptually informed instruction throughout the book: Carol Smith's tutorial on the particulate nature of matter (Chapter 2), Michelene Chi's on the kinetic nature of heat (Chapter 3), John Clement's on the ubiquitous nature of force (Chapter 5), Michael Ranney's on the anthropogenic nature of climate change (Chapter 7), Virginia Slaughter's on the vitalistic nature of biological activities (Chapter 8), Sarah Gripshover's on the metabolic nature of food consumption (Chapter 9), Ken Springer's on the biophysical nature of inheritance (Chapter 10), and Terry Au's on the microbial nature of illness (Chapter 11).

These tutorials have proven effective because they harness the same kind of analytic power harnessed by the chicken-sexing tutorial and the mathematical-equivalence tutorial. They are based on an analysis of the domain that takes what learners believe to be true of the domain and either challenges those beliefs (for beliefs that are wrong), refines those beliefs (for beliefs that are accurate but imprecise), or elaborates on those beliefs (for beliefs that are accurate but incomplete). Effective tutorials forge a path between a learner's intuitive theories of the domain and an expert's theory. The path that is forged is rarely the only path—others are possible—but it is a path nonetheless. Forms of instruction that do not forge such paths include plug-and-chug problem sets, free exploration of microworlds, and unguided experimentation (recall the failure of such approaches from Chapter 5). These forms of instruction allow students to remain absorbed in their intuitive theories and do not, therefore, challenge the theories or refine them.

Also ineffective is fostering general abilities like critical analysis, quantitative reasoning, or inquiry skills, as these abilities do not address the conceptual problems inherent in an intuitive theory. Learning how to analyze a text on astronomy will not help a flat-earth theorist become a spherical-earth theorist, just as learning how to run a controlled physics experiment will not help an impetus theorist become a Newtonian theorist. Students need an explication of their intuitive theories, an explanation for why those theories are flawed, and a demonstration of how scientific theories of the same phenomena fare much better. Critical analysis, quantitative reasoning, and inquiry skills are important to develop, of course, but they are not remedies for domain-specific scientific misconceptions.

By its very nature, science is a domain-specific enterprise. Specific kinds of scientists (e.g., paleontologists) run specific kinds of experiments (e.g., carbon dating) to test specific kinds of hypotheses (e.g., that one fossil is older than another) with specific kinds of data (e.g., differential rates of radioactive decay). Just as doing science is domain-specific, *learning* science is domain-specific as well. Students in specific kinds of classes (e.g., microbiology) must learn specific kinds of concepts (e.g., bacteria, RNA, mitochondria) embedded in specific kinds of theories (e.g., germ theory, cell theory) relevant to specific kinds of phenomena (e.g., fermentation, decomposition, disease). Instruction that neglects the domain-specific nature of intuitive theories and their scientific counterparts has about as much chance of working as the chance of a nuclear physicist making an important discovery in immunology, or an immunologist making an important discovery in nuclear physics. It could happen, but I wouldn't hold my breath.

✦ ✦ ✦

MOVING FROM INTUITIVE theories to scientific theories is difficult, but that difficulty is compounded by our frequent failure to recognize the limitations of our intuitive theories. These theories give us a sense of understanding—a sense that feels appropriate and sufficient—and we rarely seek to improve that understanding on our own.

Consider the phenomenon of rainbows. You've probably seen several rainbows in your life. You know their shape, their colors, and the order of the colors. You know that rainbows are fleeting and can't be touched. You probably even know the conditions under which rainbows appear. Would you say that you understand rainbows well? On a scale from 1 to 7, where 1 indicates "poor understanding" and 7 indicates "expert-level understanding," where would you locate yourself?

As someone who has read an entire book on the limitations of our intuitive theories, you may be wary of your knowledge of rainbows, recognizing that your intuitive theories of light and optics may be inadequate for capturing the true nature of a rainbow. But adults, in general, are not wary. They think they know much more than they actually do. If asked to rate their understanding of rainbows or any other natural phenomena (e.g., earthquakes, comets, tides), most adults rate their understanding as "moderate"—that is, a 4 on a scale from 1 to 7. If you then ask adults to write out an explanation of these phenomena ("So tell me: how *do* rainbows form?"), their confidence in their understanding drops from a 4 to a 3. And if you then ask a diagnostic question about their understanding ("Why are rainbows curved rather than straight? Why do the colors of the rainbow always appear in the same order?"), their confidence drops from a 3 to a 2.

This tendency to overrate our understanding of natural phenomena has been labeled the *illusion of explanatory depth*. It is the illusion that our explanatory knowledge, as grounded in intuitive theories, runs much deeper than it actually does. This illusion has been documented in people of varying ages, from four-year-olds to forty-year-olds, and with varying levels of education, from minimal exposure to science to graduate-level training in

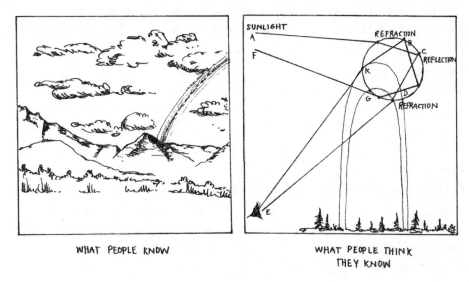

WHAT PEOPLE KNOW   WHAT PEOPLE THINK
                                    THEY KNOW

Our knowledge of the causal origins of natural phenomena, like rainbows, is sparser than we think it is.

science. It has even been documented in people who have significant first-hand experience with the domain under consideration (e.g., cycling experts asked to explain the mechanics of a bicycle). As someone who holds a PhD in psychology, I qualify as an expert in the field, yet I fall prey to the illusion of explanatory depth every time I prepare a new lecture on a psychological topic. I start my preparation convinced I know enough about the topic to occupy a full hour's worth of class but soon discover I know only enough to occupy five minutes' worth. My first year of teaching was one long foray into the illusion of explanatory depth.

Researchers who have studied this illusion have determined that it's not just a matter of general overconfidence, on par with overconfidence in our driving ability or our financial investments. It's specific to complex causal systems—systems with multiple causal pathways, multiple levels of analysis, nonvisible mechanisms, and indeterminate end states. Consequently, the illusion does not pertain to forms of knowledge that lack such properties, like knowledge of procedures (e.g., how to bake chocolate chip cookies) or knowledge of narratives (e.g., the plot of *Star Wars*). If you think you can bake chocolate chip cookies or recount the plot of *Star Wars*, you probably can.

Our knowledge of natural phenomena thus suffers on two fronts: from our limited ability to explain these phenomena (in accurate terms) and from our limited recognition of this limited ability. We are blind to our own blindness.

Another complication in moving from intuitive theories of the world to scientific theories is that our intuitive views are surprisingly resilient. As the economist John Maynard Keynes once noted about the process of theory revision, "The difficulty lies not so much in developing new ideas as in escaping from old ones." Throughout the book, we've seen many examples of old ideas constraining our appreciation of new ones, even when we can fully articulate the new ones. In the domain of physics, for instance, adults who know that buoyancy is determined by density still have trouble discounting an object's weight when making judgments of sinking and floating (see Chapter 2). Adults who know that it takes two wires to complete an electric circuit still have trouble denying that electricity could flow from an electric source to an electric device through a single wire (Chapter 3). Adults who know that two objects of different mass fall to the ground at the same rate still have trouble denying that a lead ball will fall faster than a wooden ball (Chapter 5). And remarkably, adults who know that the earth is a sphere still estimate distances between cities as if the earth were flat (Chapter 6).

We exhibit the same tendencies in the domain of biology. Adults who know that plants are alive still classify them as "not alive" when rushed or mentally preoccupied (Chapter 8). Adults who understand that aspects of their personal identity have changed with age still deny that those aspects will change in the future (Chapter 9). Adults who have learned that infectious disease is spread through germs will nevertheless blame supernatural forces for making them sick (Chapter 11). And adults who accept that humans evolved from nonhuman ancestors still deny that humans are related to *all* organisms through common ancestry, even a lowly paramecium (Chapter 13).

These findings suggest that scientific knowledge does not improve our understanding of the world as it much as it complicates our understanding, adding a new layer of interpretation atop an older one. This way of thinking about conceptual change is relatively new, only being described within the last decade. Before that time, researchers interested in conceptual change tended to assume that scientific theories *overwrite* intuitive theories, most likely because the investigators were focused on characterizing differences between science novices (e.g., ninth-graders) and science experts (e.g., physics PhDs) rather than testing the stability of those differences when experts are rushed, burdened, or distracted. Given that researchers have only begun to study this new phenomenon, there is still much we do not know. Why aren't intuitive theories erased by scientific ones? What contexts trigger intuitive theories, and what contexts trigger scientific theories? What skills are needed to recognize the difference between reasoning based on intuition and reasoning based on science? What skills are needed to prioritize science over intuition?

With respect to the last question, it would seem that knowing a lot of scientific facts is not enough; we must actively *think* like scientists. We know, for instance, that appreciating humans' place in the biological world requires more than just knowing that species are related through common ancestry; it also requires the ability to discern patterns of genetic relatedness from the branches of an evolutionary tree. Likewise, we cannot understand the biological underpinnings of infectious disease just by knowing that germs exist; we need the ability to think of germs as living, breeding organisms. If thinking like a scientist is critical to reaping the benefits of science, then educators may need to introduce scientific ideas as methods of reasoning rather than just bodies of knowledge, as approaches to problems rather than just their solutions. Intuitive theories provide us with everyday approaches to everyday problems—that's their raison d'être—and the reason we default to those theories when rushed or distracted may be that we never learned to use our scientific theories in the same way.

✦ ✦ ✦

IN GRADUATE SCHOOL, I helped teach a psychology course on cognitive development, from the development of scientific cognition to the development of moral cognition. Moral cognition was the last topic covered, and the instructor who lectured on moral cognition concluded her lecture by noting that the development of moral cognition is more socially significant than the development of scientific cognition. It matters whether your neighbor has a sense of moral virtue and treats you with moral dignity, she argued, but it doesn't matter whether your neighbor holds an accurate understanding of biology or an accurate understanding of physics. Her view was that errors in moral reasoning are public and impactful, whereas errors in scientific reasoning are private and inconsequential.

That comparison struck me as wrong. It was wrong not because the instructor overemphasized the importance of moral reasoning but because she underemphasized the importance of scientific reasoning. Our understanding of natural phenomena has widespread implications for how we act on the world and react to it: how we decide whether a surface is safe to walk on, how we decide whether an object is safe to touch, how we lift objects, how we stack objects, how we plan for an earthquake, how we plan for a flood, how we select the foods we eat, how we select the garments we wear, how we cope with aging, how we cope with death, how we interpret the results of a blood test, how we interpret the results of a genetic screening, how we avoid illness, how we treat illness, and how we treat other animals—just to name a few examples.

Our understanding of natural phenomena has widespread social implications as well. Vaccination, pasteurization, stem cell research, cloning, fertility treatment, genetic modification of food, genetic modification of microbes, antibiotics, pesticides, cryogenics, space exploration, nuclear power, climate change: these science-laden issues affect society as a whole. It is important not just that scientists understand them but that everyone understands them, as we must collectively decide what policies are needed to address these issues and what resources are needed to investigate them.

Vaccination provides one of the clearest examples of the importance of collective understanding and collective action. Vaccination was pioneered by Edward Jenner in 1796 as a method of inducing immunity to life-threatening viruses, like smallpox and polio. It entails injecting dead or inactivated virus cells into the body to encourage the body's immune system to develop antibodies specific to that virus prior to infection by a live strain. If enough people are vaccinated against a particular disease, its transmission will be curtailed to the point of eradication. Measles were eradicated from the United States in the late 1990s, less than forty years after the introduction of a measles vaccine. The disease that had once infected nearly all American children—and killed hundreds of them yearly—had virtually ceased to exist within America's shores.

Then, in 2014, measles reemerged with a vengeance, infecting over 600 people in two major outbreaks. It reemerged not among those who were

too young to receive the vaccine or whose immune systems were too com-
promised to receive the vaccine but among those who had intentionally
avoided the vaccine—or, in many cases, among those *whose parents* had intentionally avoided vaccinating their children. Those parents couldn't wrap
their minds around the idea of injecting their children with an inactivated
virus, suspended in mysterious "chemicals," so they entrusted their children's well-being to nature or to God. And the result was a public health
disaster. Hundreds of children suffered, or even died, from a problem we've
known how to fix for over 200 years. Thankfully, the most recent set of outbreaks have stirred action. Laws limiting personal or religious exemption
to vaccination are being passed in more and more states, and programs for
educating the public on the dangers of nonvaccination are being developed
in more and more communities.

As the vaccination debacle illustrates, modern developments in science
and technology cannot be understood on the basis of intuitive theories
alone. Reliance on intuitive theories will surely undermine our pursuit
of a more productive economy, a more healthful society, and a more liv-
able environment. Bill Nye, "the science guy," has argued as much from
an educational point of view. He sees science denial as a threat not just to
our intellectual lives but to the wellbeing of society as a whole. "To the
grownups," he has argued, "if you want to deny [science] and live in your
world that's completely inconsistent with everything we've observed in the
universe, that's fine. But don't make your kids do it, because we need them.
We need scientifically literate voters and taxpayers for the future. We need
engineers that can build stuff and can solve problems."

While science denial is problematic from a sociological point of view,
it's unavoidable from a psychological point of view. There is a fundamental
disconnect between the cognitive abilities of individual humans and the
cognitive demands of modern society. Over the past two thousand years,
humans have created societies that require mastery of high-level cognitive
procedures, like reading and writing, as well as high-level cognitive structures, like scientific concepts and scientific theories. Concepts and theories that were once at the forefront of scientific inquiry are now routinely
taught to young children. A person ignorant of those ideas could get along
just fine in societies of the past but not in today's society. In today's society,
getting by requires a basic proficiency in science as much as it requires a
basic proficiency in cooking, cleaning, grooming, and mending.

Our modern way of life is thoroughly dependent on science, so we must take obstacles to understanding science seriously. We must take *intuitive theories* seriously. We must create environments that help us become aware of those theories and craft instruction that helps us overcome them, in the classroom and beyond. Intuitive theories will be with us forever, as they are reinvented by every child in every generation. Let's not let the theories we construct as children constrain the opportunities we pursue as adults.

Acknowledgments

IN THIS BOOK, I've argued that an apt metaphor for learning counterintuitive scientific ideas is Neurath's boat: a boat discovered to be unseaworthy while at sea and is thus restructured and rejiggered as it continues its voyage. Neurath's boat is an apt metaphor for this book as well. It has been restructured and rejiggered several times midvoyage, and I would not have been able to do so without the guidance and assistance of many friends and colleagues.

First, there are the people who helped launch this boat of a book. I am indebted to Paul Bloom, Alison Gopnik, Steve Pinker, Michael Shermer, and Carlo Valdesolo for helping me navigate the world of literary agents and trade book publishers. I am particularly grateful to Steve Pinker for providing valuable advice about when and how to write a trade book and for providing inroads into this foreign world.

Second, there are several people who saw potential in this work and helped me shape it into something seaworthy: Max Brockman, TJ Kelleher, and Helene Barthelemy. Max, my agent, was instrumental in helping me refine and articulate my ideas. TJ, my editor, helped me make my writing more interesting and accessible. And Helene, my editor's assistant, guided me through the process of procuring (legal) illustrations.

Third, there are the people who provided feedback on early drafts of the manuscript: Max Rattner, Sharang Tickoo, Josh Valcarcel, Andrea Villalobos, and Neil Young. Special thanks are due to Sharang, Andrea, and Neil for reading and commenting on the entire book. Their feedback has made the book significantly better.

Finally, there are the people who made my book more visually appealing: Ian Silverstein and Summer Peet. Ian made drawings of cartoons, popular artwork, and brains, and Summer made drawings of tasks, materials, and diagrams. Their drawings are more vivid and more creative than anything I had in mind when I brought them on as illustrators.

In addition to the people who helped me write the book, many others helped me think through its ideas. I am grateful to numerous colleagues with whom I've discussed research on intuitive theories and conceptual change over the years, including Elizabeth Allen, Melissa Allen, Eric Amsel, Dave Barner, Andy Baron, Hilary Barth, Igor Bascandziev, Jake Beck, Jonathan Beier, Peter Blake, Stefaan Blancke, Liz Bonawitz, Daphna Buchsbaum, Luke Butler, Prassede Calabi, Maureen Callanan, Eric Cheries, Micki Chi, John Coley, Sara Cordes, Kathleen Corriveau, Steve Croker, Fiery Cushman, Judith Danovitch, Yarrow Dunham, Natalie Emmons, Lisa Feigenson, Anna Fisher, Jason French, Ori Friedman, Erin Furtak, Patricia Ganea, Susan Gelman, Tamsin German, Will Gervais, Thalia Goldstein, Noah Goodman, Sara Gottlieb, Tom Griffiths, Justin Halberda, Kiley Hamlin, Paul Harris, Pat Hawley, Ben Heddy, Barbara Hofer, Bruce Hood, Jen Jipson, Suzie Johnson, Chuck Kalish, Deb Kelemen, Katie Kinzler, Josh Knobe, Melissa Koenig, Barbara Koslowski, Tamar Kushnir, Asheley Landrum, Jon Lane, Mathieu Le Corre, Sang Ah Lee, Cristine Legare, Marjaana Lindeman, Doug Lombardi, Tania Lombrozo, Jessecae Marsh, Amy Masnick, Koleen McCrink, Brad Morris, Stellan Ohlsson, Kristina Olson, John Opfer, Jonathan Phillips, Patrice Potvin, Lindsey Powell, Sandeep Prasada, Mike Ranney, Marjorie Rhodes, Bekah Richert, Reba Rosenberg, Karl Rosengren, Josh Rottman, Mark Sabbagh, Dylan Sabo, Bill Sandoval, Laurie Santos, Barbara Sarnecka, Rebecca Saxe, Michael Schneider, Laura Schulz, Ann Senghas, Viviane Seyrayani, Carissa Shafto, Pat Shafto, Anna Shusterman, Kristin Shutts, Gale Sinatra, Carol Smith, Erin Smith, Jesse Snedeker, Dave Sobel, Gregg Solomon, Liz Spelke, Mahesh Srinivasan, Christina Starmans, Elsbeth Stern, Josh Tenenbaum, Eric Thiessen, J. D. Trout, David Uttal, Tessa van Schijndel, Stella Vosniadou, Laura Wagner, Caren Walker, Sandy Waxman, Deena Weisberg, Michael Weisberg, Joseph Jay Williams, Nathan Winkler-Rhodes, Justin Wood, Jacki Woolley, Debbie Zaitchik, and Corinne Zimmerman.

I also would like to thank the many students who assisted me in studying intuitive theories and conceptual change over the years, including Katie

Abelson, Ella Afkhamnejad, Sarah Aronow-Werner, Alison Ban, Sarah Berkoff, Gillian Binnie, Sam Boland, Valerie Bourassa, Isabel Checa, Liza Comart, Alexander Flood-Bryzman, Jessica Gale, Rosie Glicklich, Ilana Glosser, Tori Halote, Julia Hamilton, Kelsey Harrington, Harper Hayes, Rourke Healey, Sarah Hennessy, Jen Hichar, Isabel Hubbard, Nick Hung, Jess Ingle, Mariam Kandil, Catherine Kiang, William Krause, Tori Leon, Alex Levin, Jai Levin, Gabrielle Lindquist, Madalyn Long, Lisa Matsukata, Kate McCallum, Caitlin Morgan, Roxie Myhrum, Anisha Narayan, Cara Neal, Allison Powers, Madeline Rasch, Max Rattner, Heidi Reiner, Lee Richardson, Dan Rubin-Wills, Amanda Schlitt, Tom Selstad, Columbia Shafer, Ilana Share, Devin Shermer, Rosie Silber-Marker, Debra Skinner, Jack Strelich, Lea Theodorou, Evan Thomas, Sharang Tickoo, Lester Tong, Josh Valcarcel, Andrea Villalobos, Linneen Warren, Dan Watson, Rachel Yoo, and Stefanie Young.

I must also acknowledge my colleagues in the Occidental College Psychology Department and the Occidental College Cognitive Science Department for their support and encouragement. Financial support was provided by the National Science Foundation (through a Faculty Early Career Award, DRL-0953384) and the James S. McDonnell Foundation (through an Understanding Human Cognition Scholar Award).

The support of my family was also invaluable. My parents, Joe and Marilyn, have always encouraged my academic pursuits and may be the only people who have read all my academic papers. My wife, Katie, has not read as many of my papers, but she too has been incredibly supportive and influential. Katie has probably influenced my thinking more than any of my professional colleagues, as she is the first person I talk to about anything and everything I find important.

Finally, one person stands out as the true inspiration for this book: Susan Carey. Susan was my graduate adviser and my reason for studying intuitive theories and conceptual change. Almost everything I know about the topic I learned from Susan. Indeed, almost everything anyone knows about the topic we learned from Susan. She broke new ground in defining and studying conceptual change, bringing the phenomenon to the fore in developmental research. This book would not have been possible without Susan, either in the proximate sense of her being my mentor or in the ultimate sense of her being a pioneering researcher. Thank you, Susan, for showing us all the power and importance of conceptual change.

Notes

Chapter 1: Why We Get the World Wrong

1 **this combination of factors:** Hotchkiss, 2001.

2 **Milk in the nineteenth:** Stenn, 1980.

2 **After pasteurization was introduced:** Hotchkiss, 2001; Potter, Kaufmann, Blake, and Feldman, 1984.

3 **Between 2010 and 2012** Olsen, MacKinnon, Goulding, Bean, and Slutsker, 2000; Mungai, Behravesh, and Gould, 2015.

3 **People are increasingly:** Potter, Kaufmann, Blake, and Feldman, 1984.

3 **Only 50 percent of American adults:** Pew Research Center, 2015.

4 **Most people denied:** Barber, 1961; Kuhn, 1962; Thagard, 1992.

4 **Conservatives are less likely:** Pew Research Center, 2009; Leiserowitz, Maibach, Roser-Renouf, Feinberg, and Howe, 2013; Lewandowsky, Ecker, Seifert, Schwarz, and Cook, 2012; Miller, Scott, and Okamoto, 2006.

5 **Galileo once decreed:** Galilei, 1632/1953.

5 **While few of us can articulate:** Gopnik, 1997; Keil, 1992; Murphy and Medin, 1985; Wellman and Gelman, 1992.

6 **It allows us to make inferences:** Gopnik and Wellman, 2012.

6 **Much of the causal knowledge:** Carey, 2009; Shtulman, 2008; Vosniadou, 1994a.

6 **Most theories posit causal:** Evans and Lane, 2011; Gelman and Legare, 2011; Shtulman and Lombrozo, 2016.

7 **To understand the scientific:** Chi, Roscoe, Slotta, Roy, and Chase, 2012; Wiser and Amin, 2001.

8   **What differentiates conceptual change:** Carey, 1991; Chi, 1992; Nersessian, 1989; Vosniadou and Brewer, 1987.

9   **Many people believe:** Jarrett, 2014; O'Connor, 2008.

10 **Third, intuitive theories:** Chi, 2005; Vosniadou, 1994a. For a contrary view, see DiSessa, 2008.

11 **They are also incredibly:** Clark, D'Angelo, and Schleigh, 2011; Eckstein and Kozhevnikov, 1997; Halloun and Hestenes, 1985; Howe, Tavares, and Devine, 2012; Kaiser, Proffitt, and McCloskey, 1985; Kaiser, McCloskey, and Proffitt, 1986; Liu and MacIsaac, 2005.

11 **Galileo, for instance, explained:** Galilei, 1590/1960.

13 **Yet, if we are asked to draw:** Kaiser, Jonides, and Alexander, 1986; Mc-Closkey, Caramazza, and Green, 1980.

13 **Four-year-olds thus deny:** Piaget, 1929/2007; Opfer and Siegler, 2004; Stavy and Wax, 1989.

13 **They are also less accurate:** Babai, Sekal, and Stavy, 2010; Goldberg and Thompson-Schill, 2009.

13 **Findings like these:** Shtulman and Harrington, 2016; Shtulman and Lombrozo, 2016; Shtulman and Valcarcel, 2012.

13 **discovery that scientific theories:** Chai-Elsholz, Carruthers, and Silec, 2011.

14 **In some cases, our scientific:** Foisy, Potvin, Riopel, and Masson, 2015; Masson, Potvin, Riopel, and Foisy, 2014.

14 **"I'm not stupid:** Buchholz, 2015.

15 **Most science deniers:** Kahan, Peters, Wittlin, Slovic, Ouelette, Braman, and Mandel, 2012.

16 **Studies have shown:** Au, Chan, Chan, Cheung, Ho, and Ip, 2008.

16 **better we understand thermal:** Kempton, 1986.

16 **better we understand how the body:** McFerran and Mukhopadhyay, 2013.

Chapter 2: Matter

20 **If you have ever:** Piaget, 1941/2000.

21 **Not until middle school:** Elkind, 1961; Gottesman, 1973; Miller, 1973.

21 **children master the logic:** Siegler, DeLoache, and Eisenberg, 2010.

21 **Even within the domain:** Elkind, 1961.

22 **Piaget's successors:** Field, 1987.

22 **In one study:** Mermelstein and Meyer, 1969.

22 **Surprisingly, the instruction:** Brainerd and Allen, 1971; Field, 1987.

23 **Children cannot perceive atoms:** Toulmin and Goodfield, 1982.

23 **This collection of perceptions:** Smith, 2007.

24 **They also vacillate:** Ibid.

24 **They also claim that air:** Carey, 1991.

24 **four-year-olds were shown:** Kohn, 1993.

24   **children can be prompted:** Hardy, Jonen, Möller, and Stern, 2006; Kloos, Fisher, and Van Orden, 2010; Rappolt-Schlichtmann, Tenenbaum, Koepke, and Fischer, 2007.

25   **even purer demonstration:** Smith, Solomon, and Carey, 2005.

26   **This notion leads them:** Nakhleh, Samarapungavan, and Saglam, 2005; Novick and Nussbaum, 1981.

28   **Finally, between twelve:** Piaget, 1937/1954.

28   **Infants may fail:** Diamond and Goldman-Rakic, 1989.

28   **Their eyes reveal:** Diamond, 1985.

29   **They look longer:** Baillargeon, Spelke, and Wasserman, 1985.

29   **Young infants thus demonstrate:** Baillargeon, 1987.

29   **Such events:** Spelke, 1994.

30   **eight-month-old infants:** Huntley-Fenner, Carey, and Solimando, 2002; see also Rosenberg, 2008.

30   **lemurs form precise expectations:** Mahajan, Barnes, Blanco, and Santos, 2009.

30   **We can trace:** Scholl, 2001.

32   **This "mystery material" task:** Smith, Carey, and Wiser, 1985.

32   **Smith introduced the concept:** Smith and Unger, 1997.

33   **In follow-up studies, Smith:** Smith, 2007; Smith, Maclin, Grosslight, and Davis, 1997.

35   **Highlighting these parallels:** Moss and Case, 1999.

36   **They interfere with:** Shtulman and Valcarcel, 2012; Shtulman and Harrington, 2016.

36   **Even though we may recognize:** Potvin, Masson, Lafortune, and Cyr, 2015.

36   **one speeded-classification study:** Shtulman, unpublished data.

36   **Antoine Lavoisier:** Bynum, 2012.

Chapter 3: Energy

39   **members of the academy:** Middleton, 1971.

40   **their understanding of freezing:** Wiser and Carey, 1983.

41   **Florentine experimenters' view:** Ibid.

42   **This substance, termed *caloric*:** Fox, 1971.

42   **Researcher: You just:** Chiou and Anderson, 2010.

43   **"Some of the cold:** Chang and Linn, 2013; Erickson, 1979.

43   **dueling-substance view:** Erickson, 1979.

44   **Most of us assume:** Clough and Driver, 1985; Clark, 2006.

44   **Pound for pound:** Cross and Rotkin, 1975.

45   **At 200° Fahrenheit:** Corlett, Wilson, and Corlett, 1995.

45   **Physics experts claim:** Slotta, Chi, and Joram, 1995.

45   **Chi and her colleagues:** Chi, Slotta, and De Leeuw, 1994.

46   **they are *ongoing*:** Chi, Roscoe, Slotta, Roy, and Chase, 2012; Slotta and Chi, 2006.

47   **chicken-and-egg problem:** Slotta and Chi, 2006.

48   **Many people actually think:** Hrepic, Zollman, and Rebello, 2010.

48   **"As the sound moves:** Hrepic, Zollman, and Rebello, 2010.

49   **children between six and ten:** Mazens and Lautrey, 2003.

49   **same pattern:** Lautrey and Mazens, 2004.

50   **Child: Your ear sends:** Barman, Barman, and Miller, 1996.

50   **Extramissionist beliefs:** Cottrell and Winer, 1994.

51   **Like most adults:** Lindberg, 1976.

51   **conviction of our extramissionist:** Winer, Cottrell, Karefilaki, and Gregg, 1996; Winer and Cottrell, 1996; Winer, Cottrell, Karefilaki, and Chronister, 1996.

52   **researchers devised a tutorial:** Gregg, Winer, Cottrell, Hedman, and Fournier, 2001.

52   **Studies that have directly probed:** Reiner, Slotta, Chi, and Resnick, 2000.

53   **Most burns each year:** American Burn Association, 2013; Mayo Clinic, 2014; Dokov and Dokova, 2011.

53   **PhDs in physics:** Lewis and Linn, 1994.

54   **This anecdote fits:** Shtulman and Harrington, 2016; Kelemen, Rottman, and Seston, 2013; Goldberg and Thompson-Schill, 2009.

54   **monitored scientists' brains:** Dunbar, Fugelsang, and Stein, 2007; Foisy, Potvin, Riopel, and Masson, 2015.

55   **one fMRI study:** Masson, Potvin, Riopel, and Foisy, 2014.

Chapter 4: Gravity

57   **William James:** James, 1890/1950.

57   **Four decades of research:** Spelke and Kinzler, 2007.

58   **they look longer:** Spelke, Breinlinger, Macomber, and Jacobson, 1992.

59   **infants were shown two boxes:** Needham and Baillargeon, 1993.

59   **Nevertheless, infants:** Baillargeon, Needham, and DeVos, 1992.

59   **Nine-month-olds:** Baillargeon and Hanko-Summers, 1990.

59   **expectations about how much:** Krist, 2010.

60   **two toy pigs:** Hespos and Baillargeon, 2008.

61   **Both expectations:** Spelke, 1994.

61   **Monkeys and apes:** Mendes, Rakoczy, and Call, 2008; Santos, 2004.

61   **They are surprised:** Cacchione and Krist, 2004.

62   **psychologist Bruce Hood:** Hood, 1995.

64   **Hood considered both:** Hood, 1998; Hood, Santos, and Fieselman, 2000.

64   **solid plank of wood:** Hood, Carey, and Prasada, 2000.

64   **They ignore the barrier:** Berthier, DeBlois, Poirier, Novak, and Clifton, 2000; Shutts, Keen, and Spelke, 2006.

66   **track toddlers' gaze:** Lee and Kuhlmeier, 2013.

66 **likelihood that solidity:** Bascandziev and Harris, 2011; Hood, Wilson, and Dyson, 2006.

66 **Human toddlers are not:** Cacchione and Call, 2010; Hood, Hauser, Anderson, and Santos, 1999; Osthaus, Slater, and Lea, 2003.

66 **gravity errors:** Santos, 2004; Santos, Seelig, and Hauser, 2006.

66 **one ambitious study:** Cacchione, Call, and Zingg, 2009.

67 **apes' eyes reveal:** Cacchione and Burkart, 2012; Santos and Hauser, 2002; Santos, Seelig, and Hauser, 2006.

67 **When nonhuman animals:** Hood, Hauser, Anderson, and Santos, 1999; Osthaus, Slater, and Lea, 2003.

68 **Other animals can watch:** Tomasello and Carpenter, 2007; Tomasello and Herrmann, 2010.

68 **Nor can they be talked into:** Jaswal, 2010.

68 **Another way to help:** Bascandziev and Harris, 2010; Joh, Jaswal, and Keen, 2011.

68 **Around 7 percent:** Public Policy Polling, 2013.

68 **US National Aeronautics and Space Administration:** Shermer, 2001.

69 **We think about falling:** Frappart, Raijmakers, and Frède, 2014; Galili, 2001.

70 **Imagine that you have:** Blown and Bryce, 2013.

72 **"We cannot start:** Neurath, 1973.

Chapter 5: Motion

73 **Medieval physicists:** Fischbein, Stavy, and Ma-Naim, 1989; McCloskey, 1983b.

74 **Many of us have memorized:** Champagne, Klopfer, and Anderson, 1980; Halloun and Hestenes, 1985.

76 **Take the task of drawing:** Eckstein and Kozhevnikov, 1997; Kaiser, Proffitt, and McCloskey, 1985; McCloskey, 1983b.

77 **They appear to believe:** Kaiser, McCloskey, and Proffitt, 1986; McCloskey, Caramazza, and Green, 1980.

77 **participants were asked:** Kaiser, Jonides, and Alexander, 1986.

78 **Quite often:** Clement, 1982; Palmer and Flanagan, 1997.

79 **On the other hand:** Clement, 1993; Minstrell, 1982.

79 **"The momentum from:** McCloskey, 1983b; Steinberg, Brown, and Clement, 1990.

79 **"In moving:** Clagett, 1961.

79 **"motion is not continued:** Steinberg, Brown, and Clement, 1990.

80 **golf ball:** McCloskey, 1983a.

81 **Wile E. Coyote–esque:** Roser, Fugelsang, Handy, Dunbar, and Gazzaniga, 2009.

81 **But if those paths:** Kaiser, Proffitt, and Anderson, 1985.

81   **Likewise, if asked:** Kaiser, Proffitt, Whelan, and Hecht, 1992.
81   **elementary-schoolers were asked:** Howe, Tavares, and Devine, 2012.
82   **Even two-year-olds show:** Kim and Spelke, 1999.
82   **One compelling demonstration:** Freyd and Jones, 1994; Kozhevnikov and Hegarty, 2001.
83   **Researchers recruited physics students:** Kim and Pak, 2002.
83   **Microworlds are virtual:** Masson and Vázquez-Abad, 2006; White, 1984.
83   **popular video game *Enigmo*:** Masson, Bub, and Lalonde, 2011.
84   **Similar results have been obtained:** Miller, Lehman, and Koedinger, 1999; Renken and Nunez, 2013; Zacharia and Olympiou, 2011.
85   **gravity, in general, works:** Orwig, 2015.
85   **The problem is that abstract:** Kirschner, Sweller, and Clark, 2006.
85   **Education researcher Maggie Renken:** Renken and Nunez, 2010; see also Klahr and Nigam, 2004.
86   **One such method:** Clement, 1993.
87   **Clement has compared lessons:** Ibid.
88   **"Not All Preconceptions:** Clement, Brown, and Zietsman, 1989.
88   **"too many talks:** DiSessa, 2008.

Chapter 6: Cosmos

91   **Questions like these:** Harrison, 1981.
92   **Humans as a species** Couprie, 2011.
93   **"Round like a ball":** Nussbaum and Novak, 1976; Vosniadou and Brewer, 1992.
93   **For decades, Vosniadou:** Vosniadou and Brewer, 1992, 1994; Vosniadou, Skopeliti, and Ikospentaki, 2004, 2005; Diakidoy, Vosniadou and Hawks, 1997; Samarapungavan, Vosniadou and Brewer, 1996.
97   **Younger children tend:** Vosniadou, 1994a.
97   **Some psychologists:** Hannust and Kikas, 2010; Nobes, Martin, and Panagiotaki, 2005.
98   **They select responses:** Panagiotaki, Nobes, and Banerjee, 2006; Straatemeier, van der Maas, and Jansen, 2008; Vosniadou, Skopeliti, and Ikospentaki, 2004.
98   **multiple-choice tests:** Vosniadou, Skopeliti, and Ikospentaki, 2005.
99   **child-friendly tutorials:** Hayes, Goodhew, Heit, and Gillan, 2003.
100   **Indian children's mental models:** Samarapungavan, Vosniadou and Brewer, 1996.
100   **Native American children:** Diakidoy, Vosniadou and Hawks, 1997.
101   **Samoan children project:** Vosniadou, 1994b.
101   **Cross-cultural diversity:** Siegal, Butterworth, and Newcombe, 2004.
102   **"Well, what would it:** Anscombe, 1959.
103   **Prior to that discovery:** Vosniadou and Brewer, 1994.

104 **This progression in children's:** Harlow, Swanson, Nylund-Gibson, and Truxler, 2011.

106 **over 90 percent:** Schneps, Sadler, Woll, and Crouse, 1988.

106 **researchers attempted to correct:** Dunbar, Fugelsang, and Stein, 2007.

106 **One study found that adults:** Carbon, 2010.

Chapter 7: Earth

109 **Far from our everyday:** Marshak, 2009.

110 **prevailing intuition:** Le Grand, 1988; Marvin, 1973; Oreskes, 1999.

110 **"Lemuria":** Sclater, 1864.

111 **"It is just as if:** Wegener, 1929/1966.

112 **They already knew:** Oreskes, 1999.

112 **By what mechanism:** Gould, 1992.

112 **"The great ocean basins:** Willis, 1910.

112 **"If we are to believe:** Chamberlin, 1928.

113 **One wide-scale study:** Libarkin and Anderson, 2005.

114 **common misconceptions:** Libarkin, Anderson, Dahl, Beilfuss, Boone, and Kurdziel, 2005; Marques and Thompson, 1997.

115 **researchers taught a group:** Sanchez and Wiley, 2014.

117 **"It's possible for dirt:** Libarkin and Schneps, 2012.

117 **"We are always:** Darwin, 1859.

118 **event that occurred:** Catley and Novick, 2009.

118 **Our estimates are off:** Lee, Liu, Price, and Kendall, 2011; Trend, 2001.

118 **amount of time:** National Science Board, 2014.

119 **It is now abundantly clear:** Kolbert, 2006.

120 **Climate is considered:** Lombardi and Sinatra, 2012.

120 **"We keep hearing:** Sheppard, 2015.

120 **researchers asked people:** Li, Johnson, and Zaval, 2011.

121 **same findings:** Donner and McDaniels, 2013.

121 **Commonly cited green activities:** Boyes and Stanisstreet, 1993; Punter, Ochando-Pardo, and Garcia, 2011.

122 **we are significantly more inclined:** Skamp, Boyes, and Stanisstreet, 2013.

122 **America is deeply divided:** Leiserowitz, Maibach, Roser-Renouf, Feinberg, and Howe, 2013.

123 **Clearly, there are:** National Academies of Sciences, Engineering, and Medicine, 2016b.

123 **psychologist Michael Ranney:** Ranney and Clark, 2016.

124 **Nevertheless, when told:** Lewandowsky, Gignac, and Vaughan, 2013; Myers, Maibach, Peters, and Leiserowitz, 2015.

124 **The more widespread:** Cialdini and Goldstein, 2004; Shtulman, 2013.

124 **participants were asked:** Ding, Maibach, Zhao, Roser-Renouf, and Leiserowitz, 2011; see also Van der Linden, Leiserowitz, Feinberg, and Maibach, 2015.

125 **"Wednesday is Earth Day:** Obama, 2015.

Chapter 8: Life

133   **five-year-olds proved:** Callanan and Oakes, 1992.

133   **If their parents:** Carey, 1985.

135   **Both videos:** Bidet-Ildei, Kitromilides, Orliaguet, Pavlova, and Gentaz, 2014; see also Kuhlmeier, Troje, and Lee, 2010.

136   **This pattern:** Anggoro, Waxman, and Medin, 2008; Hatano, Siegler, Richards, Inagaki, Stavy, and Wax, 1993; Piaget, 1929/2007.

136   **"worms have:** Carey, 1988.

136   **Lucy's reluctance:** Carey, 1985; Gutheil, Vera, and Keil, 1998; Herrmann, Waxman, and Medin, 2010; Stavy and Wax, 1989.

139   **Indeed, urban children's:** Coley, 2012; Medin, Waxman, Woodring, and Washinawatok, 2010; Ross, Medin, Coley, and Atran, 2003.

140   **They are also more likely:** Geerdts, Van de Walle, and LoBue, 2015.

140   **"The best news:** Strohminger, personal communication.

140   **five biological principles:** Lazar and Torney-Purta, 1991; Panagiotaki, Nobes, Ashraf, and Aubby, 2015; Speece and Brent, 1984; Slaughter and Griffiths, 2007.

141   **Children in modern:** Rosengren, Miller, Gutiérrez, Chow, Schein, and Anderson, 2014.

141   **children's books on death:** Ibid.; Poling and Hupp, 2008.

142   **If young children:** Astuti and Harris, 2008; Harris and Giménez, 2005.

142   **religious testimony:** Bering, 2006.

143   **They know that flowers:** Zaitchik, Iqbal, and Carey, 2014.

143   **psychologist Virginia Slaughter:** Slaughter and Lyons, 2003.

144   **study is reminiscent:** Onion, 2010.

145   **Slaughter and her colleagues:** Slaughter and Griffiths, 2007.

145   **finding is consistent:** Webb, 1993.

146   **A great example is:** MacAvoy, 2015.

146   **Most of us never:** Bering, 2002.

147   **In conversations:** Leddon, Waxman, and Medin, 2011.

147   **We know far less:** Coley, Medin, Proffitt, Lynch, and Atran, 1999.

147   **when asked explicitly:** Shtulman, unpublished data.

147   **Perhaps the most striking:** Goldberg and Thompson-Schill, 2009.

148   **When these people:** Zaitchik and Solomon, 2008.

Chapter 9: Growth

150   **When this thought experiment:** Klavir and Leiser, 2002.

150   **In the history of biology:** Bechtel and Richardson, 1998.

151   **Many years before:** Inagaki and Hatano, 1993; Morris, Taplin, and Gelman, 2000.

152   **But to preschoolers:** Anggoro, Waxman, and Medin, 2008.

152 **Several years before:** Inagaki and Hatano, 1996.

152 **it's common practice:** Opfer and Siegler, 2004.

154 **researchers asked four-year-olds:** Nguyen, McCullough, and Noble, 2011.

154 **In a follow-up study:** Ibid.

156 **We know this from studies:** Johnson and Carey, 1998.

158 **But children can:** Gripshover and Markman, 2013.

158 **Connections between healthy:** McFerran and Mukhopadhyay, 2013.

159 **Medical experts cite:** Livingston and Zylke, 2012.

159 **they asked participants:** McFerran and Mukhopadhyay, 2013.

160 **"I'm going to tell you:** Gelman and Wellman, 1991.

161 **Researchers have posed:** Astuti, Solomon, and Carey, 2004; Atran, Medin, Lynch, Vapnarsky, Ek, and Sousa, 2001; Sousa, Atran, and Medin, 2002; Diesendruck and Haber, 2009; Waxman, Medin, and Ross, 2007.

161 **human sociology:** Diesendruck and Haber, 2009; Donovan, 2014; Haslam, Rothschild and Ernst, 2000; Kimel, Huesmann, Kunst, and Halperin, 2016.

162 **organ donation:** Meyer, Leslie, Gelman and Stilwell, 2013; Sanner, 2001.

162 **"A Change of Heart":** Sylvia, 1997.

163 **Daughter: When I grow up:** Carey, 1985.

165 **Even as adults:** Quoidbach, Gilbert, and Wilson, 2013.

Chapter 10: Inheritance

168 **Most people are wary:** Priest, Bonfadelli, and Rusanen, 2003.

168 **In one recent survey:** Lusk, 2015.

169 **Most people judge:** Christensen, Jayaratne, Roberts, Kardia, and Petty, 2010.

169 **There is no single gene:** Rosenberg, Pritchard, Weber, Cann, Kidd, Zhivotovsky, and Feldman, 2002.

169 **race a social construct:** United Nations Educational, Scientific and Cultural Organization, 1970.

169 **One reason people lack:** Blancke, Van Breusegem, De Jaeger, Braeckman, and Van Montagu, 2015; Dar-Nimrod and Heine, 2011.

169 **Children believe that:** Gelman and Wellman, 1991.

170 **link between genes:** Dar-Nimrod and Heine, 2011; Kronberger, Wagner, and Nagata, 2014.

170 **we are loath:** National Academies of Sciences, Engineering, and Medicine, 2016a.

170 **Children know that parents:** Johnson and Solomon, 1997.

171 **Psychologist Gregg Solomon:** Solomon, Johnson, Zaitchik, and Carey, 1996.

172 **In a follow-up study:** Solomon, 2002.

174 **But even these children:** Byers-Heinlein and Garcia, 2015.

176 **This point is nicely:** Keil and Batterman, 1984.

178   **"Suppose doctors took:** Keil, 1992.

179   **Child: They messed it up:** Ibid.

180   **Indeed, this gradient:** Zaitchik and Solomon, 2009.

181   **psychologist Ken Springer:** Springer, 1995.

182   **But they have no conception:** Venville, Gribble, and Donovan, 2005.

182   **Most adults believe:** Duncan and Tseng, 2011.

182   **simple trait-based understanding:** Shea, 2015.

184   **Merely reading:** Dar-Nimrod, Cheung, Ruby, and Heine, 2014.

184   **Equally problematic:** Dar-Nimrod and Heine, 2006.

184   **mathematics achievement:** Spelke, 2005; Spencer, Steele, and Quinn, 1999.

Chapter 11: Illness

186   **Curiously, the insular cortex:** Wicker, Keysers, Plailly, Royet, Gallese, and Rizzolatti, 2003.

186   **We produce more:** Schaller, Miller, Gervais, Yager, and Chen, 2010.

186   **one far-ranging study:** Curtis, Aunger, and Rabie, 2004.

187   **evolutionary logic behind disgust:** Haidt, McCauley, and Rozin, 1994.

187   **Our hypersensitivity:** Rozin, Millman, and Nemeroff, 1986.

188   **They are not keen:** Stevenson, Oaten, Case, Repacholi, and Wagland, 2010.

188   **Children also have:** Widen and Russell, 2013.

189   **"A grasshopper is washing:** Fallon, Rozin, and Pliner, 1984.

190   **To circumvent this:** Rozin, Fallon, and Augustoni-Ziskind, 1985.

191   **Food picks up:** Dawson, Han, Cox, Black, and Simmons, 2007.

191   **Ravens, for instance:** Heinrich, 1999.

191   **rule we seem:** Rozin, 1990.

193   **"humors":** Thagard, 1999.

193   **Bloodletting:** Miton, Claidière, and Mercier, 2015.

193   **Of course, bad air:** Johnson, 2007.

194   **Its successor:** Lederberg, 2000; Thagard, 1999.

195   **All this talk:** Au, Sidle, and Rollins, 1993; Blacker and LoBue, 2016; Kalish, 1996; Siegal and Share, 1990; Springer, Nguyen, and Samaniego, 1996.

195   **one shocking demonstration:** DeJesus, Shutts, and Kinzler, 2015.

196   **This point:** Solomon and Cassimatis, 1999.

196   **Another study:** Raman and Gelman, 2005.

197   **Immunologists have found:** Zuger, 2003.

198   **Think Biology:** Au, Chan, Chan, Cheung, Ho, and Ip, 2008.

199   **Au and her colleagues:** Zamora, Romo, and Au, 2006.

200   **Christians and Jews:** Bearon and Koenig, 1990.

200   **folk belief:** Legare and Gelman, 2008; Legare and Gelman, 2009.

201   **similar developmental pattern:** Nguyen and Rosengren, 2004; Raman and Gelman, 2004.

202   **"Peter and Mark:** Raman and Winer, 2004.

202 **Cancer looms:** Cancer Research UK, 2015.

Chapter 12: Adaptation

203 **Evolution had been contemplated:** Mayr, 1982.
203 **What Darwin discovered:** Gregory, 2009; Mayr, 1982.
204 **Darwin himself:** Darwin, 1859.
205 **They treated species:** Gould, 1996; Mayr, 2001.
206 **Fifty years after:** Bowler, 1992.
206 **"Nothing in biology:** Dobzhansky, 1973.
207 **This question is:** Shtulman, 2006; Shtulman and Calabi, 2013; Shtulman and Schulz, 2008.
209 **Consistent with this idea:** Coley and Tanner, 2015; Gregory, 2009; Shtulman and Calabi, 2012.
209 **The problem is:** Bishop and Anderson, 1990; Shtulman, 2006; Ware and Gelman, 2014.
210 **Physicists tell us:** Roughgarden, 2004.
210 **His voyage:** Lack, 1947/1983.
211 **Hans Christian Andersen's:** Andersen, 1844/1981.
212 **We refer to biological:** Gelman, Ware, and Kleinberg, 2010.
212 **children (ages four to nine):** Shtulman and Schulz, 2008.
213 **In a follow-up study:** Emmons and Kelemen, 2015.
214 **"natural selection left:** Onion, 2015.
214 **Darwin gleaned:** Millman and Smith, 1997; Gruber, 1981.
215 **introductory ecology students:** Zimmerman and Cuddington, 2007.
215 **recognized as true:** Shtulman and Valcarcel, 2012.
215 **Inspired by this finding:** Shtulman, 2014.
216 **empirical point of view:** De Waal, 2006.
217 **public's reaction:** Brulliard, 2016.
218 **US National Science Teachers Association:** National Science Teachers Association, 2013.
218 **In some school systems:** Berkman and Plutzer, 2011; Mead and Mates, 2009.
218 **Sometimes adaptation:** Evans, Spiegel, Gram, Frazier, Tare, Thompson, and Diamond, 2010; Opfer, Nehm, and Ha, 2012.

Chapter 13: Ancestry

221 **Teddy assumed:** Catley, Novick, and Shade, 2010; Shtulman, 2006.
225 **It's conceivable:** Poling and Evans, 2004; Shtulman, 2006.
225 **visual representations:** Gould, 1997.
225 **In recent years, cladograms:** Catley and Novick, 2008; MacDonald and Wiley, 2012.
227 **Accordingly, they misinterpret:** Meir, Perry, Herron, and Kingsolver, 2007; Novick and Catley, 2007; Phillips, Novick, Catley, and Funk, 2012.

228   **Further complicating matters:** Catley and Novick, 2008; MacDonald and Wiley, 2012.

229   **indiscriminate extra features:** Tufte, 2001.

229   **As a consequence:** MacDonald and Wiley, 2012; MacFadden, Oviedo, Seymour, and Ellis, 2012.

229   **likelihood that an extinct species:** Mayr, 2001.

230   **In a study I conducted:** Shtulman and Checa, 2012.

232   **"tree of life":** Gould, 1997.

233   **Primates are:** Mora, Tittensor, Adl, Simpson, and Worm, 2011.

233   **Even though this cladogram:** Pennisi, 2003.

234   **ask a preschooler:** Evans, 2001; Kelemen, 2004; Samarapungavan and Wiers, 1997.

235   **religious beliefs:** Miller, Scott, and Okamoto, 2006; see also Gervais, 2015; Poling and Evans, 2004.

235   **Countries with high levels:** Heddy and Nadelson, 2012.

235   **These findings hold:** Heddy and Nadelson, 2013.

235   **That fervor:** IFLScience, 2015.

236   **This hostile reaction:** Berkman and Plutzer, 2011.

236   **Religion and evolution:** Mayr, 1982.

237   **"I am almost:** Darwin, 1844.

237   **Gallup has polled:** Newport, 2010.

237   **40 to 45 percent:** Ibid.

Chapter 14: How to Get the World Right

241   **In 1802:** Pemberton, Gingras, and MacEachern, 2007.

244   **Historically, the reclassification:** Thagard, 2014.

244   **such reclassifications:** Chi, Slotta, and De Leeuw, 1994; Chi, Roscoe, Slotta, Roy, and Chase, 2012.

246   **One nice example:** Biederman and Shiffrar, 1987.

248   **researchers created:** McNeil, Fyfe, and Dunwiddie, 2015.

250   **This illusion:** Rozenblit and Keil, 2002; Mills and Keil, 2004; Keil, 2003.

251   **It has even been documented:** Lawson, 2006.

252   **"The difficulty lies:** Keynes, 1936.

254   **It entails injecting:** Riedel, 2005.

254   **disease that had once:** Orenstein, Papania, and Wharton, 2004.

254   **Then, in 2014:** Centers for Disease Control, 2015.

255   **Laws limiting personal:** National Conference of State Legislatures, 2016; Horne, Powell, Hummel, and Holyoak, 2015.

255   **"To the grownups:** Kuo, 2012.

References

American Burn Association (2013). *National burn repository*. Chicago: American Burn Association.

Andersen, H. C. (1844/1981). The ugly duckling. In L. Owens (ed. and trans.), *The complete Hans Christian Andersen fairy tales* (pp. 15–20). New York: Avenel Books.

Anggoro, F. K., Waxman, S. R., and Medin, D. L. (2008). Naming practices and the acquisition of key biological concepts: Evidence from English and Indonesian. *Psychological Science, 19*, 314–319.

Anscombe, G. E. M. (1959) *An introduction to Wittgenstein's Tractatus*. New York: Harper.

Astuti, R., and Harris, P. L. (2008). Understanding mortality and the life of the ancestors in rural Madagascar. *Cognitive Science, 32*, 713–740.

Astuti, R., Solomon, G. E., and Carey, S. (2004). Constraints on conceptual development: A case study of the acquisition of folkbiological and folksociological knowledge in Madagascar. *Monographs of the Society for Research in Child Development*, 1–161.

Atran, S., Medin, D., Lynch, E., Vapnarsky, V., Ek, E. U., and Sousa, P. (2001). Folkbiology doesn't come from folkpsychology: Evidence from Yukatek Maya in cross-cultural perspective. *Journal of Cognition and Culture, 1*, 3–42.

Au, T. K. F., Chan, C. K., Chan, T. K., Cheung, M. W., Ho, J. Y., and Ip, G. W. (2008). Folkbiology meets microbiology: A study of conceptual and behavioral change. *Cognitive Psychology, 57*, 1–19.

Au, T. K., Sidle, A. L., and Rollins, K. B. (1993). Developing an intuitive understanding of conservation and contamination: Invisible particles as a plausible mechanism. *Developmental Psychology, 29*, 286–299.

Babai, R., Sekal, R., and Stavy, R. (2010). Persistence of the intuitive conception of living things in adolescence. *Journal of Science Education and Technology, 19*, 20–26.

Baillargeon, R. (1987). Object permanence in 3½- and 4½-month-old infants. *Developmental Psychology, 23*, 655–664.

Baillargeon, R., and Hanko-Summers, S. (1990). Is the top object adequately supported by the bottom object? Young infants' understanding of support relations. *Cognitive Development, 5*, 29–53.

Baillargeon, R., Needham, A., and DeVos, J. (1992). The development of young infants' intuitions about support. *Early Development and Parenting, 1*, 69–78.

Baillargeon, R., Spelke, E. S., and Wasserman, S. (1985). Object permanence in five-month-old infants. *Cognition, 20*, 191–208.

Barber, B. (1961). Resistance by scientists to scientific discovery. *Science, 134*, 596–602.

Barman, C. R., Barman, N. S., and Miller, J. A. (1996). Two teaching methods and students' understanding of sound. *School Science and Mathematics, 96*, 63–67.

Bascandziev, I., and Harris, P. L. (2010). The role of testimony in young children's solution of a gravity-driven invisible displacement task. *Cognitive Development, 25*, 233–246.

Bascandziev, I., and Harris, P. L. (2011). Gravity is not the only ruler for falling events: Young children stop making the gravity error after receiving additional perceptual information about the tubes mechanism. *Journal of Experimental Child Psychology, 109*, 468–477.

Bearon, L. B., and Koenig, H. G. (1990). Religious cognitions and use of prayer in health and illness. *Gerontologist, 30*, 249–253.

Bechtel, W., and Richardson, R. C. (1998). Vitalism. In E. Craig (ed.), *Routledge encyclopedia of philosophy* (pp. 639–643). London: Routledge.

Bering, J. M. (2002). Intuitive conceptions of dead agents' minds: The natural foundations of afterlife beliefs as phenomenological boundary. *Journal of Cognition and Culture, 2*, 263–308.

———(2006). The folk psychology of souls. *Behavioral and Brain Sciences, 29*, 453–498.

Berkman, M. B., and Plutzer, E. (2011). Defeating creationism in the courtroom, but not in the classroom. *Science, 331*, 404–405.

Berthier, N. E., DeBlois, S., Poirier, C. R., Novak, J. A., and Clifton, R. K. (2000). Where's the ball? Two- and three-year-olds reason about unseen events. *Developmental Psychology, 36*, 394–401.

Bidet-Ildei, C., Kitromilides, E., Orliaguet, J. P., Pavlova, M., and Gentaz, E. (2014). Preference for point-light human biological motion in newborns: Contribution of translational displacement. *Developmental Psychology, 50*, 113–120.

Biederman, I., and Shiffrar, M. M. (1987). Sexing day-old chicks: A case study and expert systems analysis of a difficult perceptual-learning task. *Journal of Experimental Psychology: Learning, Memory, and Cognition, 13*, 640–645.

Bishop, B. and Anderson, C.A. (1990). Student conceptions of natural selection and its role in evolution. *Journal of Research in Science Teaching, 27*, 415–427.

Blacker, K. A., and LoBue, V. (2016). Behavioral avoidance of contagion in children. *Journal of Experimental Child Psychology, 143*, 162–170.

Blancke, S., Van Breusegem, F., De Jaeger, G., Braeckman, J., and Van Montagu, M. (2015). Fatal attraction: The intuitive appeal of GMO opposition. *Trends in Plant Science, 22*, 1360–1385.

Blown, E. J., and Bryce, T. G. K. (2013). Thought-experiments about gravity in the history of science and in research into children's thinking. *Science and Education, 22*, 419–481.

Bowler, P. J. (1992). *The eclipse of Darwinism: Anti-Darwinian evolution theories in the decades around 1900*. Baltimore: John Hopkins University Press.

Boyes, E., and Stanisstreet, M. (1993). The greenhouse effect: children's perceptions of causes, consequences, and cures. *International Journal of Science Education, 15*, 531–552.

Brainerd, C. J., and Allen, T. W. (1971). Experimental inductions of the conservation of "first-order" quantitative invariants. *Psychological Bulletin, 75*, 128–144.

Brulliard, K. (2016, May 19). People love watching nature on nest cams—until it gets grisly. *Washington Post*. Retrieved from www.washingtonpost.com/news/animalia /wp/ 2016/05/19/when-nest-cams-get-gruesome-some-viewers-cant-take-it/.

Buchholz, L. (2015). I know what's best for the health of my family, and it's magical thinking. *Womanspiration, 11*. Retrieved from http://reductress.com/post /i-know-whats-best-for-the-health-of-my-family-and-its-magical-thinking/.

Byers-Heinlein, K., and Garcia, B. (2015). Bilingualism changes children's beliefs about what is innate. *Developmental Science, 18*, 344–350.

Bynum, W. (2012). *A little history of science*. New Haven, CT: Yale University Press.

Cacchione, T., and Burkart, J. M. (2012). Dissociation between seeing and acting: Insights from common marmosets (*Callithrix jacchus*). *Behavioural Processes, 89*, 52–60.

Cacchione, T., and Call, J. (2010). Intuitions about gravity and solidity in great apes: The tubes task. *Developmental Science, 13*, 320–330.

Cacchione, T., Call, J., and Zingg, R. (2009). Gravity and solidity in four great ape species (*Gorilla gorilla, Pongo pygmaeus, Pan troglodytes, Pan paniscus*): Vertical and horizontal variations of the table task. *Journal of Comparative Psychology, 123*, 168–180.

Cacchione, T., and Krist, H. (2004). Recognizing impossible object relations: intuitions about support in chimpanzees (*Pan troglodytes*). *Journal of Comparative Psychology, 118*, 140–148.

Callanan, M. A., and Oakes, L. M. (1992). Preschoolers' questions and parents' explanations: Causal thinking in everyday activity. *Cognitive Development, 7*, 213–233.

Cancer Research UK (2015, Oct. 26). Ten persistent myths about cancer that are false. *The Intendent*. Retrieved from www.independent.co.uk/author/cancer -research-uk.

Carbon, C. C. (2010). The earth is flat when personally significant experiences with the sphericity of the earth are absent. *Cognition, 116*, 130–135.

Carey, S. (1985). *Conceptual change in childhood*. Cambridge, MA: MIT Press.

———(1988). Conceptual differences between children and adults. *Mind and Language, 3*, 167–181.

———(1991). Knowledge acquisition: Enrichment or conceptual change? In S. Carey and R. Gelman (eds.), *The epigenesis of mind: Essays in biology and cognition* (pp. 257–291). Hillsdale, NJ: Lawrence Erlbaum.

———(2009). *The origin of concepts*. Oxford, UK: Oxford University Press.

Catley, K. M., and Novick, L. R. (2008). Seeing the wood for the trees: An analysis of evolutionary diagrams in biology textbooks. *BioScience, 58*, 976–987.

———(2009). Digging deep: Exploring college students' knowledge of macroevolutionary time. *Journal of Research in Science Teaching, 46*, 311–332.

Catley, K. M., Novick, L. R., and Shade, C. K. (2010). Interpreting evolutionary diagrams: When topology and process conflict. *Journal of Research in Science Teaching, 47*, 861–882.

Centers for Disease Control (2015). *Measles cases and outbreaks*. Retrieved from www.cdc.gov/measles/cases-outbreaks.html.

Chai-Elsholz, R., Carruthers, L., and Silec, T. (2011). *Palimpsests and the literary imagination of medieval England: Collected essays*. London: Palgrave Macmillan.

Chamberlin, R. T. (1928). Some of the objections to Wegener's theory. In W. A. J. M. van Waterschoot van der Gracht (ed.), *The theory of continental drift: A symposium* (pp. 83–87). Tulsa, OK: American Association of Petroleum Geologists.

Champagne, A. B., Klopfer, L. E., and Anderson, J. H. (1980). Factors influencing the learning of classical mechanics. *American Journal of Physics, 48*, 1074–1079.

Chang, H. Y., and Linn, M. C. (2013). Scaffolding learning from molecular visualizations. *Journal of Research in Science Teaching, 50*, 858–886.

Chi, M. (1992). Conceptual change within and across ontological categories: Examples from learning and discovery in science. In R. Giere (ed.), *Cognitive models of science* (pp. 129–186). Minneapolis: University of Minnesota Press.

Chi, M. T. H. (2005). Commonsense conceptions of emergent processes: Why some misconceptions are robust. *Journal of the Learning Sciences, 14*, 161–199.

Chi, M. T. H., Roscoe, R. D., Slotta, J. D., Roy, M., and Chase, C. C. (2012). Misconceived causal explanations for emergent processes. *Cognitive Science, 36*, 1–61.

Chi, M. T. H., Slotta, J. D., and De Leeuw, N. (1994). From things to processes: A theory of conceptual change for learning science concepts. *Learning and Instruction, 4*, 27–43.

Chiou, G. L., and Anderson, O. R. (2010). A study of undergraduate physics students' understanding of heat conduction based on mental model theory and an ontology-process analysis. *Science Education, 94*, 825–854.

Christensen, K. D., Jayaratne, T. E., Roberts, J. S., Kardia, S. L. R., and Petty, E. M. (2010). Understandings of basic genetics in the United States: Results from a national survey of black and white men and women. *Public Health Genomics, 13*, 467–476.

Cialdini, R. B., and Goldstein, N. J. (2004). Social influence: Compliance and conformity. *Annual Review of Psychology, 55*, 591–621.

Clagett, M. (1961). *The science of mechanics in the Middle Ages*. Madison: University of Wisconsin Press.

Clark, D. B. (2006). Longitudinal conceptual change in students' understanding of thermal equilibrium: An examination of the process of conceptual restructuring. *Cognition and Instruction, 24*, 467–563.

Clark, D. B., D'Angelo, C. M., and Schleigh, S. P. (2011). Comparison of students' knowledge structure coherence and understanding of force in the Philippines, Turkey, China, Mexico, and the United States. *Journal of the Learning Sciences, 20*, 207–261.

Clement, J. (1982). Students' preconceptions in introductory mechanics. *American Journal of Physics, 50*, 66–71.

———(1993). Using bridging analogies and anchoring intuitions to deal with students' preconceptions in physics. *Journal of Research in Science Teaching, 30*, 1241–1257.

Clement, J., Brown, D. E., and Zietsman, A. (1989). Not all preconceptions are misconceptions: finding "anchoring conceptions" for grounding instruction on students' intuitions. *International Journal of Science Education, 11*, 554–565.

Clough, E. E., and Driver, R. (1985). Secondary students' conceptions of the conduction of heat: Bringing together scientific and personal views. *Physics Education, 20*, 176–182.

Coley, J. D. (2012). Where the wild things are: Informal experience and ecological reasoning. *Child Development, 83*, 992–1006.

Coley, J. D., Medin, D., Proffitt, J., Lynch, E., and Atran, S. (1999). Inductive reasoning in folkbiological thought. In D. Medin and S. Atran (eds.), *Folkbiology* (pp. 205–232). Cambridge, MA: MIT Press.

Coley, J. D., and Tanner, K. (2015). Relations between intuitive biological thinking and biological misconceptions in biology majors and nonmajors. *CBE-Life Sciences Education, 14*, ar8, 1–19.

Corlett, E. N., and Wilson, J. R., and Corlett, N. (1995). *Evaluation of human work*. London: Taylor and Francis.

Cottrell, J. E., and Winer, G. A. (1994). Development in the understanding of perception: The decline of extramission perception beliefs. *Developmental Psychology, 30*, 218–228.

Couprie, D. L. (2011). *Heaven and earth in ancient Greek cosmology*. New York: Springer.

Cross, D. V., and Rotkin, L. (1975). The relation between size and apparent heaviness. *Perception and Psychophysics, 18*, 79–87.

Curtis, V., Aunger, R., and Rabie, T. (2004). Evidence that disgust evolved to protect from risk of disease. *Proceedings of the Royal Society of London B: Biological Sciences, 271*, S131-S133.

Dar-Nimrod, I., Cheung, B. Y., Ruby, M. B., and Heine, S. J. (2014). Can merely learning about obesity genes affect eating behavior? *Appetite, 81*, 269–276.

Dar-Nimrod, I., and Heine, S. J. (2006). Exposure to scientific theories affects women's math performance. *Science, 314*, 435–435.

———(2011). Genetic essentialism: On the deceptive determinism of DNA. *Psychological Bulletin, 137*, 800–818.

Darwin, C. (1844, January 11). *Letter to Joseph Dalton Hooker*. Retrieved from www.darwinproject.ac.uk/letter/entry-729.

———(1859). *On the origin of species by means of natural selection*. London: John Murray.

Dawson, P., Han, I., Cox, M., Black, C., and Simmons, L. (2007). Residence time and food contact time effects on transfer of *Salmonella* Typhimurium from tile, wood and carpet: testing the five-second rule. *Journal of Applied Microbiology, 102*, 945–953.

De Waal, F. (2006). Morally evolved: Primate social instincts, human morality, and the rise and fall of "Veneer Theory." In S. Macedo and J. Ober (eds.), *Primates and philosophers: How morality evolved* (pp. 1–58). Princeton, NJ: Princeton University Press.

DeJesus, J. M., Shutts, K., and Kinzler, K. D. (2015). Eww she sneezed! Contamination context affects children's food preferences and consumption. *Appetite, 87*, 303–309.

Diakidoy, I. A., Vosniadou, S., and Hawks, J. D. (1997). Conceptual change in astronomy: Models of the earth and of the day/night cycle in American-Indian children. *European Journal of Psychology of Education, 12*, 159–184.

Diamond, A. (1985). Development of the ability to use recall to guide action, as indicated by infants' performance on AB. *Child Development, 56*, 868–883.

Diamond, A., and Goldman-Rakic, P. S. (1989). Comparison of human infants and rhesus monkeys on Piaget's AB task: Evidence for dependence on dorsolateral prefrontal cortex. *Experimental Brain Research, 74*, 24–40.

Diesendruck, G., and Haber, L. (2009). God's categories: The effect of religiosity on children's teleological and essentialist beliefs about categories. *Cognition, 110*, 100–114.

Ding, D., Maibach, E. W., Zhao, X., Roser-Renouf, C., and Leiserowitz, A. (2011). Support for climate policy and societal action are linked to perceptions about scientific agreement. *Nature Climate Change, 1*, 462–466.

DiSessa, A. A. (2008). A bird's-eye view of the "pieces" vs. "coherence" controversy (from the "pieces" side of the fence). In S. Vosniadou (ed.), *International handbook of research on conceptual change* (pp. 35–60). New York: Routledge.

Dobzhansky, T. (1973). Nothing in biology makes sense except in the light of evolution. *American Biology Teacher, 35*, 125–129.

Dokov, W., and Dokova, K. (2011). Epidemiology and diagnostic problems of electrical injury in forensic medicine. In D. N. Vieira (ed.), *Forensic medicine: From old problems to new challenges* (pp. 121–136). Rijeka, Croatia: InTech.

Donner, S. D., and McDaniels, J. (2013). The influence of national temperature fluctuations on opinions about climate change in the U.S. since 1990. *Climatic Change, 118*, 537–550.

Donovan, B. M. (2014). Playing with fire? The impact of the hidden curriculum in school genetics on essentialist conceptions of race. *Journal of Research in Science Teaching, 51*, 462–496.

Dunbar, K., Fugelsang, J., and Stein, C. (2007). Do naïve theories ever go away? Using brain and behavior to understand changes in concepts. In M. Lovett and P. Shah (eds.), *Thinking with data* (pp. 193–206). New York: Lawrence Erlbaum Associates.

Duncan, R. G., and Tseng, K. A. (2011). Designing project-based instruction to foster generative and mechanistic understandings in genetics. *Science Education, 95*, 21–56.

Eckstein, S. G., and Kozhevnikov, M. (1997). Parallelism in the development of children's ideas and the historical development of projectile motion theories. *International Journal of Science Education, 19*, 1057–1073.

Elkind, D. (1961). Children's discovery of the conservation of mass, weight, and volume: Piaget replication study II. *Journal of Genetic Psychology, 98*, 219–227.

Emmons, N. A., and Kelemen, D. A. (2015). Young children's acceptance of within-species variation: Implications for essentialism and teaching evolution. *Journal of Experimental Child Psychology, 139*, 148–160.

Erickson, G. L. (1979). Children's conceptions of heat and temperature. *Science Education, 63*, 221–230.

Evans, E. M. (2001). Cognitive and contextual factors in the emergence of diverse belief systems: creation versus evolution. *Cognitive Psychology, 42*, 217–266.

Evans, E. M., and Lane, J. D. (2011). Contradictory or complementary? Creationist and evolutionist explanations of the origin(s) of species. *Human Development, 54*, 144–159.

Evans, E. M., Spiegel, A. N., Gram, W., Frazier, B. N., Tare, M., Thompson, S., and Diamond, J. (2010). A conceptual guide to natural history museum visitors' understanding of evolution. *Journal of Research in Science Teaching, 47*, 326–353.

Fallon, A. E., Rozin, P., and Pliner, P. (1984). The child's conception of food: The development of food rejections with special reference to disgust and contamination sensitivity. *Child Development, 55*, 566–575.

Field, D. (1987). A review of preschool conservation training: An analysis of analyses. *Developmental Review, 7,* 210–251.

Fischbein, E., Stavy, R., and Ma-Naim, H. (1989). The psychological structure of naïve impetus conceptions. *International Journal of Science Education, 11,* 71–81.

Foisy, L. M. B., Potvin, P., Riopel, M., and Masson, S. (2015). Is inhibition involved in overcoming a common physics misconception in mechanics? *Trends in Neuroscience and Education, 4,* 26–36.

Fox, R. (1971). *The caloric theory of gases: From Lavoisier to Regnault.* Oxford, UK: Clarendon.

Frappart, S., Raijmakers, M., and Frède, V. (2014). What do children know and understand about universal gravitation? Structural and developmental aspects. *Journal of Experimental Child Psychology, 120,* 17–38.

Freyd, J. J., and Jones, K. T. (1994). Representational momentum for a spiral path. *Journal of Experimental Psychology: Learning, Memory, and Cognition, 20,* 968–976.

Galilei, G. (1590/1960). *On motion.* Madison: University of Wisconsin Press.

———(1632/1953). *Dialogue concerning the two chief world systems, Ptolemaic and Copernican.* Oakland: University of California Press.

Galili, I. (2001). Weight versus gravitational force: Historical and educational perspectives. *International Journal of Science Education, 23,* 1073–1093.

Geerdts, M. S., Van de Walle, G. A., and LoBue, V. (2015). Daily animal exposure and children's biological concepts. *Journal of Experimental Child Psychology, 130,* 132–146.

Gelman, S. A., and Legare, C. H. (2011). Concepts and folk theories. *Annual Review of Anthropology, 40,* 379–398.

Gelman, S. A., Ware, E. A., and Kleinberg, F. (2010). Effects of generic language on category content and structure. *Cognitive Psychology, 61,* 273–301.

Gelman, S. A., and Wellman, H. M. (1991). Insides and essences: Early understandings of the non-obvious. *Cognition, 38,* 213–244.

Gervais, W. M. (2015). Override the controversy: Analytic thinking predicts endorsement of evolution. *Cognition, 142,* 312–321.

Goldberg, R. F., and Thompson-Schill, S. L. (2009). Developmental "roots" in mature biological knowledge. *Psychological Science, 20,* 480–487.

Gopnik, A. (1997). *Words, thoughts, and theories.* Cambridge, MA: MIT Press.

Gopnik, A., and Wellman, H. M. (2012). Reconstructing constructivism: Causal models, Bayesian learning mechanisms, and the theory theory. *Psychological Bulletin, 138,* 1085–1108.

Gottesman, M. (1973). Conservation development in blind children. *Child Development, 44,* 824–827.

Gould, S. J. (1992). *Ever since Darwin: Reflections in natural history.* New York: Norton.

————(1996). *Full house: The spread of excellence from Plato to Darwin.* New York: Three Rivers Press.

————(1997). Redrafting the tree of life. *Proceedings of the American Philosophical Society, 141,* 30–54.

Gregg, V. R., Winer, G. A., Cottrell, J. E., Hedman, K. E., and Fournier, J. S. (2001). The persistence of a misconception about vision after educational interventions. *Psychonomic Bulletin and Review, 8,* 622–626.

Gregory, T. R. (2009). Understanding natural selection: Essential concepts and common misconceptions. *Evolution: Education and Outreach, 2,* 156–175.

Gripshover, S. J., and Markman, E. M. (2013). Teaching young children a theory of nutrition: Conceptual change and the potential for increased vegetable consumption. *Psychological Science, 24,* 1541–1553.

Gruber, H. E. (1981). *Darwin on man: A psychological study of scientific creativity.* Chicago: University of Chicago Press.

Gutheil, G., Vera, A., and Keil, F. C. (1998). Do houseflies think? Patterns of induction and biological beliefs in development. *Cognition, 66,* 33–49.

Haidt, J., McCauley, C., and Rozin, P. (1994). Individual differences in sensitivity to disgust: A scale sampling seven domains of disgust elicitors. *Personality and Individual Differences, 16,* 701–713.

Halloun, I. A., and Hestenes, D. (1985). Common sense concepts about motion. *American Journal of Physics, 53,* 1056–1065.

Hannust, T., and Kikas, E. (2010). Young children's acquisition of knowledge about the earth: A longitudinal study. *Journal of Experimental Child Psychology, 107,* 164–180.

Hardy, I., Jonen, A., Möller, K., and Stern, E. (2006). Effects of instructional support within constructivist learning environments for elementary school students' understanding of floating and sinking. *Journal of Educational Psychology, 98,* 307–326.

Harlow, D. B., Swanson, L. H., Nylund-Gibson, K., and Truxler, A. (2011). Using latent class analysis to analyze children's responses to the question, "What is a day?" *Science Education, 95,* 477–496.

Harris, P. L., and Giménez, M. (2005). Children's acceptance of conflicting testimony: The case of death. *Journal of Cognition and Culture, 5,* 143–164.

Harrison, E. R. (1981). *Cosmology.* Cambridge, UK: Cambridge University Press.

Haslam, N., Rothschild, L., and Ernst, D. (2000). Essentialist beliefs about social categories. *British Journal of Social Psychology, 39,* 113–127.

Hatano, G., Siegler, R. S., Richards, D. D., Inagaki, K., Stavy, R., and Wax, N. (1993). The development of biological knowledge: A multi-national study. *Cognitive Development, 8,* 47–62.

Hayes, B. K., Goodhew, A., Heit, E., and Gillan, J. (2003). The role of diverse instruction in conceptual change. *Journal of Experimental Child Psychology*, *86*, 253–276.

Heddy, B. C., and Nadelson, L. S. (2012). A global perspective of the variables associated with acceptance of evolution. *Evolution: Education and Outreach*, *5*, 412–418.

———(2013). The variables related to public acceptance of evolution in the United States. *Evolution: Education and Outreach*, *6*, 1–14.

Heinrich, B. (1999). *Mind of the raven*. New York: Harper Collins.

Herrmann, P., Waxman, S. R., and Medin, D. L. (2010). Anthropocentrism is not the first step in children's reasoning about the natural world. *Proceedings of the National Academy of Sciences*, *107*, 9979–9984.

Hespos, S. J., and Baillargeon, R. (2008). Young infants' actions reveal their developing knowledge of support variables: Converging evidence for violation-of-expectation findings. *Cognition*, *107*, 304–316.

Hood, B. M. (1995). Gravity rules for 2- to 4-year olds? *Cognitive Development*, *10*, 577–598.

———(1998). Gravity does rule for falling events. *Developmental Science*, *1*, 59–63.

Hood, B., Carey, S., and Prasada, S. (2000). Predicting the outcomes of physical events: Two-year-olds fail to reveal knowledge of solidity and support. *Child Development*, *71*, 1540–1554.

Hood, B. M., Hauser, M. D., Anderson, L., and Santos, L. (1999). Gravity biases in a non-human primate? *Developmental Science*, *2*, 35–41.

Hood, B. M., Santos, L., and Fieselman, S. (2000). Two-year-olds' naive predictions for horizontal trajectories. *Developmental Science*, *3*, 328–332.

Hood, B. M., Wilson, A., and Dyson, S. (2006). The effect of divided attention on inhibiting the gravity error. *Developmental Science*, *9*, 303–308.

Horne, Z., Powell, D., Hummel, J. E., and Holyoak, K. J. (2015). Countering antivaccination attitudes. *Proceedings of the National Academy of Sciences*, *112*, 10321–10324.

Hotchkiss, J. H. (2001). Lambasting Louis: Lessons from pasteurization. In A. Eaglesham, S. G. Pueppke, and R. W. F. Hardy (eds.), *Genetically modified food and the consumer* (pp. 51–68). Ithaca, NY: National Agricultural Biotechnology Council.

Howe, C., Tavares, J. T., and Devine, A. (2012). Everyday conceptions of object fall: Explicit and tacit understanding during middle childhood. *Journal of Experimental Child Psychology*, *111*, 351–366.

Hrepic, Z., Zollman, D. A., and Rebello, N. S. (2010). Identifying students' mental models of sound propagation: The role of conceptual blending in understanding conceptual change. *Physical Review Special Topics: Physics Education Research*, *6*, 1–18.

Huntley-Fenner, G., Carey, S., and Solimando, A. (2002). Objects are individuals but stuff doesn't count: Perceived rigidity and cohesiveness influence infants' representations of small groups of discrete entities. *Cognition, 85*, 203–221.

IFLScience (2015, January 29). Richard Dawkins reads hate mail from "fans." Retrieved from www.iflscience.com/editors-blog/richard-dawkins-reads-hate-mail -fans.

Inagaki, K., and Hatano, G. (1993). Young children's understanding of the mind-body distinction. *Child Development, 64*, 1534–1549.

————(1996). Young children's recognition of commonalities between animals and plants. *Child Development, 67*, 2823–2840.

James, W. (1890/1950). *The principles of psychology*. Mineola, NY: Dover Publications.

Jarrett, C. (2014). *Great myths of the brain*. Hoboken, NJ: Wiley-Blackwell.

Jaswal, V. K. (2010). Believing what you're told: Young children's trust in unexpected testimony about the physical world. *Cognitive Psychology, 61*, 248–272.

Joh, A. S., Jaswal, V. K., and Keen, R. (2011). Imagining a way out of the gravity bias: Preschoolers can visualize the solution to a spatial problem. *Child Development, 82*, 744–750.

Johnson, S. (2007). *The ghost map*. New York: Riverhead Books.

Johnson, S. C., and Carey, S. (1998). Knowledge enrichment and conceptual change in folkbiology: Evidence from Williams syndrome. *Cognitive Psychology, 37*, 156–200.

Johnson, S. C., and Solomon, G. E. (1997). Why dogs have puppies and cats have kittens: The role of birth in young children's understanding of biological origins. *Child Development, 68*, 404–419.

Kahan, D. M., Peters, E., Wittlin, M., Slovic, P., Ouellette, L. L., Braman, D., and Mandel, G. (2012). The polarizing impact of science literacy and numeracy on perceived climate change risks. *Nature Climate Change, 2*, 732–735.

Kaiser, M. K., Jonides, J., and Alexander, J. (1986). Intuitive reasoning about abstract and familiar physics problems. *Memory and Cognition, 14*, 308–312.

Kaiser, M. K., McCloskey, M., and Proffitt, D. R. (1986). Development of intuitive theories of motion: Curvilinear motion in the absence of external forces. *Developmental Psychology, 22*, 67–71.

Kaiser, M. K., Proffitt, D. R., and Anderson, K. (1985). Judgments of natural and anomalous trajectories in the presence and absence of motion. *Journal of Experimental Psychology: Learning, Memory, and Cognition, 11*, 795–803.

Kaiser, M. K., Proffitt, D. R., and McCloskey, M. (1985). The development of beliefs about falling objects. *Perception and Psychophysics, 38*, 533–539.

Kaiser, M. K., Proffitt, D. R., Whelan, S. M., and Hecht, H. (1992). Influence of animation on dynamical judgments. *Journal of Experimental Psychology: Human Perception and Performance, 18*, 669–689.

Kalish, C. W. (1996). Preschoolers' understanding of germs as invisible mechanisms. *Cognitive Development, 11*, 83–106.

Keil, F. C. (1992). *Concepts, kinds, and cognitive development.* Cambridge, MA: MIT Press.

———(2003). Folkscience: Coarse interpretations of a complex reality. *Trends in Cognitive Sciences, 7*, 368–373.

Keil, F. C., and Batterman, N. (1984). A characteristic-to-defining shift in the development of word meaning. *Journal of Verbal Learning and Verbal Behavior, 23,* 221–236.

Kelemen, D. (2004). Are children "intuitive theists"? Reasoning about purpose and design in nature. *Psychological Science, 15,* 295–301.

Kelemen, D., Rottman, J., and Seston, R. (2013). Professional physical scientists display tenacious teleological tendencies: Purpose-based reasoning as a cognitive default. *Journal of Experimental Psychology: General, 142,* 1074–1083.

Kempton, W. (1986). Two theories of home heat control. *Cognitive Science, 10,* 75–90.

Keynes, J. M. (1936). *The general theory of employment, interest, and money.* London: Macmillan.

Kim, E., and Pak, S. J. (2002). Students do not overcome conceptual difficulties after solving 1000 traditional problems. *American Journal of Physics, 70,* 759–765.

Kim, I. K., and Spelke, E. S. (1999). Perception and understanding of effects of gravity and inertia on object motion. *Developmental Science, 2,* 339–362.

Kimel, S. Y., Huesmann, R., Kunst, J. R., and Halperin, E. (2016). Living in a genetic world: How learning about interethnic genetic similarities and differences affects peace and conflict. *Personality and Social Psychology Bulletin, 42,* 688–700.

Kirschner, P. A., Sweller, J., and Clark, R. E. (2006). Why minimal guidance during instruction does not work: An analysis of the failure of constructivist, discovery, problem-based, experiential, and inquiry-based teaching. *Educational Psychologist, 41,* 75–86.

Klahr, D., and Nigam, M. (2004). The equivalence of learning paths in early science instruction: Effects of direct instruction and discovery learning. *Psychological Science, 15,* 661–667.

Klavir, R., and Leiser, D. (2002). When astronomy, biology, and culture converge: Children's conceptions about birthdays. *Journal of Genetic Psychology, 163,* 239–253.

Kloos, H., Fisher, A., and Van Orden, G. C. (2010). Situated naïve physics: Task constraints decide what children know about density. *Journal of Experimental Psychology: General, 139,* 625–637.

Kohn, A. S. (1993). Preschoolers' reasoning about density: Will it float? *Child Development, 64,* 1637–1650.

Kolbert, E. (2006). *Field notes from a catastrophe: Man, nature, and climate change.* London: Bloomsbury.

Kozhevnikov, M., and Hegarty, M. (2001). Impetus beliefs as default heuristics:

Dissociation between explicit and implicit knowledge about motion. *Psychonomic Bulletin and Review, 8,* 439–453.

Krist, H. (2010). Development of intuitions about support beyond infancy. *Developmental Psychology, 46,* 266–278.

Kronberger, N., Wagner, W., and Nagata, M. (2014). How natural is "more natural"? The role of method, type of transfer, and familiarity for public perceptions of cisgenic and transgenic modification. *Science Communication, 36,* 106–130.

Kuhlmeier, V. A., Troje, N. F., and Lee, V. (2010). Young infants detect the direction of biological motion in point-light displays. *Infancy, 15,* 83–93.

Kuhn, T. S. (1962). *The structure of scientific revolutions.* Chicago: University of Chicago Press.

Kuo, L, (2012, August 28). Bill Nye, The Science Guy, says creationism is not appropriate for children. *Huffington Post.* Retrieved from www.huffingtonpost .com/2012/08/28/ bill-nye-science-guy-creationism-evolution_n_1835208.html.

Lack, D. (1947/1983). *Darwin's finches.* Cambridge, UK: Cambridge University Press.

Lautrey, J., and Mazens, K. (2004). Is children's naïve knowledge consistent? A comparison of the concepts of sound and heat. *Learning and Instruction, 14,* 399–423.

Lawson, R. (2006). The science of cycology: Failures to understand how everyday objects work. *Memory and Cognition, 34,* 1667–1675.

Lazar, A., and Torney-Purta, J. (1991). The development of the subconcepts of death in young children: A short-term longitudinal study. *Child Development, 62,* 1321–1333.

Le Grand, H. E. (1988). *Drifting continents and shifting theories.* Cambridge, UK: Cambridge University Press.

Leddon, E. M., Waxman, S. R., and Medin, D. L. (2011). What does it mean to "live" and "die"? A cross-linguistic analysis of parent-child conversations in English and Indonesian. *British Journal of Developmental Psychology, 29,* 375–395.

Lederberg, J. (2000). Infectious history. *Science, 288,* 287–293.

Lee, H. S., Liu, O. L., Price, C. A., and Kendall, A. L. (2011). College students' temporal-magnitude recognition ability associated with durations of scientific changes. *Journal of Research in Science Teaching, 48,* 317–335.

Lee, V., and Kuhlmeier, V. A. (2013). Young children show a dissociation in looking and pointing behavior in falling events. *Cognitive Development, 28,* 21–30.

Legare, C. H., and Gelman, S. A. (2008). Bewitchment, biology, or both: The co-existence of natural and supernatural explanatory frameworks across development. *Cognitive Science, 32,* 607–642.

———(2009). South African children's understanding of AIDS and flu: Investigating conceptual understanding of cause, treatment and prevention. *Journal of Cognition and Culture, 9,* 333–346.

Leiserowitz, A., Maibach, E., Roser-Renouf, C., Feinberg, G. and Howe, P. (2013) *Global warming's six Americas*. New Haven, CT: Yale Project on Climate Change Communication.

Lewandowsky, S., Ecker, U. K., Seifert, C. M., Schwarz, N., and Cook, J. (2012). Misinformation and its correction: Continued influence and successful debiasing. *Psychological Science in the Public Interest, 13*, 106–131.

Lewandowsky, S., Gignac, G. E., and Vaughan, S. (2013). The pivotal role of perceived scientific consensus in acceptance of science. *Nature Climate Change, 3*, 399–404.

Lewis, E. L., and Linn, M. C. (1994). Heat energy and temperature concepts of adolescents, adults, and experts: Implications for curricular improvements. *Journal of Research in Science Teaching, 31*, 657–677.

Li, Y., Johnson, E. J., and Zaval, L. (2011). Local warming: Daily temperature change influences belief in global warming. *Psychological Science, 22*, 454–459.

Libarkin, J. C., and Anderson, S. W. (2005). Assessment of learning in entry-level geoscience courses: Results from the Geoscience Concept Inventory. *Journal of Geoscience Education, 53*, 394–401.

Libarkin, J. C., Anderson, S. W., Dahl, J., Beilfuss, M., Boone, W., and Kurdziel, J. P. (2005). Qualitative analysis of college students' ideas about the earth: Interviews and open-ended questionnaires. *Journal of Geoscience Education, 53*, 17–26.

Libarkin, J. C., and Schneps, M. H. (2012). Elementary children's retrodictive reasoning about earth science. *International Electronic Journal of Elementary Education, 5*, 47–62.

Lindberg, D. C. (1976). *Theories of vision from al-Kindi to Kepler*. Chicago: University of Chicago Press.

Liu, X., and MacIsaac, D. (2005). An investigation of factors affecting the degree of naïve impetus theory application. *Journal of Science Education and Technology, 14*, 101–116.

Livingston, E., and Zylke, J. W. (2012). JAMA obesity theme issue. *Journal of the American Medical Association, 307*, 970–971.

Lombardi, D., and Sinatra, G. M. (2012). College students' perceptions about the plausibility of human-induced climate change. *Research in Science Education, 42*, 201–217.

Lusk, J. (2015). *Food demand survey: January 2015*. Stillwater: Oklahoma State University Department of Agricultural Economics.

MacAvoy, A. (2015). *Pentagon plans to exhume, identify hundreds killed in bombing of Pearl Harbor*. Retrieved from www.huffingtonpost.com/2015/04/14/pentagon-pearl-harbor-identify_n_7066902.html.

MacDonald, T., and Wiley, E. O. (2012). Communicating phylogeny: Evolutionary tree diagrams in museums. *Evolution: Education and Outreach, 5*, 14–28.

MacFadden, B. J., Oviedo, L. H., Seymour, G. M., and Ellis, S. (2012). Fossil horses, orthogenesis, and communicating evolution in museums. *Evolution: Education and Outreach, 5*, 29–37.

Mahajan, N., Barnes, J. L., Blanco, M., and Santos, L. R. (2009). Enumeration of objects and substances in non-human primates: Experiments with brown lemurs (*Eulemur fulvus*). *Developmental Science, 12*, 920–928.

Marques, L., and Thompson, D. (1997). Misconceptions and conceptual changes concerning continental drift and plate tectonics among Portuguese students aged 16–17. *Research in Science and Technological Education, 15*, 195–222.

Marshak, S. (2009). *Essentials of geology*. New York: W. W. Norton and Company.

Marvin, U. (1973). *Continental drift: The evolution of a concept*. Washington, DC: Smithsonian Institution Press.

Masson, M. E., Bub, D. N., and Lalonde, C. E. (2011). Video-game training and naïve reasoning about object motion. *Applied Cognitive Psychology, 25*, 166–173.

Masson, S., Potvin, P., Riopel, M., and Foisy, L. M. B. (2014). Differences in brain activation between novices and experts in science during a task involving a common misconception in electricity. *Mind, Brain, and Education, 8*, 44–55.

Masson, S., and Vázquez-Abad, J. (2006). Integrating history of science in science education through historical microworlds to promote conceptual change. *Journal of Science Education and Technology, 15*, 257–268.

Mayo Clinic (2014). *Causes of frostbite*. Retrieved from www.mayoclinic.org /diseases-conditions/frostbite/basics/causes/con-20034608.

Mayr, E. (1982). *The growth of biological thought: Diversity, evolution, and inheritance*. Cambridge, MA: Harvard University Press.

———(2001). *What evolution is*. New York: Basic Books.

Mazens, K., and Lautrey, J. (2003). Conceptual change in physics: Children's naïve representations of sound. *Cognitive Development, 18*, 159–176.

McCloskey, M. (1983a). Intuitive physics. *Scientific American, 248*, 122–130.

———(1983b). Naïve theories of motion. In D. Gentner and A. L. Stevens (eds.), *Mental models* (pp. 299–324). Hillsdale, NJ: Erlbaum.

McCloskey, M., Caramazza, A., and Green, B. (1980). Curvilinear motion in the absence of external forces: Naive beliefs about the motion of objects. *Science. 210*, 1139–1141.

McFerran, B., and Mukhopadhyay, A. (2013). Lay theories of obesity predict actual body mass. *Psychological Science, 24*, 1428–1436.

McNeil, N. M., Fyfe, E. R., and Dunwiddie, A. E. (2015). Arithmetic practice can be modified to promote understanding of mathematical equivalence. *Journal of Educational Psychology, 107*, 423–436.

Mead, L. S., and Mates, A. (2009). Why science standards are important to a strong science curriculum and how states measure up. *Evolution: Education and Outreach, 2*, 359–371.

Medin, D., Waxman, S., Woodring, J., and Washinawatok, K. (2010). Human-centeredness is not a universal feature of young children's reasoning: Culture and experience matter when reasoning about biological entities. *Cognitive Development*, *25*, 197–207.

Meir, E., Perry, J, Herron, J. C., and Kingsolver, J. (2007). College students' misconceptions about evolutionary trees. *American Biology Teacher*, *69*, 71–76.

Mendes, N., Rakoczy, H., and Call, J. (2008). Ape metaphysics: Object individuation without language. *Cognition*, *106*, 730–749.

Mermelstein, E., and Meyer, E. (1969). Conservation training techniques and their effects on different populations. *Child Development*, *40*, 471–490.

Meyer, M., Leslie, S. J., Gelman, S. A., and Stilwell, S. M. (2013). Essentialist beliefs about bodily transplants in the United States and India. *Cognitive Science*, *37*, 668–710.

Middleton, W. E. K. (1971). *The experimenters: A study of the Accademia del Cimento*. Baltimore: Johns Hopkins Press.

Miller, C. S., Lehman, J. F., and Koedinger, K. R. (1999). Goals and learning in microworlds. *Cognitive Science*, *23*, 305–336.

Miller, J. D., Scott, E. C., and Okamoto, S. (2006). Public acceptance of evolution. *Science*, *313*, 765–766.

Miller, S. A. (1973). Contradiction, surprise, and cognitive change: The effects of disconfirmation of belief on conservers and nonconservers. *Journal of Experimental Child Psychology*, *15*, 47–62.

Millman, A. B., and Smith, C. L. (1997). Darwin's use of analogical reasoning in theory construction. *Metaphor and Symbol*, *12*, 159–187.

Mills, C. M., and Keil, F. C. (2004). Knowing the limits of one's understanding: The development of an awareness of an illusion of explanatory depth. *Journal of Experimental Child Psychology*, *87*, 1–32.

Minstrell, J. (1982). Explaining the "at rest" condition of an object. *Physics Teacher*, *20*, 10–14.

Miton, H., Claidière, N., and Mercier, H. (2015). Universal cognitive mechanisms explain the cultural success of bloodletting. *Evolution and Human Behavior*, *36*, 303–312.

Mora, C., Tittensor, D. P., Adl, S., Simpson, A. G., and Worm, B. (2011). How many species are there on Earth and in the ocean? *PLoS Biology*, *9*, e1001127.

Morris, S. C., Taplin, J. E., and Gelman, S. A. (2000). Vitalism in naïve biological thinking. *Developmental Psychology*, *36*, 582–595.

Moss, J., and Case, R. (1999). Developing children's understanding of the rational numbers: A new model and an experimental curriculum. *Journal for Research in Mathematics Education*, *30*, 122–147.

Mungai, E. A., Behravesh, C. B., and Gould, L. H. (2015). Increased outbreaks associated with nonpasteurized milk, United States, 2007–2012. *Emerging Infectious Diseases*, *21*, 119–122.

Murphy, G. L., and Medin, D. L. (1985). The role of theories in conceptual coherence. *Psychological Review*, *92*, 289–316.

Myers, T. A., Maibach, E., Peters, E., and Leiserowitz, A. (2015). Simple messages help set the record straight about scientific agreement on human-caused climate change: The results of two experiments. *PloS One, 10*, e0120985.

Nakhleh, M. B., Samarapungavan, A., and Saglam, Y. (2005). Middle school students' beliefs about matter. *Journal of Research in Science Teaching, 42*, 581–612.

National Academies of Sciences, Engineering, and Medicine (2016a). *Genetically engineered crops: Experiences and prospects*. Washington, DC: National Academies Press.

————(2016b). *Science literacy: Concepts, contexts, and consequences*. Washington, DC: National Academies Press.

National Conference of State Legislatures (2016, Aug. 23). *States with religious and philosophical exemptions from school immunization requirements*. Retrieved from www.ncsl.org/research/health/school-immunization-exemption-state-laws.aspx.

National Science Board (2014). *Science and engineering indicators*. Arlington, VA: National Science Foundation.

National Science Teachers Association (2013). *Next generation science standards*. Washington, DC: National Academies Press.

Needham, A., and Baillargeon, R. (1993). Intuitions about support in 4.5-month-old infants. *Cognition, 47*, 121–148.

Nersessian, N. J. (1989). Conceptual change in science and in science education. *Synthese, 80*, 163–183.

Neurath, O. (1973). *Empiricism and sociology*. Dordrecht: Holland: D. Reidel Publishing Company.

Newport, F. (2010). *Four in 10 Americans believe in strict creationism*. Gallup Organization.

Newton, I. (1687/1999). *The principia: Mathematical principles of natural philosophy*. Berkeley: University of California Press.

Nguyen, S. P., McCullough, M. B., and Noble, A. (2011). A theory-based approach to teaching young children about health: A recipe for understanding. *Journal of Educational Psychology, 103*, 594–606.

Nguyen, S. P., and Rosengren, K. S. (2004). Causal reasoning about illness: A comparison between European- and Vietnamese-American children. *Journal of Cognition and Culture, 4*, 51–78.

Nobes, G., Martin, A. E., and Panagiotaki, G. (2005). The development of scientific knowledge of the earth. *British Journal of Developmental Psychology, 23*, 47–64.

Novick, L. R., and Catley, K. M. (2007). Understanding phylogenies in biology: The influence of a Gestalt perceptual principle. *Journal of Experimental Psychology: Applied, 13*, 197–223.

Novick, S., and Nussbaum, J. (1981). Pupils' understanding of the particulate nature of matter: A cross-age study. *Science Education, 65*, 187–196.

Nussbaum, J., and Novak, J. D. (1976). An assessment of children's concepts of the earth utilizing structured interviews. *Science Education, 60*, 535–550.

O'Connor, A. (2008, November 10). The claim: Tongue is mapped into four areas of taste. *New York Times*, D6.

Obama, B. (2015). Climate change can no longer be ignored. *Office of the Press Secretary*. Retrieved from www.whitehouse.gov/the-press-office/2015/04/18 /weekly-address-climate-change-can-no-longer-be-ignored.

Olsen, S. J., MacKinnon, L. C., Goulding, J. S., Bean, N. H., and Slutsker, L. (2000). Surveillance for foodborne disease outbreaks: United States, 1993–1997. *Morbidity and Mortality Weekly Report, 49,* 1–62.

Onion (2010). *Scientists successfully teach gorilla it will die someday*. Retrieved from www.theonion.com/video/scientists-successfully-teach-gorilla-it-will-die-17165.

————(2015). *Natural selection kills 38 quadrillion organisms in bloodiest day yet.* Retrieved from www.theonion.com/article/natural-selection-kills-38-quadrillion -organisms-i-37873.

Opfer, J. E., Nehm, R. H., and Ha, M. (2012). Cognitive foundations for science assessment design: Knowing what students know about evolution. *Journal of Research in Science Teaching, 49,* 744–777.

Opfer, J. E., and Siegler, R. S. (2004). Revisiting preschoolers' living things concept: A microgenetic analysis of conceptual change in basic biology. *Cognitive Psychology, 49,* 301–332.

Orenstein, W. A., Papania, M. J., and Wharton, M. E. (2004). Measles elimination in the United States. *Journal of Infectious Diseases, 189,* S1–S3.

Oreskes, N. (1999). *The rejection of continental drift: Theory and method in American earth science.* Oxford, UK: Oxford University Press.

Orwig, J. (2015). The physics of Mario World show the game has a fundamental flaw. *Business Insider*. Retrieved from www.businessinsider.com/mario -brothers-physics-gravity-2015-2.

Osthaus, B., Slater, A. M., and Lea, S. E. (2003). Can dogs defy gravity? A comparison with the human infant and a non-human primate. *Developmental Science, 6,* 489–497.

Ozsoy, S. (2012). Is the earth flat or round? Primary school children's understandings of the planet earth. *International Electronic Journal of Elementary Education, 4,* 407–415.

Palmer, D. H., and Flanagan, R. B. (1997). Readiness to change the conception that "motion-implies-force": A comparison of 12-year-old and 16-year-old students. *Science Education, 81,* 317–331.

Panagiotaki, G., Nobes, G., Ashraf, A., and Aubby, H. (2015). British and Pakistani children's understanding of death: Cultural and developmental influences. *British Journal of Developmental Psychology, 33,* 31–44.

Panagiotaki, G., Nobes, G., and Banerjee, R. (2006). Children's representations of the earth: A methodological comparison. *British Journal of Developmental Psychology, 24,* 353–372.

Pemberton, S. G., Gingras, M. K., and MacEachern, J. A. (2007). Edward Hitchcock and Roland Bird: Two early titans of vertebrate ichnology in North America. In W. Miller (ed.), *Trace fossils: Concepts, problems, prospects* (pp. 30–49). Amsterdam: Elsevier.

Pennisi, E. (2003). Modernizing the tree of life. *Science, 300,* 1692–1697.

Pew Research Center (2009). *Public opinion on religion and science in the United States.* Washington, DC: Pew Research Center.

———(2015). *Public and scientists' views on science and society.* Washington, DC: Pew Research Center.

Phillips, B. C., Novick, L. R., Catley, K. M., and Funk, D. J. (2012). Teaching tree thinking to college students: It's not as easy as you think. *Evolution: Education and Outreach, 5,* 595–602.

Piaget, J. (1929/2007). *The child's conception of the world.* New York: Routledge.

———(1941/2001). *The child's conception of number.* New York: Routledge.

———(1937/1954). *The construction of reality in the child.* New York: Basic Books.

Poling, D. A., and Evans, E. M. (2004). Religious belief, scientific expertise, and folk ecology. *Journal of Cognition and Culture, 4,* 485–524.

Poling, D. A., and Hupp, J. M. (2008). Death sentences: A content analysis of children's death literature. *Journal of Genetic Psychology, 169,* 165–176.

Potter, M. E., Kaufmann, A. F., Blake, P. A., and Feldman, R. A. (1984). Unpasteurized milk: The hazards of a health fetish. *Journal of the American Medical Association, 252,* 2048–2052.

Potvin, P., Masson, S., Lafortune, S., and Cyr, G. (2015). Persistence of the intuitive conception that heavier objects sink more: A reaction time study with different levels of interference. *International Journal of Science and Mathematics Education, 13,* 21–43.

Priest, S. H., Bonfadelli, H., and Rusanen, M. (2003). The "trust gap" hypothesis: Predicting support for biotechnology across national cultures as a function of trust in actors. *Risk Analysis, 23,* 751–766.

Public Policy Polling (2013). *Democrats and Republicans differ on conspiracy theory beliefs.* Raleigh, NC: Public Policy Polling.

Punter, P., Ochando-Pardo, M., and Garcia, J. (2011). Spanish secondary school students' notions on the causes and consequences of climate change. *International Journal of Science Education, 33,* 447–464.

Quoidbach, J., Gilbert, D. T., and Wilson, T. D. (2013). The end of history illusion. *Science, 339,* 96–98.

Raman, L., and Gelman, S. A. (2004). A cross-cultural developmental analysis of children's and adults' understanding of illness in South Asia (India) and the United States. *Journal of Cognition and Culture, 4,* 293–317.

———(2005). Children's understanding of the transmission of genetic disorders and contagious illnesses. *Developmental Psychology, 41,* 171–182.

Raman, L., and Winer, G. A. (2004). Evidence of more immanent justice responding in adults than children: A challenge to traditional developmental theories. *British Journal of Developmental Psychology, 22,* 255–274.

Ranney, M. A., and Clark, D. (2016). Climate change conceptual change: Scientific information can transform attitudes. *Topics in Cognitive Science, 8,* 49–75.

Rappolt-Schlichtmann, G., Tenenbaum, H. R., Koepke, M. F., and Fischer, K. W. (2007). Transient and robust knowledge: Contextual support and the dynamics of children's reasoning about density. *Mind, Brain, and Education, 1,* 98–108.

Reiner, M., Slotta, J. D., Chi, M. T. H., and Resnick, L. B. (2000). Naïve physics reasoning: A commitment to substance-based conceptions. *Cognition and Instruction, 18,* 1–34.

Renken, M. D., and Nunez, N. (2010). Evidence for improved conclusion accuracy after reading about rather than conducting a belief-inconsistent simple physics experiment. *Applied Cognitive Psychology, 24,* 792–811.

———(2013). Computer simulations and clear observations do not guarantee conceptual understanding. *Learning and Instruction, 23,* 10–23.

Riedel, S. (2005). Edward Jenner and the history of smallpox and vaccination. *Baylor University Medical Center Proceedings, 18,* 21–25.

Rosenberg, R. D. (2008). *Infants' and young children's representations of objects and non-cohesive entities: Implications for the core cognition hypothesis* (unpublished doctoral dissertation). Harvard University, Cambridge, MA.

Rosenberg, N. A., Pritchard, J. K., Weber, J. L., Cann, H. M., Kidd, K. K., Zhivotovsky, L. A., and Feldman, M. W. (2002). Genetic structure of human populations. *Science, 298,* 2381–2385.

Rosengren, K. S., Miller, P. J., Gutiérrez, I. T., Chow, P. I., Schein, S. S., and Anderson, K. N. (2014). Children's understanding of death: Toward a contextualized and integrated account. *Monographs of the Society for Research in Child Development, 79,* 1–162.

Roser, M. E., Fugelsang, J. A., Handy, T. C., Dunbar, K. N., and Gazzaniga, M. S. (2009). Representations of physical plausibility revealed by event-related potentials. *NeuroReport, 20,* 1081–1086.

Ross, N., Medin, D., Coley, J. D., and Atran, S. (2003). Cultural and experiential differences in the development of folkbiological induction. *Cognitive Development, 18,* 25–47.

Roughgarden, J. (2004). *Evolution's rainbow: Diversity, gender, and sexuality in nature and people.* Berkeley: University of California Press.

Rozenblit, L., and Keil, F. (2002). The misunderstood limits of folk science: An illusion of explanatory depth. *Cognitive Science, 26,* 521–562.

Rozin, P. (1990). Development in the food domain. *Developmental Psychology, 26,* 555–562.

Rozin, P., Fallon, A., and Augustoni-Ziskind, M. (1985). The child's conception of food: The development of contamination sensitivity to "disgusting" substances. *Developmental Psychology, 21,* 1075–1079.

Rozin, P., Millman, L., and Nemeroff, C. (1986). Operation of the laws of sympathetic magic in disgust and other domains. *Journal of Personality and Social Psychology, 50,* 703–712.

Samarapungavan, A., Vosniadou, S., and Brewer, W. F. (1996). Mental models of the earth, sun, and moon: Indian children's cosmologies. *Cognitive Development, 11,* 491–521.

Samarapungavan, A. and Wiers, R. W. (1997). Children's thoughts on the origin of species: A study of explanatory coherence. *Cognitive Science, 21,* 147–177.

Sanchez, C. A., and Wiley, J. (2014). The role of dynamic spatial ability in geoscience text comprehension. *Learning and Instruction, 31,* 33–45.

Sanner, M. A. (2001). People's feelings and beliefs about receiving transplants of different origins: Questions of life and death, identity, and nature's border. *Clinical Transplantation, 15,* 19–27.

Santos, L. R. (2004). Core knowledges: A dissociation between spatiotemporal knowledge and contact-mechanics in a non-human primate? *Developmental Science, 7,* 167–174.

Santos, L. R., and Hauser, M. D. (2002). A non-human primate's understanding of solidity: Dissociations between seeing and acting. *Developmental Science, 5,* F1–F7.

Santos, L. R., Seelig, D., and Hauser, M. D. (2006). Cotton-top tamarins' (*Saguinus oedipus*) expectations about occluded objects: A dissociation between looking and reaching tasks. *Infancy, 9,* 147–171.

Schaller, M., Miller, G. E., Gervais, W. M., Yager, S., and Chen, E. (2010). Mere visual perception of other people's disease symptoms facilitates a more aggressive immune response. *Psychological Science, 21,* 649–652.

Schneps, M. H., Sadler, P. M., Woll, S., and Crouse, L. (1988). *A private universe.* Santa Monica, CA: Pyramid Films.

Scholl, B. J. (2001). Objects and attention: The state of the art. *Cognition, 80,* 1–46.

Sclater, P. L. (1864). The mammals of Madagascar. *Quarterly Journal of Science, 1,* 213–219.

Shea, N. A. (2015). Examining the nexus of science communication and science education: A content analysis of genetics news articles. *Journal of Research in Science Teaching, 52,* 397–409.

Sheppard, K. (2015). Watch a U.S. Senator use a snowball to deny global warming. *Mother Jones.* Retrieved from www.motherjones.com/blue-marble/2015/02/inhofe-snowball-climate-change.

Shermer, M. (2001). Fox's Flapdoodle: Tabloid television offers a lesson in uncritical thinking. *Scientific American, 284,* 37.

Shtulman, A. (2006). Qualitative differences between naive and scientific theories of evolution. *Cognitive Psychology, 52,* 170–194.

————(2008). The development of core knowledge domains. In E. M. Anderman and L. Anderman (eds.), *Psychology of classroom learning: An encyclopedia* (pp. 320–325). Farmington Hills, MI: Thompson Gale.

————(2013). Epistemic similarities between students' scientific and supernatural beliefs. *Journal of Educational Psychology, 105,* 199–212.

————(2014). *Using the history of science to identify conceptual prerequisites to understanding evolution.* Poster presented at the 40th meeting of the Society for Philosophy and Psychology, Vancouver, Canada.

Shtulman, A., and Calabi, P. (2012). Cognitive constraints on the understanding and acceptance of evolution. In K. S. Rosengren, S. Brem, E. M. Evans, and G. Sinatra (eds.), *Evolution challenges: Integrating research and practice in teaching and learning about evolution* (pp. 47–65). Cambridge, UK: Oxford University Press.

————(2013). Tuition vs. intuition: Effects of instruction on naïve theories of evolution. *Merrill-Palmer Quarterly, 59,* 141–167.

Shtulman, A., and Checa, I. (2012). Parent-child conversations about evolution in the context of an interactive museum display. *International Electronic Journal of Elementary Education, 5,* 27–46.

Shtulman, A., and Harrington, K. (2016). Tensions between science and intuition across the lifespan. *Topics in Cognitive Science, 8,* 118–137.

Shtulman, A., and Lombrozo, T. (2016). Bundles of contradiction: A coexistence view of conceptual change. In D. Barner and A. Baron (eds.), *Core knowledge and conceptual change* (pp. 49–67). Oxford, UK: Oxford University Press.

Shtulman, A., and Schulz, L. (2008). The relationship between essentialist beliefs and evolutionary reasoning. *Cognitive Science, 32,* 1049–1062.

Shtulman, A., and Valcarcel, J. (2012). Scientific knowledge suppresses but does not supplant earlier intuitions. *Cognition, 124,* 209–215.

Shutts, K., Keen, R., and Spelke, E. S. (2006). Object boundaries influence toddlers' performance in a search task. *Developmental Science, 9,* 97–107.

Siegal, M., Butterworth, G., and Newcombe, P. A. (2004). Culture and children's cosmology. *Developmental Science, 7,* 308–324.

Siegal, M., and Share, D. L. (1990). Contamination sensitivity in young children. *Developmental Psychology, 26,* 455–458.

Siegler, R. S., DeLoache, J. S., and Eisenberg, N. (2010). *How children develop.* New York: Macmillan.

Skamp, K., Boyes, E., and Stanisstreet, M. (2013). Beliefs and willingness to act about global warming: Where to focus science pedagogy? *Science Education, 97,* 191–217.

Slaughter, V., and Griffiths, M. (2007). Death understanding and fear of death in young children. *Clinical Child Psychology and Psychiatry, 12,* 525–535.

Slaughter, V., and Lyons, M. (2003). Learning about life and death in early childhood. *Cognitive Psychology, 46,* 1–30.

Slotta, J. D., and Chi, M. T. (2006). Helping students understand challenging topics in science through ontology training. *Cognition and Instruction, 24,* 261–289.

Slotta, J. D., Chi, M. T., and Joram, E. (1995). Assessing students' misclassifications of physics concepts: An ontological basis for conceptual change. *Cognition and Instruction, 13,* 373–400.

Smith, C. (2007). Bootstrapping processes in the development of students' commonsense matter theories: Using analogical mappings, thought experiments, and learning to measure to promote conceptual restructuring. *Cognition and Instruction, 25,* 337–398.

Smith, C., Carey, S., and Wiser, M. (1985). On differentiation: A case study of the development of the concepts of size, weight, and density. *Cognition, 21,* 177–237.

Smith, C., Maclin, D., Grosslight, L., and Davis, H. (1997). Teaching for understanding: A comparison of two approaches to teaching students about matter and density. *Cognition and Instruction, 15,* 317–393.

Smith, C., Solomon, G. E., and Carey, S. (2005). Never getting to zero: Elementary school students' understanding of the infinite divisibility of number and matter. *Cognitive Psychology, 51,* 101–140.

Smith, C., and Unger, C. (1997). What's in dots-per-box? Conceptual bootstrapping with stripped-down visual analogs. *Journal of the Learning Sciences, 6,* 143–181.

Solomon, G. E. (2002). Birth, kind and naïve biology. *Developmental Science, 5,* 213–218.

Solomon, G. E., and Cassimatis, N. L. (1999). On facts and conceptual systems: Young children's integration of their understandings of germs and contagion. *Developmental Psychology, 35,* 113–126.

Solomon, G. E., Johnson, S. C., Zaitchik, D., and Carey, S. (1996). Like father, like son: Young children's understanding of how and why offspring resemble their parents. *Child Development, 67,* 151–171.

Sousa, P., Atran, S., and Medin, D. (2002). Essentialism and folkbiology: Evidence from Brazil. *Journal of Cognition and Culture, 2,* 195–223.

Speece, M. W., and Brent, S. B. (1984). Children's understanding of death: A review of three components of a death concept. *Child Development, 55,* 1671–1686.

Spelke, E. S. (1994). Initial knowledge: Six suggestions. *Cognition, 50,* 431–445.

———(2005). Sex differences in intrinsic aptitude for mathematics and science? A critical review. *American Psychologist, 60,* 950–958.

Spelke, E. S., Breinlinger, K., Macomber, J., and Jacobson, K. (1992). Origins of knowledge. *Psychological Review, 99,* 605–632.

Spelke, E. S., and Kinzler, K. D. (2007). Core knowledge. *Developmental Science, 10,* 89–96.

Spencer, S. J., Steele, C. M., and Quinn, D. M. (1999). Stereotype threat and women's math performance. *Journal of Experimental Social Psychology, 35,* 4–28.

Springer, K. (1995). Acquiring a naive theory of kinship through inference. *Child Development, 66*, 547–558.

Springer, K., Ngyuen, T., and Samaniego, R. (1996). Early understanding of age-and environment-related noxiousness in biological kinds: Evidence for a naive theory. *Cognitive Development, 11*, 65–82.

Stavy, R., and Wax, N. (1989). Children's conceptions of plants as living things. *Human Development, 32*, 88–94.

Steinberg, M. S., Brown, D. E., and Clement, J. (1990). Genius is not immune to persistent misconceptions: Conceptual difficulties impeding Isaac Newton and contemporary physics students. *International Journal of Science Education, 12*, 265–273.

Stenn, F. (1980). Nurture turned to poison. *Perspectives in Biology and Medicine, 24*, 69–80.

Stevenson, R. J., Oaten, M. J., Case, T. I., Repacholi, B. M., and Wagland, P. (2010). Children's response to adult disgust elicitors: Development and acquisition. *Developmental Psychology, 46*, 165–177.

Straatemeier, M., van der Maas, H. L., and Jansen, B. R. (2008). Children's knowledge of the earth: A new methodological and statistical approach. *Journal of Experimental Child Psychology, 100*, 276–296.

Sylvia, C. (1997). *A change of heart: A memoir*. New York: Time Warner.

Thagard, P. (1992). *Conceptual revolutions*. Princeton, NJ: Princeton University Press.

Thagard, P. (1999). *How scientists explain disease*. Princeton, NJ: Princeton University Press.

———(2014). Explanatory identities and conceptual change. *Science and Education, 23*, 1531–1548.

Tomasello, M., and Carpenter, M. (2007). Shared intentionality. *Developmental Science, 10*, 121–125.

Tomasello, M., and Herrmann, E. (2010). Ape and human cognition: What's the Difference? *Current Directions in Psychological Science, 19*, 3–8.

Toulmin, S., and Goodfield, J. (1982). *The architecture of matter*. Chicago: University of Chicago Press.

Trend, R. D. (2001). Deep time framework: A preliminary study of UK primary teachers' conceptions of geological time and perceptions of geoscience. *Journal of Research in Science Teaching, 38*, 191–221.

Tufte, E. R. (2001). *The visual display of quantitative information* (2nd ed.). Cheshire, CT: Graphics Press.

United Nations Educational, Scientific and Cultural Organization (1970). *The race concept: Results of an inquiry*. Westport, CT: Greenwood Press.

Van der Linden, S., Leiserowitz, A. A., Feinberg, G. D., and Maibach, E. W. (2015). The scientific consensus on climate change as a gateway belief: Experimental evidence. *PloS One, 10*, e0118489.

Venville, G., Gribble, S. J., and Donovan, J. (2005). An exploration of young children's understandings of genetics concepts from ontological and epistemological perspectives. *Science Education, 89*, 614–633.

Vosniadou, S. (1994a). Capturing and modeling the process of conceptual change. *Learning and Instruction, 4*, 45–69.

———(1994b). Universal and culture-specific properties of children's mental models of the earth. In L. A. Hirschfeld and S. A. Gelman (eds.), *Mapping the mind: Domain specificity in cognition and culture* (pp. 412–430). Cambridge, UK: Cambridge University Press.

Vosniadou, S., and Brewer, W. F. (1987). Theories of knowledge restructuring in development. *Review of Educational Research, 57*, 51–67.

———(1992). Mental models of the earth: A study of conceptual change in childhood. *Cognitive Psychology, 24*, 535–585.

———(1994). Mental models of the day/night cycle. *Cognitive Science, 18*, 123–183.

Vosniadou, S., Skopeliti, I., and Ikospentaki, K. (2004). Modes of knowing and ways of reasoning in elementary astronomy. *Cognitive Development, 19*, 203–222.

———(2005). Reconsidering the role of artifacts in reasoning: Children's understanding of the globe as a model of the earth. *Learning and Instruction, 15*, 333–351.

Ware, E. A., and Gelman, S. A. (2014). You get what you need: An examination of purpose-based inheritance reasoning in undergraduates, preschoolers, and biological experts. *Cognitive Science, 38*, 197–243.

Waxman, S., Medin, D., and Ross, N. (2007). Folkbiological reasoning from a cross-cultural developmental perspective: Early essentialist notions are shaped by cultural beliefs. *Developmental Psychology, 43*, 294–308.

Webb, N. (1993). *Helping bereaved children: A handbook for practitioners*. New York: Guilford.

Wegener, A. (1929/1966). *The origin of continents and oceans*. New York: Dover.

Wellman, H. M., and Gelman, S. A. (1992). Cognitive development: Foundational theories of core domains. *Annual Review of Psychology, 43*, 337–375.

White, B. Y. (1984). Designing computer games to help physics students understand Newton's laws of motion. *Cognition and Instruction, 1*, 69–108.

Wicker, B., Keysers, C., Plailly, J., Royet, J. P., Gallese, V., and Rizzolatti, G. (2003). Both of us disgusted in my insula: The common neural basis of seeing and feeling disgust. *Neuron, 40*, 655–664.

Widen, S. C., and Russell, J. A. (2013). Children's recognition of disgust in others. *Psychological Bulletin, 139*, 271–299.

Willis, B. (1910). Principles of paleogeography. *Science, 31*, 241–260.

Winer, G. A., and Cottrell, J. E. (1996). Effects of drawing on directional representations of the process of vision. *Journal of Educational Psychology, 88*, 704–714.

Winer, G. A., Cottrell, J. E., Karefilaki, K. D., and Chronister, M. (1996). Conditions affecting beliefs about visual perception among children and adults. *Journal of Experimental Child Psychology, 61*, 93–115.

Winer, G. A., Cottrell, J. E., Karefilaki, K. D., and Gregg, V. R. (1996). Images, words, and questions: Variables that influence beliefs about vision in children and adults. *Journal of Experimental Child Psychology, 63*, 499–525.

Wiser, M., and Amin, T. (2001). "Is heat hot?" Inducing conceptual change by integrating everyday and scientific perspectives on thermal phenomena. *Learning and Instruction, 11*, 331–355.

Wiser, M., and Carey, S. (1983). When heat and temperature were one. In D. Gentner and A. L. Stevens (eds.), *Mental models* (pp. 267–297). Hillsdale, NJ: Erlbaum.

Zacharia, Z. C., and Olympiou, G. (2011). Physical versus virtual manipulative experimentation in physics learning. *Learning and Instruction, 21*, 317–331.

Zaitchik, D., Iqbal, Y., and Carey, S. (2014). The effect of executive function on biological reasoning in young children: An individual differences study. *Child Development, 85*, 160–175.

Zaitchik, D., and Solomon, G. E. (2008). Animist thinking in the elderly and in patients with Alzheimer's disease. *Cognitive Neuropsychology, 25*, 27–37.

———(2009). Conservation of species, volume, and belief in patients with Alzheimer's disease: The issue of domain specificity and conceptual impairment. *Cognitive Neuropsychology, 26*, 511–526.

Zamora, A., Romo, L. F., and Au, T. K. F. (2006). Using biology to teach adolescents about STD transmission and self-protective behaviors. *Journal of Applied Developmental Psychology, 27*, 109–124.

Zimmerman, C., and Cuddington, K. (2007). Ambiguous, circular and polysemous: Students' definitions of the "balance of nature" metaphor. *Public Understanding of Science, 16*, 393–406.

Zuger, A. (2003, March 4). "You'll catch your death!" An old wives' tale? *New York Times*, F1.

Index

Max S. Gerber

ANDREW SHTULMAN is an associate professor of psychology and cognitive science at Occidental College, where he directs the Thinking Lab. He holds degrees in psychology from Princeton and Harvard and has published several dozen scholarly articles on conceptual development and conceptual change. His work has been featured in *Scientific American*, *National Geographic*, and *The New Yorker*. He lives in Pasadena, California.